Lindsey Mar

The School Fundraising Handbook

How to maximise your income from grants, sponsorship and many other sources of finance

NOMINATION SCHEMES

EMPLOYEE VOLUNTEERS

CROWDFUNDING

FUNDRAISING EVENTS

FREE RESOURCES

PRODUCT DONATIONS

COMMISSION SCHEMES

GRANTS

CLUBS

MONEY-SAVING IDEAS

SPONSORSHIP

MATCH FUNDING

Crown House Publishing Limited
www.crownhouse.co.uk

HIRE SCHEMES

SPORTS

FREE EDUCATIONAL SPEAKERS

First published by
Crown House Publishing
Crown Buildings, Bancyfelin, Carmarthen, Wales, SA33 5ND, UK
www.crownhouse.co.uk

and

Crown House Publishing Company LLC
PO Box 2223, Williston, VT 05495, USA
www.crownhousepublishing.com

Cover image © stickasa – fotolia.com

First published 2019.

Quotes from Ofsted and Department for Education documents used in this publication have been approved under an Open Government Licence. Please see: http://www.nationalarchives.gov.uk/doc/open-government-licence/version/3/.

All information correct at the time of going to press.

British Library of Cataloguing-in-Publication Data
A catalogue entry for this book is available from the British Library.

Print ISBN 978-178583426-4
Mobi ISBN 978-178583469-1
ePub ISBN 978-178583470-7
ePDF ISBN 978-178583471-4

LCCN 2019949584

Printed in the UK by
TJ International, Padstow, Cornwall

Preface

School budgets are tight and school leaders are under increasing pressure to generate their own income. There are over 32,000 schools in the UK alone, all being challenged to find new ways to raise and save money in areas such as ICT, the arts, environmental projects, sport and extra-curricular activities.

The government has a statutory responsibility to fund education in England, so state schools should only need to fundraise to provide *extra* income, not to subsidise core services. However, according to the Institute for Fiscal Studies, schools have experienced a real terms cut of 8% in per pupil funding since 2010.[1] As a result, many schools are reportedly turning to crowdfunding to raise money for basics such as textbooks, pens and pencils, as well as sports facilities and playgrounds.[2] Understandably, many charitable trusts are unwilling to step in to fund services that should be paid for by government.

Although most schools are aware of the benefits of fundraising, many aren't fully informed about the range of grants, schemes and other support available. While it is the role of the school business manager to generate income, many are often so overloaded with other essential tasks that there is often limited time to spend on fundraising. Teachers, support staff, governors, students and other members of the school community can also apply for help for their school. However, if they are not fully aware of the opportunities on offer, or do not feel sufficiently confident to apply for such schemes, then valuable funding sources can be missed.

The research shows that not all schools are utilising the opportunities available to them. For example, a report by Kellogg's suggests that more than three-quarters of schools (78%) never use food redistribution charities.[3] This is a shame because by accessing this type of support schools can redirect their finances into teaching and learning.

This book aims to help schools become better informed about the resources available to them, and to raise awareness of all the wonderful charities and organisations that are willing to support schools and other educational establishments. *The School Fundraising Handbook* offers key contact information for over a hundred grants, as well as tips, statistics and key information, so that even the most inexperienced fundraiser can feel confident when raising money for their school.

---

1 L. Tickle, School Cuts: 'Children Now Raise Money for Their Own Education', *The Guardian* (14 August 2018). Available at: www.theguardian.com/education/2018/aug/14/school-cuts-children-raise-money-own-education.

2 N. McIntyre and R. Adams, More Than 1,000 English Schools Turn to Online Donations to Raise Funds, *The Guardian* (9 April 2019). Available at: www.theguardian.com/education/2019/apr/09/cash-strapped-english-schools-turn-to-online-donations-to-close-funding-gap.

3 Kellogg's, *No Food for Thought: The Impact of Hunger in UK Classrooms* (2014), p. 23. Available at: www. kelloggs.co.uk/content/dam/europe/kelloggs_gb/pdf/R1_Kelloggs%20No%20food%20for%20thought.pdf.

Grants have the potential to generate the biggest supplementary income for schools, so Part I is dedicated to this area. Part II offers more specific help for fundraising and managing key school projects, and Part III offers ideas to help your school not only to raise money but to save money too. Although it is predominately written for schools, most of the information provided is also relevant to nurseries, pre-schools, colleges, universities and other education providers. The tips provided in this book will not automatically lead to your funding application being accepted; however, they will improve your chances of success. Always make sure that you follow the funder's guidelines when submitting your bid.

Transparency and ethics matter in an era of instant communication, so schools should consider any philanthropic funding very carefully. Businesses often provide donations, goods and services as part of their corporate social responsibility (CSR) policy, the purpose of which can be both altruistic and strategic. Positive public relations can raise the profile of a company in the minds of consumers *and* boost long-term profits. This issue is particularly acute in schools where there is a captive young audience of potential future customers. There is no reason why schools should not take advantage of the funding and support on offer from businesses, but they should also be aware of what the company is getting in return. Thoughtful evaluation and due diligence are required to ensure that the principles, goals and values of the donor match those of the school.

By regularly devoting time to fundraising, schools can open the door to new money that can help to raise standards and enable transformations to happen. Fundraising doesn't have to be complicated or take up too much time, but if done on a regular basis it can be very valuable, breathing life into projects so that students can continue to recieve the very best education possible.

Funding programmes often inspire creativity – and donors like to fund exciting and unusual ideas! This can motivate schools to develop innovative solutions and groundbreaking ideas that will not only help their school but support other schools too.

Fundraising can also encourage schools to forge stronger partnerships with members of the wider community. By applying for grants, for example, schools are inviting potential funders to work with them on projects in areas where they both have a mutual interest. This gives charities and other donors the opportunity to use their money to be part of the school community and to make a real difference.

Not only can fundraising be a positive challenge but it can also be very rewarding, especially when bids are won, ideas become a reality, fun events are organised, improvements are made and successes are celebrated.

Disclaimer: The details in this book are provided as guidance only. It is advisable to contact the relevant organisations for full, up-to-date information and to assess each opportunity for your school or context (be sure to seek professional advice where necessary). The author is not responsible for the content of third-party websites and is not affiliated with any of the organisations listed.

Acknowledgements

I would like to dedicate this book to my family, in particular my two beautiful children – Shannon and Danny. I love you both more than words can say.

I would also like to say a special thank you to my mom and dad for being so supportive.

Also, thank you to my lovely friend and school business manager mentor, Hayley Dunn. Thanks for your friendship and for teaching me so much.

Contents

Part I
Applying for Grants

NOMINATION SCHEMES

EMPLOYEE VOLUNTEERS

CROWDFUNDING

FUNDRAISING EVENTS

FREE RESOURCES

PRODUCT DONATIONS

COMMISSION SCHEMES

GRANTS

CLUBS

MONEY-SAVING IDEAS

SPONSORSHIP

MATCH FUNDING

HIRE SCHEMES

SPORTS

FREE EDUCATIONAL SPEAKERS

Chapter 1
Introduction to grants

There are lots of grants available to schools. Grants are non-repayable sums of money, so they do not have to be paid back. They are usually a form of restricted funding, which means that the money must be used for the specific purpose for which it was donated. Grants can be awarded for a range of purposes – for example:

- Promote sports activities and exercise.
- Buy equipment such as computers and photocopiers.
- Install energy efficient technologies like photovoltaic (PV) solar panels.
- Buy resources to help young people with special educational needs and disabilities.
- Improve the school building and grounds.
- Support staff with professional development opportunities.
- Enhance the teaching of specific subjects such as maths, English and science.

A range of different grants are available. Here are some key terms you are likely to come across:

- Capital grants: These are awarded to help recipients purchase tangible goods which become assets, such as vehicles and buildings.
- Project cost grants: These are given to help cover the cost of running a specific project. This may include staff salaries, equipment and a small percentage towards any direct overheads.
- Revenue grants: These are awarded to help cover the costs of key outgoings, such as rent, rates and utilities (these are sometimes referred to as 'core costs').
- In-kind support: This is a non-cash contribution to a project, which might include materials and services, consultancy, the use of company facilities and product donations.
- Match funding: This refers to funds that are awarded to equal the amount raised by another source or activity. The value of in-kind contributions is often accepted as match funding too.

Grants can be given by individuals or organisations such as charities, businesses and local councils.

Charitable trusts and foundations are non-profit organisations which give voluntary help to those in need. Schools can usually apply for support from both national and regional charities, including local educational trusts. The help on offer varies, but may include monetary grants and donations of goods or time. As well as donating gifts, many charities also aim to raise awareness of the causes they care about and the difference they are making.

There are over 168,000 charities in England and Wales alone, donating approximately £30 billion annually.[1] Charities derive their income from a variety of sources, including legacies, shares, fundraising events, Gift Aid donations, payroll giving, charity shop sales and so on. Some charities also distribute and administer funds on behalf of others. Most charities are run by a dedicated team of employees, alongside volunteers who give up their time to help others. Each charity is overseen by a board of trustees which works in accordance with a governing document. This is a legal document which sets out the charity's objective or purpose and how it will be administered. Most charities are regulated by the Charity Commission, a statutory body which holds them to account in accordance with the law.[2]

Each year charities must, by law, submit their annual returns (if their income is above a certain threshold) to a central register of charities, which are maintained by the Charity Commissions for each of the UK regions (their websites are listed below). The register can be searched online (for free) and is a quality source of information for any fundraiser. It provides details about charities' work and aims, along with finance information, trustee details, contact information and more.[3]

Here are the details of the Charity Commissions for England and Wales, Northern Ireland and Scotland:

Charity Commission for England and Wales
www.gov.uk/government/organisations/charity-commission
0300 066 9197

Charity Commission for Northern Ireland
www.charitycommissionni.org.uk
0283 832 0220

Scottish Charity Regulator
www.oscr.org.uk
01382 220446

You can find more information about grant-makers (including details about what they fund) by visiting the 360 Giving website: www.threesixtygiving.org.

---

1 See www.gov.uk/government/publications/charity-register-statistics/recent-charity-register-statistics-charity-commission and www.channel4.com/news/factcheck/how-much-charities-spend-good-causes.
2 This law is set out under the Charities Act 2011. See www.legislation.gov.uk/ukpga/2011/25/contents.
3 The register can be found at: www.gov.uk/find-charity-information.

You can learn more about the voluntary sector and access a range of data and statistics via the National Council for Voluntary Organisations (NCVO) website: www.ncvo.org.uk. Funding Central also provides information on grants from local, national and international funding sources: www.fundingcentral.org.uk.

Aside from charities, many businesses offer grants as part of their corporate social responsibility (CSR) commitments. Not all companies are in a position to give, but those that do give for a variety of reasons, including giving something back to the area they serve, helping good causes and being seen to be doing the right thing. As well as donating money, many offer product donations, the use of company facilities, employee volunteers, expertise and more.

Grants are also awarded by lotteries. For example, since 1994 the National Lottery has raised over £40 billion for good causes across the UK.[4] These funds are distributed by 12 independent organisations and are given to a variety of arts, sports, heritage, charitable, voluntary, health, education and environmental projects. To learn more about lottery funding and to access a list of lottery distributors contact:

National Lottery Good Causes
www.lotterygoodcauses.org.uk
0845 275 0000

Grants are also awarded by local Community Foundations[5] and by the Council for Voluntary Service organisations, details of which can be found here:

National Association for Voluntary and Community Action (NAVCA) (England)
https://navca.org.uk
0114 278 6636

Northern Ireland Council for Voluntary Action (NICVA)
www.nicva.org
0289 087 7777

Scottish Council for Voluntary Organisations (SCVO)
https://scvo.org.uk
enquiries@scvo.org.uk
0131 474 8000

---

4 See www.lotterygoodcauses.org.uk.
5 See www.ukcommunityfoundations.org.

Wales Council for Voluntary Action (WCVA)
www.wcva.org.uk
funding@wcva.org.uk
0300 111 0124

As well as providing advice and support, charities often distribute funds on behalf of donors and award grants to address local needs.

Each year local councils set aside a budget to help causes within their locality. Councils are local government organisations and include county councils, city councils, town councils, parish councils and so on. According to the National Association of Local Councils, there are 10,000 councils in England.[6] Councils usually receive funds through the Council Tax paid by local residents and from other income streams, such as hiring out council facilities. Council grants can range from £20 to £2,000 and may be used to organise events, purchase equipment, cover running costs, or fund training programmes and trip transport costs.

Schools can also contact local councillors, who often have a Pride Fund for community projects in their area. Grants typically range from £50 to £2,000. You can usually find their contact details (including email address) via your local council website.

As well as all these grant-giving organisations, grants are also distributed through government bodies and agencies. They are also offered by town mayors, Lions Clubs, Rotary Clubs and more.

---

6 See www.nalc.gov.uk/about/who-we-are.

Chapter 2

Overview of the grant application process

If you are new to applying for grants, then you may like to know what is involved in the process. This chapter will take you through the steps an applicant may need to take to apply for a grant and successfully manage the award.

1. Research potential funders and learn about any grants available. For example:
    - Visit the funder's website.
    - Read any grant policies.
    - Read any guidance notes.
    - Check the answers to any frequently asked questions.
2. Assess how well the project meets the funder's priorities. For example:
    - View the award criteria.
    - Take an eligibility test (if offered).
    - Contact the funder for further information (if the funder invites this).

If a potential grant has been identified:

3. Applicant applies for the grant, following the funder's instructions. For example:
    - Stage 1: Submit an expression of interest.
    - Stage 2: Submit a full application (including any requested documents).
4. Grant assessor reviews the application and requests any additional information. They may telephone or write and even request to visit your establishment.
5. Trustees discuss the application at the next board meeting and make a decision (sometimes the applicant is required to be present at the meeting).
6. Applicant receives a decision (or follows this up).

If the application is successful:

7. Applicant receives notice of the grant award (usually by email).

8. Applicant responds by:
    - Reading the terms and conditions.
    - Signing any grant agreements.
    - Sending an appreciation letter and inviting the grant-maker to visit the school.

9. Grant is transferred into the agreed bank account (i.e. usually by bank transfer within 30-days of award notice). Alternatively, a representative of the organisation may prefer to award a cheque at a presentation ceremony.

10. Applicant uses the grant and manages the project as agreed, ensuring to:
    - Publicise the award.
    - Take photographs of the different stages of the project.
    - Monitor the project and measure the outcomes.
    - Keep receipts and any evidence of how the grant has been spent.

11. Applicant keeps the funder updated and submits grant progress reports (e.g. every six months).

12. Once the project is complete, the applicant:
    - Evaluates the project.
    - Completes a post-grant report to give an account of the project and present the outcomes.
    - Submits any information the funder requests (e.g. copies of receipts).
    - Celebrates the work achieved.

13. The funder officially closes the grant.

14. The applicant manages the relationship well and checks whether they are eligible to apply again.

As every grant-giving organisation is unique, they will all have their own distinct set of rules which applicants must follow, so you will need to clarify the process with each funder.

Chapter 3

Identifying grants

With so many grants available, seeking out the ones which are most relevant to your school can seem like a daunting task. Not all organisations accept applications from schools, some only cover a certain geographical area and others only support certain projects. While this book provides details of over a hundred grants, there are many more out there beyond these for which schools could potentially apply.

Grants can be found by:

- Searching online and visiting funders' websites or the Charity Commission website.
- Asking around – perhaps a member of your school community knows of a suitable grant.
- Reading your local newspaper, where grant opportunities may be publicised.
- Asking other schools if they know of any suitable funding programmes.
- Enquiring with any organisations your school may be part of, such as school clusters or the local authority.
- Contacting your local library, Community Foundation or Council for Voluntary Service for help, as they often have access to grant directories.
- Asking suppliers – some offer a free grant-finding service and some even have grant programmes exclusively for their customers.
- Asking grant-makers – they may be able to signpost you to other funders.
- Seeking help from professional fundraisers.
- Contacting income generation agencies for help.
- Attending fundraising training sessions, exhibitions, conferences and events.
- Reapplying to funders that you have applied to in the past.
- Reading posts or asking questions on social media sites and online forums. On Twitter, for example, you could use:
  - Educational hashtags: #SchoolBusiness, #education, #schools, #PTA, and for school leaders and business managers: #SBLtwitter, #SBMtwitter, #SBM (school business manager), #SBL (school business leader), #SLT (senior leadership team).

- Fundraising hashtags: #EdGrant, #SchoolFundraiser, #SchoolFunding, #HelpOurSchools, #fundraising, #fundraiser, #grants, #donate, #ForACause, #GoodCause, #GoFundMe.

- Hashtags relevant to your project: #children, #students, #KidsMatter, #disadvantaged, #SEND (special educational needs and disability), #SENDcrisis, #EAL (English as an additional language), #ECE (early childhood education), #inclusion, #equality, #bullying, #art, #EdSust (educational sustainability), #EdTech, #EdApp, #ICT, #STEM (science, technology, engineering and maths), #music, #HistoryTeacher, #GeographyTeacher, #PhysicsEd, #PlayOutdoors.

- Hashtags for weekly discussions and live chats: #EdChat, #EduChat, #UKEdChat, #EdFinChat, #SpEdChat (special educational needs), #SLTchat, #CharityTuesday, #TT (teacher Tuesday), #TLChat (teacher librarians).

- Your local area's dedicated hashtag: e.g. #WestMidlandsHour is on Tuesdays between 8 and 9pm.

- You can also connect with others and share tips by using the official hashtag for this book: #SchoolFundraisingHandbook.

- Some Twitter accounts you may like to follow include: @fundraising, @FundingCentral, @FundEd4schools, @Get_Grants, @GRANTfinder_uk, @GrantFunders, @Grants4Schools, @GrantsOnline, @IoFtweets, @PTApatter, @SchoolFundingUK, @UKCF_tweets, @ukfundraising.

There are also grant databases, magazines and other resources that fundraisers can subscribe to or buy. Education shows also provide opportunities to network and learn more about income generation.

Grant databases

FundEd
www.funded.org.uk
info@funded.org.uk
This database offers information on funding from a range of grant-giving trusts and lists data by curriculum or interest area. There is an annual fee to access it (£90 +VAT at the time of writing). Please contact FundEd for more information.

Funding Central
www.fundingcentral.org.uk
fundingcentralhelp@ncvo.org.uk
Through one search, fundraisers can access information on thousands of grants. The database is free to access for small charitable and voluntary organisations

(such as parent–teacher associations (PTAs) and friends groups); however, there is a subscription fee for organisations with an annual income of over £100,000.

GRANTfinder

www.grantfinder.co.uk

GRANTfinder is a subscription service which offers a comprehensive database of key funding opportunities across the UK. It also provides support throughout the funding process from identification to application and management. Please use the contact form on their website to book a demo or to request further information.

Grants Online

www.grantsonline.org.uk

info@grantsonline.org.uk

This online database was established in 2001 and currently offers information on nearly 5,000 funding schemes in the UK. The organisation also provides up-to-date funding information, alerts and newsletters. There is a subscription fee to access the full list (£20 + VAT for individual access for one month).

Fundraising publications

Directory of Social Change

www.dsc.org.uk

cs@dsc.org.uk

0207 697 4200

The Directory of Social Change offer a range of useful publications, including funding directories and best practice guides. They also offer a range of grant databases and training programmes.

FundEd Magazine

www.funded.org.uk

info@funded.org.uk

01342 718679

As well as offering a grants database, FundEd publish a magazine every term. Fundraisers can either pay an annual subscription for both the magazine and database or pay a smaller fee to subscribe to the magazine only. *FundEd Magazine* offers tools and advice to help schools generate income as well as details of current grants and competitions.

Income generation agencies

ICS Funding Services

www.ics-funding.co.uk

This income generation agency offers an expert bid-writing service which works on a no-win, no-fee basis. Education sector clients include schools, academies, multi-academy trusts, special schools, sixth form colleges, nurseries and PTAs.

School Funding Service

http://schoolfundingservice.co.uk

The School Funding Service offers bid-writing and fundraising manager services for schools in the UK. They also run bid-writing and fundraising skills workshops. Visit their website to read their blog and subscribe to free grant updates.

Education shows

Education shows provide a great way to network with colleagues and find out how to get the best out of your school budget.

Childcare Expo

www.childcareexpo.co.uk

The Childcare Expo is the longest-running exhibition for the early years and primary education sector. Events are free to attend and are held in London, Manchester and the Midlands. Delegates can discover new resources, meet suppliers, attend seminars and workshops, and network with other professionals.

Eastern Education Show

http://easterneducationshow.uk

The Eastern Education Show, which takes place at Newmarket in February, is the region's leading event for the promotion and development of effective teaching and learning and school management. Delegates from all types of schools are welcome to attend, including those from infant, junior, primary, secondary and special schools, and also colleges and academies across Suffolk, Norfolk, Essex, Cambridgeshire, Bedfordshire, Hertfordshire, Peterborough, Rutland and Lincolnshire.

Education Show

https://www.bettshow.com/educationshow

The Education Show at ExCeL London is a one-stop shop for supplies and information. The show usually takes place in January and is free to attend. From 2020 it will be held within the Bett (formerly British Technology and Training) Show. Please use the contact form on their website to request further information.

National Education Show

www.nationaleducationshow.com

The National Education Show offers school teachers and education staff the knowledge, resources and expert guidance they need to improve, enhance and raise standards in the education sector. This annual conference takes place every year in Wales, and provides an opportunity to share knowledge, watch demonstrations, attend seminars and find out about educational products and supplies.

Northern Education Show

http://northerneducationshow.uk

The Northern Education Show takes place in Manchester and attracts more than 250 school decision-makers and over 100 exhibitors. It usually takes place in October and is free to attend for head teachers, deputy head teachers, finance directors, bursars, business managers, governors, local authority leaders, PTAs, IT managers and school leadership teams.

Schools and Academies Show

https://saashow.london

The Schools and Academies Show (formerly the Academies Show) is a free-to-attend event which is designed to support school business management. It usually takes place in April at ExCeL London.

Southern Education Show

www.southerneducationshow.uk

The Southern Education Show takes place in February at Newbury Racecourse. It includes inspirational keynotes, interactive workshops and a range of exhibitors. Register online for free tickets.

Local support

Local library services

England, Wales and Northern Ireland: www.gov.uk/local-library-services
Scotland: https://scottishlibraries.org/find-a-library

UK Community Foundations

www.ukcommunityfoundations.org

Community Foundations are a national network dedicated to working locally and inspiring people to give. For details of local grants, contact your local Community Foundation.

Schools can find information about grants by using the Key for School Leaders website: https://schoolleaders.thekeysupport.com. There is the opportunity to 'ask a question' via their website (please note that there may be a charge to access this service).

Schools can also put systems in place to invite supporters to come forward, thereby helping to save time researching potential funders. For example, you could:

■ Make fundraising ideas an agenda item for your team meetings. This can encourage staff to look out for fundraising opportunities and share information with you on a regular basis.

■ Establish a permanent fundraising section in your school newsletter or on your website to raise awareness of projects you need help with and to invite support.

■ Communicate your needs by sending a press release to local newspapers and radio stations. This can help to attract the attention of funders, particularly those that prefer to find projects to fund themselves or don't accept unsolicited applications.

Searching for funders

Before you begin searching for funding, it is useful to know what different funders can potentially offer:

■ While some funders offer a one-off grant; others offer ongoing support.

■ Some funders will only offer match funding or part-fund projects; others are willing to cover all of the project costs.

■ Some funders are willing to pay for things like salaries and running costs; others prefer to finance something more tangible like equipment and resources.

■ Some funders will fund individual schools; others prefer to fund a group of schools.

■ Some grants are awarded to help certain beneficiaries only (e.g. children within a certain age range); others have a more open grants policy.

■ Some funders will finance projects within a certain region; others will accept applications from across the UK.

With this mind, it is beneficial to look out for funders that:

■ Offer the level and type of funding you need.

■ You haven't received a grant from in the past year.

■ Share your values.

■ Have funding priorities which align with yours.

■ Are keen to help the type of students at which your project is aimed.

■ Are local.

Grant-making trusts don't usually like generic requests. Grants are typically awarded for specific reasons, such as tackling a particular problem or promoting a certain area, so look out for funders whose aims and interests match your own.

When searching for grants, think about your niche: reflect on your project themes and identify any wider funding that may be available. For example, if students at your breakfast club are kept entertained with sporting activities, then consider looking for grants related to sports education as well as those for breakfast clubs. If your school operates in a rural area or where there is deprivation, you might wish to factor this into your search. For instance, if want to purchase new computers, rural schools are eligible for the Computers for Rural People scheme: https://germinate.net/mission/computers-for-rural-people.

When researching funders, you will notice that grants of varying amounts are offered. Don't let this put you off. Large projects can often be broken down into smaller projects, so you can apply for smaller grants instead. Likewise, if you are fundraising for a number of small projects (all helping the same beneficiaries), then you can group these together and apply for one large grant. Make sure the amount of funding you request matches the level of funding offered. If the funder makes grants of £10,000 or more, for instance, then don't be tempted to apply for less than this amount.

When searching for grants, you will need to take into account when you need the funding, as you will need to allow enough time to write the application, for the application to be assessed (at each stage), for the decision to be made and for the grant to be paid.

Grant applications can often be time-consuming, so make sure you set aside enough time to complete each stage of the process. While some funders have a straightforward application form, others require applicants to first submit an expression of interest, which is then followed by a number of application rounds.

Find out when applications are accepted and make sure this date works for you. While some funders accept applications on a rolling basis, others stipulate a certain deadline, so be aware of this when looking for relevant grants.

Depending on which funder you apply to, it can take anything from one month to a year for them to reach a decision. Applications are often considered by a grants committee, and how often the committee meets will depend on the individual organisation (some meet monthly, others quarterly). Most funders will offer information about timescales on their website, so this should help you to determine whether or not the grant is suitable for your school.

If you need funding urgently, then you may wish to consider applying for smaller grants, as the application forms are usually shorter and decisions are made more rapidly. The more money you ask for, the longer the application will take to write, the more evidence you will need to submit and the longer it will take to receive a decision. If you are requesting funding for multiple years, then this will also add to the length of the application process.

If you are looking to fund a new project, you might like to consider piloting it first. Not only can this help you to test out ideas before fully committing to the final proposal, but it also enables you to apply for smaller grants. (Funders prefer to support projects that have been successfully trialled.) Similarly, if you are fundraising for a major project and need to raise a large sum of money, you could consider phasing it in gradually and apply for smaller grants relating to each stage of its development.

Remember: grants are not usually awarded retrospectively, so always plan ahead and avoid starting your project until you have received official confirmation of a grant.

Learn about the funder

Once you have discovered a suitable grant, it is important to take steps to learn more about the funder and explore whether or not they are the right match for your project. The majority of funders have a website where they will publish lots of useful information to help applicants determine whether they meet the organisation's funding aims. If not, you can usually find the relevant information by viewing their annual accounts on the website of the Charity Commission with whom they are registered.

As well as information about the history and structure of the organisation and their contact details, a grant-maker's website should provide you with the following:

- Information about any funding programmes they are running, including their strategic priorities and deadlines.
- Details of any grant criteria.
- An online eligibility test.
- Guidelines about how to apply.
- Application forms.
- Answers to frequently asked questions.
- Annual reports.
- Impact reports.
- Grant policies.
- Details of previous grant recipients.
- Case studies.

Alternatively, if you are using a charity's annual accounts then you should be able to find out the following information:

- Contact details.
- Details of their aims and objectives.
- Information about the organisation's structure, governance and management.
- Background information about the charity.
- Trustees' annual reports.
- Independent examiner's reports.
- Financial information (including a balance sheet and details of income and expenditure).
- Statement of financial activities.
- Information about previously awarded grants.

Grant-makers often provide a range of tools via their website to help applicants assess their funding bid, so be sure to read the grant criteria and take the eligibility test (if available). Some charities also run webinars to give fundraisers the opportunity to participate in live online chats to learn more about the work of the organisation and ask questions. Check what support is on offer.

If you still need help after reading the guidance materials, then contact the funder for more information. This is especially important if you are requesting a large sum of money. Never be afraid to ask questions – it can save you a lot of time spent applying to the wrong funder. Some funders state on their website how they prefer to be contacted, so check this out before communicating with them. Due to the high volume of applications they receive not all grant-makers are able to answer queries, so don't be disappointed if you are unable to speak to anyone.

Remember that charities are established because they are keen to make a difference in key areas, so try to find out what is important to them and make sure your project is relevant to their work. Tell them why your plan is interesting and different, describe the difference(s) you are trying to make and enquire whether this is something they would be interested in supporting. If they can't help, maybe they will know of a funder who can, or perhaps there will be an opportunity for you to get involved with other projects they have funded instead.

Know what is expected

Once you have found a grant that you are interested in applying for, you will need to find out about the funder's expectations of the applicant. You can usually find this information on their website and by reading their terms and conditions. It is important that you fully understand their criteria; if you can't meet these, then your application may be rejected or they may request that any grants awarded are repaid.

Here are some examples of what funders can expect from applicants:

- They may require you to deliver a short presentation to their grants committee.
- They will often expect you to publicly acknowledge the grant.
- They will insist that you use the grant as agreed and within a specified time period.
- They can expect you to follow certain procedures for evaluation and monitoring.
- They may expect you to complete an end-of-grant report that outlines how the grant has been spent and the difference it has made.

Chapter 4
Getting prepared

Before you begin searching and applying for grants, make sure you have all the information and tech you will need ready to hand.

- A calendar will help you to record key dates and note down deadlines.
- A project noticeboard near your desk will enable you to post information as you go along.
- You could consider placing a vision board in the staffroom to invite ideas from staff.

Technology will be well-established in most schools, but there some pieces of software that may be useful:

- If you are operating a Microsoft Windows system, you can use OneNote to create a project workbook. Use this app to write down and capture ideas, organise your project, share ideas, and create to-do lists and checklists.
- If you need to send large documents with your grant application, you can use a free file sharing platform like WeTransfer, Dropbox or Google Drive.
- If you want to carry out your own surveys or questionnaires, there are lots of free online tools to help you create these, including SurveyMonkey and Google Forms.

Social media can be a great way to find out information and connect with other people:

- Consider registering with LinkedIn (if you haven't already). It is a professional networking platform which can help you to connect and nurture relationships with key decision-makers. There are currently over 500 million members on LinkedIn.
- Twitter is a savvy way to keep up-to-date and interact with key people and organisations in the industry.
- Pinterest is a useful tool for sharing visual ideas. You could create a board per project and encourage staff to contribute 'pins' to it.

If you apply for lots of grants, you will find that most organisations request similar information. Here is a list of what you should keep readily accessible:

- Your school contact details:
  - School name.
  - Address.
  - Phone number.

- Email.
- Website.
- Social media sites.
- Details about the school:
  - The type of school (foundation, academy, etc.).
  - The date it was established and when it adopted its current legal status (you can find this information in your governing document).
  - The name, address and details of the organisation ultimately responsible for the school (i.e. local authority or academy trust).
  - The name of the head teacher.
  - How many governors or trustees the school has and the name of the chairperson.
  - A statement about the school's values, ethos and aims (including the school motto).
  - Details about the catchment area the school serves.
- Key reference numbers (as applicable):
  - Local authority number and establishment number.
  - Department for Education number.
  - Ofsted unique reference number (URN).
  - Charity registration number.
  - VAT registration number.
- Details about your students:
  - The school capacity rate.
  - Number of students currently on roll.
  - The number of students per year group and their age ranges.
  - Percentage of students on free school meals and/or pupil premium.
- Your bank account details (for the account you would like the grant to be paid into if your application is successful).

If you need help finding the information you require about the school you are fundraising for, then here are some tips:

- Try to obtain copies of any old grant applications which should contain the key information.

- Check what information is provided on the school website. This will usually feature an e-prospectus, exam results, pupil premium reports, PE and sports premium reports, SEND information and so on. You can see a list of what maintained schools must publish online at: www.gov.uk/guidance/what-maintained-schools-must-publish-online.

- Get a copy of the latest Ofsted school inspection report from the school website or by visiting: https://reports.ofsted.gov.uk.

- Check what information is provided in the Department for Education's online register (formerly known as Edubase), which is available at: www.gov.uk/guidance/get-information-about-schools.

If you need a copy of your school catchment area map, then visit the Primary School Catchment Area website at www.schoolcatchment.co.uk. Alternatively, try your local authority's website or contact the local schools admissions team for help.

If you would like to access data to compare your school's Ofsted performance against other schools locally, regionally and nationally, then take a look at Data View: www.gov.uk/government/publications/exploring-ofsted-inspection-data-with-data-view. Ofsted data are presented in interactive graphs and maps which allow users to compare school ratings and deprivation levels over several years.

You can compare your school's income and expenditure with other schools by checking out the school's financial benchmarking data. Schools in England can use the schools financial benchmarking service at: https://schools-financial-benchmarking.service.gov.uk.

If you would like to provide demographic information about the area in which your school operates, you can get this information from Nomis (a service provided by the Office for National Statistics): www.nomisweb.co.uk. The website provides key data about the local population, employment, unemployment, qualifications, earnings, benefit claimants and businesses. You can access statistics for the local authority and the ward in which your school is based.

You can find area profiles, parish and town council statistics, census information and a whole range of other statistics for health and well-being, environment, population, unemployment and household data via your county council's website. To find your local council visit: www.gov.uk/find-local-council.

Useful documents

As well as the information listed above, funders may request to see other documents as part of your application, to ensure that you have the relevant structures in place.

These documents could include:

- Your annual accounts or financial statements. (If your organisation has been running for less than 15 months, then you could provide a projection of your income and expenditure instead.) You will usually need to attach a note to explain any carry forward or deficit.
- Details of any key budgets (e.g. your school's annual budget and any relevant departmental budgets).
- A copy of your governing documents. This may also be known as a constitution, memorandum and articles of association, set of rules or trust deed.
- Details of any relevant school policies (e.g. child protection, equal opportunities, health and safety).
- Details of any key insurance policies.
- Details about any staff responsible for delivering your project (e.g. a copy of the CV of the music teacher who will be delivering your project).

Funders may also request additional information depending on the nature of your project.

Make sure that any documents you send are the most up-to-date versions. You should also ensure that any information you send is consistent with what is available in the public domain – for example, details about trustees in your published annual accounts should match the information you have provided to the funder.

Chapter 5

Writing your grant application

Once you have identified a grant that you would like to apply for, you will then need to find out about the funder's preferred system for accepting applications. Some require applicants to complete an interactive form via their website, but most have an official application form for applicants to download, complete and return by email or post. Others simply accept written requests by post. For example, the Edge Foundation (www. edge.co.uk) only accepts applications via their website and does not accept unsolicited funding requests outside of their biennial grant offers, whereas the DM Thomas Foundation for Young People (https://dmthomasfoundation.org) states that applications must be sent both via email and in writing. Be sure to check this out properly and read any guidance notes before applying. Some funders update their application forms regularly, so make sure you have the correct version before you begin writing your application.

Decide who will apply

Make sure the right person completes your application – someone who knows the school well and is passionate about the project. The National Lottery Awards for All, for example, only accepts grant applications submitted directly by the organisation and not by a third party. Ideally the applicant will be employed by your school (e.g. a teacher, administrator or school business manager). It is not usually necessary for the head teacher to complete the application, although they should know about it and have approved it. If a volunteer is applying for a grant on behalf of the school, then the school should make it clear that it has sanctioned this.

Schools can usually apply for grants:

- As an individual school.
- In a partnership with other schools.
- Via any umbrella organisations they are part of (such as a multi-academy trust).
- Via a third party (such as an income generation agency).

Some funders only accept applications from registered charities or organisations with a smaller annual income, so if your school has a PTA or friends group, then you could consider submitting an application through them instead. It is also worth remembering that some funders (such as the Foyle Foundation – www.foylefoundation.org.uk) preferentially support projects which have received support from their own school PTA or friends group, so try to get them on board!

Sometimes you may come across a grant that your school is not eligible to apply for, but a partner organisation or individual is, such as grants for outreach work. If this is the case, you could consider informing any partners or professionals you are planning to work with and ask if they could apply instead.

Complete the application

When writing the grant application, you will usually be led through a series of questions to help the funder extract key information to assess your proposal.

To begin with, you will be asked to give your project a name. Ideally this should be memorable so it grabs the funder's attention and entices them to learn more. For example, 'Say Pants to Poverty' was the name of a recent campaign by the Scottish charity Smalls for All, which appealed for pants and underwear to be sent to disadvantaged women and children in Africa and the UK.

Here are some ideas to help you create an effective project name:

- Try to make it short and snappy. The National Lottery Awards for All online application, for instance, allows names of no more than 40 characters.
- Think about any verbs that you would like to include in your name in order to create a call to action – for example, 'Save our School' if you are fundraising to keep your school open.
- Consider adding a personal touch by including the name of your school or the name of a teacher or class trying to raise the money.
- Make sure that any message you are attempting to convey is clearly communicated.
- Aim to make the name distinctive and catchy. You could use alliteration or an exclamation mark to make it more powerful!
- Make sure the tone of your name matches the project – use wit and humour or a more respectful tone as appropriate.
- Make sure the name aligns with your school policies, values and ethos.
- Ensure the head teacher agrees with the name and that it doesn't include any insensitive or offensive language.

Once you have decided on a project title, you will then need to write an executive summary to describe your project, the context of your work and how much money you are requesting. Often the funder will request this information within a given word count, so be sure to meet this when completing your application. Aim to describe your project in a compelling way and offer information about the five Ws: who, why, what, where and when.

If your project is creative and innovative, then let the funder know how it is different. Many funding bodies like to support fresh and unusual proposals rather than ideas they have heard about before. Write passionately about your project – make it sound worthy of investment and inspire the funder to want to be involved. If you aren't excited about your project, how can you expect the funder to be?

Remember that applying for grants can be very competitive, so try to make your application stand out. The Esmée Fairbairn Foundation, for example, receives approximately 2,000 grant applications every year, of which only one in ten are typically funded.[1]

Describe the need

As part of the application, you will need to explain why the project is important. An effective way of doing this is to describe a problem or issue within your school or a situation that needs to change. For example:

- Are your current resources old, inadequate and in need of updating?
- Is something broken and/or needs to be replaced?
- Do your school premises need to be improved?
- Has a lack of facility, service or activity been identified in your school?
- Is your school underperforming in a certain area?
- Has there been a rise in student numbers?
- Have there been changes in legislation or to the school curriculum to which you need to respond?
- Do you need to prepare your school for future changes in the educational landscape?

As well as discussing the issues relevant to your project, you may also want to inform the funder of the scale of the problem and what impact it is having on your school and wider community. For example:

- Is the problem impacting on exam results?
- Is a club under threat of closure?
- Will you have to reduce the number of school trips?
- Will you have to limit the range of subjects on offer?
- Is there a health and safety or safeguarding concern?

---

1 Esmée Fairbairn Foundation, *Guidance for Grant Applicants* (June 2019), p. 14. Available at: https:// esmeefairbairn.org.uk/apply-for-funding.

Aim to look at the problem from different viewpoints to offer a good all-round perspective on the issues involved – for instance, from point of view of students, teachers, parents, governors and other stakeholders. If you are seeking funding to replace a broken computer, for example, then consider the impact it is having on individuals, teams, the school and even the wider community.

Offer evidence

To back up your claims, you may need to provide evidence for the problem(s) described. The information you gather will depend on the nature of your project and what details you have available. However, you should aim to capture and highlight any relevant data from:

- Meeting minutes.
- School inspection reports.
- Governor reports.
- School audits.
- Risk assessments.
- Site surveys.
- Strategic school plans.
- Schools statistics (for literacy, numeracy, attainment, attendance, etc.).
- Student and parent and carer surveys.
- School letters (such as complaints or resignation letters).
- Review platforms (such as comments left on Parent View and other social media channels).

Parent View is an online platform which gives parents and carers the opportunity to tell Ofsted what they think about their children's school (although it is not designed to log complaints). Questions range from asking whether or not parents feel their children are safe at school to asking if they feel the homework set is appropriate for their age. You can access Parent View for free at: https://parentview.ofsted.gov.uk. Simply enter your school name and address to see the results, which will be available when enough parents have answered the questionnaire.

As well as gathering any existing evidence for the problems you have outlined, you may also need to gather fresh support. For example, you could:

- Carry out your own surveys and audits.
- Take photographic evidence of anything relevant.

- Sit in on lessons and take notes on any problems.
- Capture statements from key people.
- Carry out your own review by using business tools such as:
  - PESTEL analysis: This framework enables schools to look at the *political*, *economic*, *social*, *technological*, *environmental* and *legal* factors affecting the institution.
  - Process-mapping: This technique encourages users to take a holistic view of their organisation by encouraging them to map out and examine the processes used within the school.
  - SWOT analysis: This tool can help schools to strategically analyse the *strengths*, *weaknesses*, *opportunities* and *threats* relating to their organisation.

If you would like to gather wider evidence of the problem, you could:

- Research the issue. You can search for academic research on a variety of topics by using the search engine Google Scholar: https://scholar.google.co.uk.
- Review statistics and reports published by any relevant charities.
- Check out government statistics (locally, regionally and nationally).
- Read education green papers/white papers.

Define the outcomes

Most funders will want to learn about your intended outcomes in order to understand the overall difference that you would like to make. It's usually a good idea to give between three and five outcomes per project. Make sure that your goals are SMART: *specific*, *measurable*, *achievable*, *realistic* and *time bound*. Examples of a SMART outcome could be to help 100 students improve their knowledge of the Vikings over the autumn term or to enhance the visual appearance of your Key Stage 1 playground before the next school open day in January.

Aim to describe how your outcomes relate to the funder's own objectives, as they will generally have their own set of outcomes which they are working towards. Find out what is important to the grant-maker (ask questions if necessary) and justify how your project will help them to achieve their own objectives.

Discuss the project in further detail

As part of your application, you will also need to illustrate how you plan to achieve the desired outcomes, so the funder knows about any activities you intend to carry out and any purchases you intend to make. You will also need to think about:

- The location of your project.
- Staffing requirements.
- Health and safety.
- Financial planning.
- Legal aspects.
- Marketing and promotion.
- Contingency plans.
- Timescales.

Discuss the beneficiaries

Funders often request information about the people who will benefit from their funding, so be sure to clarify who the beneficiaries of your project will be and how many will benefit: will this be an individual, a group of people, a class, a department, the whole school or the local community? You may also like to summarise any supplementary information about the beneficiaries that you feel is relevant, such as their demographic characteristics, what similarities they share and why you want to help this group in particular.

If possible, try to provide a case study or capture a story to share with the funder to help them understand any issues the beneficiaries are facing. Never share personal information about the recipients (always anonymise names) and only include photographs if you have received prior consent. You should consult your school's data protection policy for further details.

Where possible, try to open up the project to as many people as you can. Not only is it important to promote inclusion and equality, but it is usually the case that the more people who will benefit from the project, the more successful your bid will be.

Confirm who has been involved in shaping the project

Funders like to learn about the individuals who have contributed to the project – they often favour applications which have engaged the beneficiaries. The National Lottery Community Fund, for example, is keen to support projects where the recipients are fully involved in the development, design, running and evaluation of the project, so let the funder know who has been involved and how they have contributed.

If you can, aim to position students at the centre of your project and always try to give them a voice, especially if the project is for their benefit. Explain to the funder how you have listened to your students, their parents and/or carers and any community groups that support them. There are lots of ways in which students can be engaged in a project – for example, they could suggest project ideas, help to run a club, draw up designs for your scheme or paint a mural for an outdoor learning space.

Funders also like to know that you have a good range of support for the project. This could include:

- Students (e.g. student council).
- Parents and carers (e.g. parent forum).
- Members of staff and subject coordinators.
- School governors.
- The PTA or friends group.
- Volunteers.
- Members of your alumni.
- Schools with whom you have collaborated.
- External advisors, subject matter experts and members of the wider community (e.g. consultants, experts from the local authority, businesses, the local mayor, charity ambassadors, legal experts).

There are lots of ways in which other people can potentially help to support your project, such as contributing ideas or donating their time, skills, expertise and/or resources.

Let the funder know if you have held meetings or established teams to work on the project. If you do organise any meetings, then make sure the minutes are recorded, as this will provide evidence of the meeting and the ideas discussed. It may also be useful to capture and record any direct quotes from individuals that you feel could be used to support your application. Don't forget to log any actions or contributions that people make too, as this can all be useful information to relay back to the funder.

Whoever you decide to involve in your project, make sure you surround yourself with a passionate, capable and energetic team, who are keen to work together to make a difference. Try to include a diverse range of people (from both inside and outside of the school) to offer their experiences, insights and perspectives on the matters discussed. Involve individuals who can challenge your ideas and strengthen your thinking. Remember that funders favour applications which demonstrate that they have the right people working on the project.

There are lots of reasons why having a strong and diverse team is important:

- It gives individuals the opportunity to be part of something that is going to make a difference to people's lives.
- It is a chance for you to connect with people who are equally passionate about the changes you are keen to make.
- It can help to raise awareness of your project and the issues concerned.
- It can help to make people feel included and that their voice is being heard and valued.
- The more helpers you have, the more you can potentially share the workload, and the quicker you can get things done.
- People can feel a sense of ownership if they have been involved with a project from the early stages. This can help you to implement the scheme more strategically – for example, students are more likely to use a club if their ideas have been used to create it.
- The more people who help, the bigger the pool of pride when the project is completed.

Explain why you are confident that your proposal will work

Funders like applications which demonstrate how the project will achieve its aims. They need to ensure that any grants they award will be used to make the greatest impact possible, so try to provide a convincing explanation to show how your project will work. For example:

- Let the funder know if you have trialled an idea prior to your application. Your project is more likely to win funding if you have successfully piloted the idea.
- Refer the funder to any case studies which evidence how a similar project has worked for other schools. This can help to demonstrate that your project is likely to succeed too.

- Capture any support you have from those who will benefit from the project and illustrate how keen they are for the project to be delivered.

- Summarise any supporting information provided by third-party professionals. For instance, sales reps may be able to provide information, statistics or evidence to help you communicate the value of the product or service.

It is also important to consider any risks which could potentially scupper your project, so let the funder know how you have attempted to identify and manage risks. For example:

- Communicate any risk assessments you have completed.

- Describe any due diligence you have carried out when choosing suppliers or service providers.

- Give particulars of any insurance plans you have organised.

- Provide details if you have consulted with any professionals about your project, such as legal experts or health and safety advisors.

- Describe any contingency plans you have put in place.

As well as describing how the project will work, the most successful applications also describe why the organisation is best placed to deliver it. You could provide information about yourself and your team, such as your skills, training, qualifications and any prior experience you have in managing a fundraising project. Funders also need to know that your organisation is properly set up and managed, so give them background information about your school. It can be useful to explain what policies and procedures you have in place (e.g. details about your finance policy or whether your PTA is registered with the Charity Commission) to give the funder reassurance that you are a professionally run organisation.

Communicate plans for monitoring and evaluation

Grant-makers need to feel confident that any projects they help fund will be managed responsibly, so you may like to describe how you will monitor and evaluate your project. Ideally, it will be assessed on an ongoing basis to determine whether or not the desired outcomes are being achieved, and to ensure that if a problem does emerge or the looked-for results are not being reached, then action will be taken.

Assuming that you are successful in obtaining funding, you will need to gather data during your project to keep track of progress. For example, if you are planning to offer students a new ten-week cooking course you could:

- Run Q&A sessions to gauge the students' level of learning.

- Invite participants to complete a self-assessment at the start and at regular intervals during the course to track progress.
- Take photographs of any work produced.
- Observe students in class and keep a record of their performance.
- Encourage students (and any helpers) to give regular feedback during the course.
- Monitor attendance levels to make sure numbers don't drop.
- Invite students to complete an evaluation form at the end of the course.

Once you have collected the information, the next challenge is to analyse and interpret it so that you can establish whether your project has achieved the desired outcomes. When interpreting the data, make sure to evaluate what is going well and what could be improved, as this can be used to guide your next steps (and even future projects).

To manage your relationship with the funder well, it is essential that you report back to them on a regular basis (or as contractually agreed). They need to see evidence that you are using their grant as agreed and learn about the progress you are making. Funders will usually stipulate how often they would like to be updated and what information they would like to be sent, so make sure you meet the criteria.

When communicating with funders, aim to share information in a clear, concise and professional way. Images can be a great way to demonstrate progress (where appropriate) and can often save a thousand words.

If any problems occur during the delivery of your project, or you identify something major that needs to be changed, then immediately inform the funder about this.

Confirm how you will acknowledge the grant

As part of the application, you will usually need to let the funder know in what ways you are willing to acknowledge their support. Not only are most grants awarded on the condition that they are publicised but it is also good manners to show your appreciation – and a great way to build a lasting relationship. As well as thanking the funder directly, aim to announce the grant publicly on social media or in the local press. If you plan to write a press release you may want to:

- Describe the grant.
- Thank the funder.
- Communicate the difference the grant will make.
- Describe the good work you intend to do.
- Raise awareness of the funder's work.

Depending on the project you could also publicise the grant by:

▪ Staging a grand opening ceremony or launch event.

▪ Arranging for students to write a thank-you letter or card.

▪ Thanking the funder on your social media channels.

▪ Writing a series of blogs (for a large project).

▪ Submitting an article to a recognised industry publication (e.g. *FundEd Magazine*).

▪ Updating your school website, blog/vlog, newsletter, app, indoor/outdoor noticeboards or TV/radio station.

▪ Acknowledging the funder in your school prospectus.

Make sure you keep the funder up-to-date with the positive messages you disseminate about them. When sharing information on social media, don't forget to tag the funder in your posts and use their Twitter hashtags, so they can see and retweet your messages. Also be sure to forward copies of any press releases to the funder as well as any press coverage you receive.

Most funders have a logo which they are happy for schools to use when publicising the grant – just email them to request a copy. Some funders even provide branded items to help grant recipients advertise the award, so find out if they have any resources that you can use.

Detail the finances

When writing your grant application, you will need to outline the project finances with the funder. Most grant-makers will want you to provide the following information:

▪ A breakdown of the costs.

▪ Confirmation of the total cost of the project.

▪ Copies of quotations (if appropriate).

When planning the budget, you will need to take into account costs such as:

▪ Salaries.	▪ Promotion.	▪ Consultancy fees.
▪ Training.	▪ Equipment.	▪ Teaching resources.
▪ Insurance.	▪ Utility costs.	▪ Volunteer expenses.
▪ Stationery.	▪ Activity costs.	
▪ Transport.	▪ Food and drink.	

Don't forget to consider any hidden costs, such as fees connected to anyone helping you write the grant application.

It is important to take time to plan the budget properly and avoid any potential over-sights. If you fail to allocate enough money for the project, then you may be unable to achieve your intended outcomes. Endeavour to break the project down into small steps and identify everything you need for it to be a success. If you are fundraising for an activity, for example, then ascertain everything you need to start it up, run it and close it down. Identify what the must-haves and the nice-to-haves are. It is essential that your costs are realistic and based on actual quotations.

Once you have calculated the cost of the project, you will need to decide how much money you are going to apply for. Be specific and let the funder know:

- The amount of money you are requesting.
- What the grant will be spent on.
- What your priorities are (in case they can't fund everything).

If you can claim back VAT, then you will not need to include VAT in your grant request. If you need help regarding VAT matters contact:

HM Revenue and Customs

www.gov.uk/government/organisations/hm-revenue-customs/contact/vat-enquiries

Most funders have a list of things they can and cannot fund, so make sure you read any guidance notes carefully to ensure they can fund everything you are requesting. Most grant programmes stipulate a minimum and maximum amount which applicants can apply for, so you should also ensure that your request is within this limit.

If you are applying for part funding, it can be useful to explain in your application how you plan to fund the rest of the costs. For example:

- Will the school contribute towards the project? If so, how much?
- Will the school PTA or friends group commit any resources?
- Will you be going for match funding? If so, from whom?

If you are applying to multiple funders, make sure you keep track of the amount you are requesting from each one and the outcomes of any decisions. Most funders (particularly the smaller ones) like to see evidence that you are applying to multiple funders. Not only can this increase the odds of success and the level of support you can achieve, but it can also make your project more financially secure and sustainable over the longer term.

Some funders favour applications where the school is contributing financially towards the project, as this shows you are serious about it. Other funders like to know that the school PTA or friends group is supporting the project, or require an explanation if this is not possible.

If you are successful in receiving an award, then remember that each grant should always be treated as a one-off, unless otherwise agreed with the funder. Therefore, if you intend to continue the project once the funding has come to an end, then you will usually need to explain how you plan to fund it in future.

Tips for writing a grant application

- Always follow the grant-maker's guidelines.
- Don't simply copy old applications. Each funder will have their own unique criteria and you will need to demonstrate how well you meet it.
- Don't overwhelm the funder with too much material. Only send quality information that is requested and relevant. Remember the acronym KISS: Keep It Short and Simple.
- Use subheadings to break up the text and use bullet points to list key ideas.
- Use facts, figures and evidence to support your application.
- Check that your finances add up.
- Avoid using jargon and acronyms such as SEND, KS1 and ICT without explanation; if you need to include acronyms then include a glossary.
- Make sure you complete the application form fully before sending it off or it may be rejected or sent back.
- Proofread your application. If possible, try to get someone else to check it too.
- Don't forget to save your work regularly as you go along.

Tips for writing a grant letter application

- Send your request on letterheaded paper and make sure that it is signed by the head teacher.
- Summarise your project and its goals, how much money you need and what difference the funding will make to the beneficiaries.
- Use the layout of your application to help grant assessors skim and review your request – for example, emphasise key words in bold, use subheadings and bullet points, and select a typeface like Times New Roman or Calibri that is clear to read.
- How long your letter should be will depend on the level of funding you are requesting. For amounts under £3,000 usually one to two sides of A4 paper is sufficient.
- When posting your letter, don't forget to include a stamped, self-addressed envelope to encourage the grant-maker to respond.

Part II

Fundraising for Specific School Projects

EMPLOYEE VOLUNTEERS

NOMINATION SCHEMES

CROWDFUNDING

FUNDRAISING EVENTS

FREE RESOURCES

PRODUCT DONATIONS

COMMISSION SCHEMES

GRANTS

MONEY-SAVING IDEAS

CLUBS

SPONSORSHIP

MATCH FUNDING

HIRE SCHEMES

SPORTS

FREE EDUCATIONAL SPEAKERS

Chapter 6
ICT projects

Information and communications technology can be a powerful tool for teaching and learning, with the potential to transform the way students learn. It can be used in all areas of the curriculum, offering new learning experiences and impacting on educational targets. With virtual reality, for example, students can explore the depths of the ocean, visit mountaintops, voyage into outer space and travel back in time to walk with the dinosaurs, all without leaving the safety of the classroom. Medical students can carry out virtual procedures on virtual patients before performing them for real. New technologies are enabling schools and universities to do more and more wonderful things.

ICT can also impact on other areas of the school. Teachers no longer have to travel lengthy distances to attend training courses because they can conveniently access online webinars. Administrators no longer have to spend hours typing up financial reports because they can be generated at the click of a button. Parents no longer have to take cash into the school office because payments for lunch, school trips and after-school clubs can be made online.

Funding is available for educational ICT projects. This is great news because ICT costs can represent one of the largest elements of a school's budget. Perhaps you want to:

- Run an after-school club for graphic design, video game design or coding.
- Introduce some digital signage into your reception area.
- Offer a distance learning course.
- Build a multimedia suite or robotics centre.
- Fund the salary of an ICT technician.
- Run an e-safety awareness session for parents and families.
- Purchase digital learning devices for every classroom.
- Offer virtual reality teaching.
- Introduce a more efficient library system.
- Invest in staff ICT training.
- Subscribe to a lesson planning app.
- Introduce digital technology for specific learner groups.
- Fund a new parent–teacher communication app.
- Run film-making or music production workshops.

- Purchase a 3D printer for your art and design department.
- Encourage students to engage in group projects by collaborating online from home.

Your ICT wish list could include:

- Digital cameras.
- Virtual reality headsets.
- Tablets or iPads.
- Laptops, netbooks or notebooks.
- Interactive whiteboards (smart boards).
- High-spec desktop computers.
- Apple Mac computers for music and creative arts projects.
- Green screen technology and film-making kits.
- Software.
- Printers (including 3D printers).
- Sound recording equipment.
- Projectors.
- Smartphones.
- Fitness trackers.
- Drones.
- Robotics kits.

Whatever your ICT project, there is a range of support available – grants, schemes, online initiatives and even competitions which schools can enter to help achieve their ICT ambitions.

Most schools have a strategic ICT plan which fundraisers should consult when tasked with a technology-related fundraising project. Every ICT strategy is unique, but it will usually describe the impact that technology is intended to have within the school, how it can be used to support teaching and learning, and how it should be integrated into the curriculum and across the school infrastructure. It may also include an inventory of the school's current ICT resources and a wish list of ICT equipment that the school would like to purchase (including a breakdown of key costs and budgets).

Aside from the range of ICT grants on offer, schools can also benefit from other support from technology-based companies. Sony, for example, is giving schools, colleges, universities and other local groups the opportunity to enjoy a tour of their manufacturing facility for free. This is great news for schools wishing to inspire the next generation of engineers, entrepreneurs and creative talent. A well-considered company site tour will deliver educational outcomes by linking to the national curriculum: be cautious of any offerings which seem more like a showcase of the company's products.

Sony UK Technology Centre
Pencoed Technology Park, Pencoed, South Wales CF35 5HZ
www.sonypencoed.co.uk/educational-visits
ukteceducationalvisits@sony.com
01656 860666
The Sony UK Technology Centre was opened by Her Majesty the Queen in 1992. The centre has won numerous awards and has been hosting regular school visits since 2012. All visits must be booked in advance. You can book a visit through their website.

Fundraising channels for ICT projects

As well as applying for grants, schools can also explore other fundraising channels to find out what equipment is available through websites such as Donate a PC. This is a free service for individuals and organisations who would like to donate unneeded IT equipment to good causes. The company aims to reduce landfill, promote reuse and help good causes. Items offered on this platform can include laptops, printers and scanners. Find out more at: www.donateapc.org.uk.

Schools and PTAs can also generate income using Rocket Fund, which is a non-profit crowdfunding platform specifically designed to help schools and PTAs fundraise for technology-related projects. It is completely free to post on the site and schools keep 100% of the donations. For more information visit: https://rocket.fund.

Did you know that BT is offering non-profit community organisations a free service that enables you to build and maintain a website? As part of the BT Community Web Kit, organisations receive free website hosting, website addresses, content templates and technical support. For more information visit: www.btck.co.uk/Default.aspx.

Is your school based near an Amazon fulfilment centre or does it have any connections with Amazon employees? Amazon employees can nominate schools to receive monetary and product donations such as Kindles and virtual reality headsets. Amazon have a range of fulfilment centres across England, Wales and Scotland (in Gourock, Dunfermline, Manchester, Doncaster, Leicester, Peterborough, Dunstable, Tilbury, Hemel Hempstead, Milton Keynes, Daventry, Coventry, Swansea and Rugeley). You can learn more about the Amazon in the Community programme at: www.aboutamazon.co.uk/amazon-in-the-community.

Pre-purchasing considerations

Before you consider making any IT purchases, here are some useful suggestions:

▤ Can you make better use of your existing resources? Schools should always maintain an up-to-date inventory (or asset register) as part of effective asset management, so check your inventory records to see if you can deploy your existing equipment more effectively. Perhaps you have perfectly serviceable computers which you could use for your new project sitting in a classroom somewhere collecting dust.

▤ Are you using your existing resources to their optimum level? How well do you know the equipment you already own? Are you getting the best out of your smartphones, for example – perhaps you can install better apps? Do you have any video cameras that also function as digital cameras, saving you the need to purchase these separately? Or will the cameras on your smartphones do the job? Can you make better use of your existing software? Find out about the equipment you already have and use it to its full potential. Even small, inexpensive gadgets come with a range of useful features, so have a look at what little treasures you already own and check what they are capable of. Why buy new equipment if your existing resources can do so much more? IT kit is only as good as the way it is used, so make sure that you invest in staff continuing professional development (CPD).

▤ Can you create an opportunity to collaborate with other schools? Is there a feeder school in your area which might be willing to share their 3D printer with you? Is there is a school in your teaching school alliance or learning network that could offer you time with their ICT expert? By collaborating with other schools you can create opportunities to share ICT resources and potentially save the costs of purchasing new equipment and services. For more information about school collaboration, see the research report *Effective School Partnerships and Collaboration for School Improvement: A Review of the Evidence*, published by the Department for Education.[1]

▤ Rather than purchasing new equipment outright, have you considered an operating lease instead? Items such as photocopiers, printers, computers, iPads and software can all be leased. Not only can this release you from the financial pressure of coming up with the capital outlay straight away, but it also relieves you of the costs of maintaining the equipment.

Schools can also help students to access cheaper computers. Axis Leasing, for example, run a programme called Laptops for Students, which aims to help bridge the home–school divide by enabling parents to enjoy better deals through bulk purchase and education pricing. For more details visit: www.axisleasing.com/services/laptops-for-students.

---

1 P. Armstrong, *Effective School Partnerships and Collaboration for School Improvement: A Review of the Evidence* (October 2015). Ref: DFE-RR466. Available at: www.gov.uk/government/publications/school-improvement-effective-school-partnerships.

Why not consider the services of an ICT consultant to help you stay up-to-date with the industry? Perhaps you could employ an in-house ICT technician or coordinator, especially if your school is large. There is even the potential to take on an apprentice to lower your costs, especially if your budget is tight. An ICT expert can help schools to stay well informed about industry developments, write ICT policies, use technology to its full potential and even access technology-related efficiency savings. They can also provide on-site support and expertise and even deliver in-house ICT training for staff (removing the cost of bringing in external training providers). If you do employ an ICT technician, don't forget to ask them to sign you up to a fundraising search engine and set up your shopping affiliate schemes (see Chapter 20).

You can also recruit student digital leaders by inviting older students to champion computing within your school. Digital leaders can help to support younger students, lend a hand at computer clubs, promote the responsible use of the internet, contribute to important ICT plans and help to support fundraising projects. Not only does this help them to build their transferable digital literacy skills, but it also enables teachers to focus on using technology to enhance learning outcomes.

Although purchasing new technology can seem like a costly upfront expense, in the long term the right purchase can be a great investment and can help your school to save money. Perhaps you have energy-hungry devices which you could replace with more efficient ones to reduce your ongoing energy costs? According to the Carbon Trust: 'UK schools could reduce energy costs by around £44 million per year which would prevent 625,000 tonnes of CO_2 from entering the atmosphere.'[2] Old monitors, desktop computers and servers, for example, can all be expensive to power, so audit your ICT equipment and identify any areas where you can reduce both costs and your carbon footprint. Flat-screen monitors, for instance, 'can reduce monitor energy use by over 65%'.[3] Perhaps you can get the students involved in recording the energy readings of your ICT devices. Some ICT companies offer free audits to help identify where efficiency savings can be made, so why not contact local companies and see what they can offer.

If you have an onsite server, then perhaps consider moving to cloud computing, where information is stored and managed at an offsite server and accessed through a web browser. This can reduce both your energy and maintenance costs.

---

2 Carbon Trust, *Schools: Learning to Improve Energy Efficiency* (March 2012), p. 3. Available at: www.carbontrust. com/media/39232/ctv019_schools.pdf.
3 Carbon Trust, *Schools*, p. 22.

Tips when purchasing ICT resources

When investing in new technology, always think things through carefully first as there will be lots of issues you will need to consider. For example, will staff and students need any training to use it? How will it be installed? Who will install it? Will the school website need to be updated? Will any school policies need to be revised? How will you plan for change as the technology evolves? Will your data be secure? Will the students be safe using it?

If you are concerned about online safety, why not get involved with Safer Internet Day? This takes place every year in February and is designed to promote safe, responsible and positive use of digital technology for children and young people. Get involved at: www. saferinternet.org.uk/safer-internet-day.

Always compare the energy ratings for any new products you intend to purchase. This is not only good for your long-term bank balance but it is also good for the environment. Replacing high-energy devices is one way in which schools can work towards the Eco-Schools National Awards. There is no cost to register your school as an Eco-School, but there is a charge of £200 (plus VAT) for a Green Flag assessor visit. Learn more about the Eco-Schools programme at: https://eco-schools.org.uk.

As well as thinking about any technology you need to purchase, it is also important to plan how it will be implemented across the school. The impact it has on learning will depend on how it is used. Allocate some time to finding out how teachers can incorporate the new technology into their lesson plans.

If you're not sure what IT kit you need, you could take a look at the products and resources that have been nominated for the Tech for Teachers award. This award celebrates the most innovative and effective technological products for teaching and learning in Key Stages 3 and 4 across a variety of curriculum-linked categories. Find out more at: www. teachwire.net/tech-for-teachers.

WonderHub is a useful online platform offering a range of teacher and parent reviews on a range of edtech products: http://wonderhub.co.uk.

If you need advice about the best technology to support learners with disabilities, then check out AbilityNet. This charity offers free support, factsheets, webinars and advice to help users with disabilities use digital technology in education, at work or at home: https://abilitynet.org.uk.

Aim to trial new hardware or software to ensure that it is suitable for your intended users and assess its compatibility with the other technology that you intend to integrate it with across the school. Always seek professional advice before entering into any contracts.

Technology shows and events

To help you keep abreast of technological trends and developments, it can be worthwhile attending technology-related events. Many events are free to attend and can offer networking, seminars, training and workshops. Some even allow you to try out the latest teaching technology. Various events run across the UK, so here is a list to help you on your way:

Bett Show (London): www.bettshow.com

Education Forum (Northamptonshire): https://education-forum.co.uk

EduTech Show (London): www.edutechshow.co.uk

School Equipment, Resources and Technology Show (Dublin): www.conorobrienevents.com

Have you heard of the magazine *Education Technology*? It is a monthly magazine and is free to view online. It features the latest edtech news, opinions and event reviews from across the education sector, including primary, secondary, further and higher education. Plus there are case studies, statistics and other useful pieces of information. Check it out at: https://edtechnology.co.uk/magazine.

Also check out Soft Egg's *School IT Blog* at: www.softegg.co.uk/blog, which offers a range of information on a variety of ICT-related topics.

Refurbished equipment

One way to reduce your outgoing costs is by purchasing refurbished rather than new equipment. For example, schools can access deals for refurbished photocopier-printers from In Kind Direct, a charity which distributes donated goods from major UK manufacturers and retailers and sells these on at low prices. There are only a small number of items available, depending on the stock that has been donated, so you may need to visit a few times to find what you're looking for. All devices come with full maintenance support. There is a one-off administration fee plus a quarterly maintenance fee per machine. Details and prices are displayed on their website and you can apply online. For full details visit: https://cat.inkinddirect.org/photocopiers.

In Kind Direct also partner with Office Depot to offer up to 80% off RRP on thousands of products for the office. For more details visit: www.inkinddirect.org/office-depot.

There are also lots of ICT recycling charities across the UK. These organisations collect redundant items and faulty equipment. They repair and refurbish where possible and then sell it on at low cost to schools, registered charities and other good causes. Not only can this help you to save money, but it also prevents thousands of products going to landfill each year. Here are some suggestions:

Computer Aid
1E Mentmore Terrace, London Fields, London E8 3DQ
www.computeraid.org/get-computers
info@computeraid.org
0208 361 5540
Supplies computers, tablets and mobile phones.

Computers for Charities
www.computersforcharities.org/lowcost
01323 848588
Supplies laptops and PCs. They also provide impartial IT advice and support.

Digital Growth – London's Computer Recycling
Unit B, Pegasus Works, 8–10 Roebuck Road, Hainault Business Park, Ilford, Essex IG6 3UF
www.londonscomputerrecycling.co.uk
0203 900 2562
Supplies IT equipment, including laptops, PCs, Apple Macs and printers.

IT for Charities have a really useful directory of almost 100 suppliers of low-cost IT equipment. You can find more at: https://itforcharities.co.uk/it-services/recycled-pcs.

Rural schools, individuals and community groups can purchase a refurbished computer for as little as £130 through the Computers for Rural People scheme. It is run by Germinate: The Arthur Rank Centre (in partnership with two other charities) and offers high-quality, internet-ready laptops and desktop computers which come pre-loaded with Microsoft software and a three-month warranty. Visit: https://germinate.net/mission/computers-for-rural-people.

Microsoft provide a directory for schools and organisations looking for professionally refurbished computers. All the PCs are pre-installed with Microsoft software. You can find an authorised Microsoft refurbisher at: www.microsoft.com/en-us/refurbishedpcs/buygenuine.

Schools can also apply to Microsoft's Showcase Schools programme. This is an initiative designed to reward schools which demonstrate a commitment to embracing technology to transform education and improve learning outcomes for students. Please note that it is only relevant to schools using Windows devices. For details visit: https://education.microsoft.com/school-leaders-toolkit/programs.

If you are purchasing hardware, check whether any of the devices you intend to buy come pre-installed with any software, as this can save you money. You can also research opportunities to purchase discounted software. For example, Entec Novare specialise in education software, networks, solutions and ICT services, which they sell at discounted rates: www.entec.co.uk.

Charity Digital Exchange is another supplier which gives eligible organisations the opportunity to access donations from leading technology companies, such as Adobe, Cisco and Symantec. This can offer schools huge savings on a wide range of products. It is free to register, although there is a small admin fee per donation taken. Organisations must have charitable tax exempt status to qualify for this scheme, so school friends groups or PTAs which are registered with the Charity Commission may apply. Please contact the organisation for more information: www.charitydigitalexchange.org.

There are also opportunities to collaborate with other schools, share knowledge of best practice, recommend vendors and discuss past experiences. Perhaps you can identify possibilities for joint purchases: by purchasing in larger volumes schools can enjoy greater buying power and negotiate better deals. Why not get involved with Twitter discussions to connect with other schools on technology projects?

If you need to purchase new equipment, then check out the Department for Education's approved frameworks for quality-checked suppliers at: www.gov.uk/guidance/find-a-dfe-approved-framework-for-your-school. The government has put together a range of purchasing frameworks to help schools save money through collective buying power. There are frameworks for a range of ICT solutions including networking equipment and support services; hardware, software and related services (including licensing); photocopiers, printers and scanners; and cloud computing services. All the frameworks offer a free quote tool, management support, a list of checked suppliers and pre-agreed terms and conditions. Government deals can be well worth a look: one local authority helped a school to achieve a saving of £100,000 on the original contract price.[4]

As well as using government frameworks, schools can access frameworks through the national Crescent Purchasing Consortium. The CPC is easy to join, free to use and it can help schools to save lots of money. Members can access over 50 framework agreements and receive free professional purchasing advice. Find out more at: www.thecpc.ac.uk.

Always buy responsibly. For help on managing your own procurement process, please see the government's advice on buying for schools at: www.gov.uk/government/collections/buying-for-schools. Don't forget to check with your local council too to see if there are any preferential rates you can access.

---

4 Department for Education, *Schools' Buying Strategy* (January 2017), p. 7. Available at: https://assets.publishing.service.gov.uk/government/uploads/system/uploads/attachment_data/file/585080/Schools_buying_strategy.pdf.

Technology-related grants

Before you begin applying for grants, check to see if your current IT supplier can offer any support. Some IT companies offer a free grant-finding service, so it's worth making some enquiries. For example, Soltech IT is an IT support company which assists schools and nurseries in Bristol and across the UK. Since 2014, they have helped schools to gain more than £705,000 of grant funding. Discover more at: www.soltechit.co.uk/school-ict-bursar-service.

You could also explore edtech suppliers that are affiliated with the British Educational Suppliers Association (BESA). These suppliers agree to BESA's Code of Practice and can be found at: www.besa.org.uk/guides-for-schools.

When applying for technology-related grants, it can be beneficial to let the funder know how the idea for your project originally came about – for example, did the student council request the new technology? If so, let them know.

Tell the grant-maker about any problems you have identified:

- Has your current ICT suite aged and so needs to be updated?
- Is your electronic hardware not performing to the standard you require and is in need of an upgrade?
- Are your PCs outdated and failing to deliver the service you require?
- Are you experiencing problems with your internet connectivity to the point that you are having to cancel lessons? Is it always slow and unreliable?
- Have students noticed a marked difference between the technology they have at home and the equipment they are given to use at school?
- Do other schools in your area have devices that you have not yet been able to introduce, and so your school is failing to keep up with the latest digital trends?
- Have student numbers been growing to the point that you now don't have enough IT resources to meet their needs?
- Are your energy bills too high, and do you believe that by upgrading to more energy-efficient equipment you will be able to bring down your long-term costs?
- Are your staff or students frustrated with out-of-date software?

Whatever issues you have identified, communicate this to the potential funder. In describing the problems, you will also want to describe your proposed solution, so be specific and let them know exactly what you need the funds for and what difference it will make to your school. Don't forget to ask your supplier for help too – they will be glad of the business! For example, sales reps can often provide an array of information to help you communicate your funding needs, such as brochures, case studies and reports. However, don't bombard the funder with too much information or technical jargon; only provide them with essential information that can assist with your application.

You might also like to give potential funders some background information on the students who will be using the new technology. Will it be aimed at improving the engagement of students with complex learning needs? Or perhaps you aim to offer students the opportunity to use digital devices they are unable to access at home? Give them some useful figures too: how many students will use the new technology, and how often will they use it? Let the funder know how the technology you intend to purchase will benefit your students and their educational prospects.

As part of your grant application, you may want to widen the benefits and tell the funder about any awards and accreditations you aim to work towards. These can also help to demonstrate how your school aims to embrace new technology and use it effectively. If your application is successful, don't forget to report back about any achievements the grant has helped you to secure. Not only is this good news for the funder, but it can also help you to build up a positive, long-lasting relationship with them.

Have you heard of the Naace Self-Review Framework? This tool helps schools to understand where they currently are in their technology strategy and to plan the next stages. There is an annual fee (currently £75) to access and use the online tool; however, schools then automatically become members of Naace and have access to key resources. Once schools have successfully completed the framework, they can also apply for the NaaceMark and the Third Millennium Learning Award. Both of these awards can offer additional recognition for your school and help you to celebrate achievements. For more information visit: www.naace.co.uk/school-improvement.html.

If you are working towards the Eco-Schools National Awards, and you are applying for a grant to replace high-energy devices, don't forget to let the funder know that this will contribute to your accreditation.

Here are some other ICT-related awards you could consider:

Best Use of Technology Award

www.isawards.co.uk

There are numerous categories in the Independent School Awards, including the Best Use of Technology Award, which recognises measurable excellence in the use of education technology by a school. Judges look for evidence that the technology has had a positive impact on the educational outcomes of students through its use inside or outside the classroom, supporting teaching and learning directly, or by easing the pressure on teachers and administrators.

Community Education Awards

www.communityeducationawards.co.uk/categories-and-individual-awards

The Community Education Awards recognise the valuable work that is undertaken in schools across the UK, especially those that deal with a range of vitally important social issues. There are lots of award categories, including the Internet Safety Award, Technology in Learning Award and STEM Innovation Award. Schools can enter for more than one award. To enter, simply fill out their brief online form.

Digital Schools Awards Scotland

www.digitalschoolsawards.co.uk

Digital Schools Awards Scotland is a national awards programme which aims to promote, recognise and encourage a whole-school approach to the use of digital technology in primary and secondary schools. The programme is supported by industry partners HP, Microsoft and Intel. Counterpart schemes are run in Northern Ireland and the Republic of Ireland.

Nursery World Awards

www.nurseryworldawards.com

Early years providers – including nurseries, schools, pre-schools and child-minders – whose website and use of social media is informative, accessible and innovative can enter the Online and Social Media Award. To apply, you will need give a brief description (approximately 400 words) and provide supporting evidence – for example, web traffic, brief testimonials from parents and photographic evidence.

TES Awards: Innovative Use of Technology to Influence Outcomes Award

www.tesawards.co.uk

This award recognises measurable excellence in the use of technology by a teacher or a school. Judges look for evidence that the technology has had a positive impact on the educational outcomes of students. School must supply any relevant data and case studies.

As well as applying for ICT awards and accreditations, schools can align fundraising projects with competitions and challenges. If you need funding to run a new after-school computer coding club, for example, then inform potential funders about how within this club you also aim to offer students the opportunity to participate in external competitions. While most challenges are just for fun, some competitions also offer prizes – which can be great news for both your students and your school!

Here are some ICT-related competitions and challenges that schools can enter:

Bebras International Challenge on Informatics and Computational Thinking

www.bebras.org

Bebras is an international initiative aiming to promote informatics (computer science) and computational thinking among school students of all ages. The emphasis is on participation, but top-performing students are awarded certificates of merit, distinction and so on.

British Informatics Olympiad

www.olympiad.org.uk

The British Informatics Olympiad is a national computing competition for schools and colleges. It aims to encourage students to take an active interest in information technology, and to meet and exchange ideas, through a challenging competition in computer programming.

FXP Festival Competition

http://fxpfestival.com

FXP Festival is a computer and mobile games design and development competition for school and college students. The competition is linked to the computer science curriculum and provides young people with an insight into what careers are on offer in the creative digital industry. The festival has two competition categories and there is a maximum of 60 spaces available to schools and colleges across East Anglia.

Grok Learning Competition

https://groklearning.com/upcoming

Grok Learning runs a number of competitions to help school students and teachers learn computer coding and web design. Check out their website for further details. The website has a useful teachers' resources section too.

Jack Petchey Foundation – Vlogstar Challenge

www.jackpetcheyfoundation.org.uk/vlogstar-challenge-0

The Vlogstar Challenge is open to 16–25-year-old vloggers from youth organisations and schools in London and Essex. The 150 semi-finalists spend a day receiving expert tuition and mentoring at YouTube's HQ in London, while the 15 finalists get to enjoy time at the company's state-of-the-art production space. The winner receives £2,000 for their school or organisation, £500 worth of equipment and one-to-one mentoring from YouTube experts.

Perse Coding Team Challenge

https://persecoding.net

UK secondary schools can enter this national competition. Teams of four students in Years 7 to 11 compete against each other in a one-hour team coding challenge. Winners receive prize money and the Braben Cup.

Raspberry Pi Competition

www.paconsulting.com/events/raspberry-pi-competition

This competition sees teams of schoolchildren show off their creativity and coding. It is open to participants from primary schools to sixth forms who compete in age-banded categories.

Technovation Challenge

https://technovationchallenge.org

The Technovation Challenge is open to teams of girls aged 10–18 from across the world who have solved a real-world problem using technology. The teams identify a problem in their community, create a mobile app solution to address the problem, and then learn how to communicate these ideas and translate them into a fully launched business.

Printers and consumables

Some suppliers run schemes to help schools access printers with minimum outlay. Here are a couple of examples. Always make sure you read the fine print and seek expert advice before entering into any contract.

Printers for Schools' Free Colour Printer Scheme

www.printersforschools.co.uk

Schools get to receive a free colour printer; however, to qualify for the scheme you must agree to keep the printer for three years. Schools must also purchase consumables from Printers for Schools (prices are available on their website), although they offer to price match these if you find can find them cheaper from another retailer. Schools can also request a free trial.

Soltech IT

www.soltechit.co.uk/lease-printers-for-education

Soltech IT offers educational establishments the opportunity to lease high-end printers for £1 a month, with a minimum contract of just three months.

Once you have your new printer set up, here are some quick tips to help you save money on printing, ink and paper supplies:

- Always encourage users to select 'Print Preview', especially when printing direct from a website, as the page will often be spread out over multiple sheets.
- Always print on both sides of the paper whenever possible. Ask your IT person to set your default settings to 'Duplex' (if your printer has this feature) or define the printer settings manually. Not only can this halve your paper costs but it also helps to save trees and waste.
- Always print in 'Draft' mode when you can, as this saves ink and prints quicker.
- Be ink-onimcal! Printing in black and white is much cheaper, so only print in colour when necessary. Again, try to set black and white as your default setting.
- Be savvy with the fonts you use: why use Tahoma if Times New Roman can help to save your school over £100 a year? For tips on choosing an appropriate font, see the

Staples guide on using your printer more frugally: www.staples.co.uk/knowledge-centre/features/how-much-could-your-business-save-by-switching-fonts.html.

▨ When it comes to paper thickness, remember that thicker paper is usually more expensive, so only print on high-quality paper when you need it. For daily use, 80 gsm is usually adequate.

▨ Most printers come with administrative controls, so aim to set print quotas for students and departments to help you stay within budget.

Virtual and augmented reality in education

More and more schools are fundraising to introduce virtual reality teaching into the class-room. This can transform the way students learn, but it doesn't have to be expensive to implement. Have you heard of Google Cardboard? Google has developed a simple, low-cost virtual reality cardboard viewer that anyone can build or buy. Schools can either buy a kit or download instructions to make their own at: https://vr.google.com/cardboard.

There is also lots of free virtual reality content on the internet – for example:

Discovery Education: www.discoveryeducation.co.uk/discoveryvr.

YouTube: www.youtube.com. Simply type in what are looking for and add 'VR 360' at the end (e.g. 'Ancient Egypt VR 360').

You can also download the free Google Expeditions app which is available on both Android and iOS: https://play.google.com/store/apps/details?id=com.google.vr.expeditions.

To introduce virtual reality into the classroom, check out *A Guide to VR & AR in Education* at: www.classvr.com/download/whitepaper-a-guide-to-ar-vr-in-education. Note that you will need to sign up to their mailing list to access this download.

Funding opportunities

Aviva Community Fund
https://community-fund.aviva.co.uk
The Aviva Fund is a funding competition which offers grants of up to £25,000.

BBC Children in Need
Grants, PO Box 649, Salford M5 0LD
www.bbcchildreninneed.co.uk
pudseygrants@bbc.co.uk
0345 609 0015

Applicants can apply to their Small Grants programme, which can potentially award up to £10,000 for three years.

Clothworkers' Foundation

Clothworkers' Hall, Dunster Court, Mincing Lane, London EC3R 7AH

https://foundation.clothworkers.co.uk

Special schools can apply to the Open Grants Programme for digital and audio visual equipment. The Small Grants programme offers grants of up to £10,000, but there is no maximum amount for the Main Grants programme. The average grant is £25,000.

Ford Britain Trust

1/623, Ford Motor Company Limited, Eagle Way, Brentwood, Essex CM13 3BW

www.ford.co.uk/fbtrust

fbtrust@ford.com

The Ford Britain Trust was created in April 1975. It offers grants for projects focusing on education, the environment, children, people with disabilities and youth activities. In particular, they are keen to help projects close to their UK locations. They offer two types of grants: small grants (offering up to £250) and large grants (of up to £3,000). Non-fee-paying and state-maintained schools are eligible to apply.

Further reading

Digital technology in education:

Higgins, S., Xiao, Z. and Katsipataki, M. (2012) *The Impact of Digital Technology on Learning: A Summary for the Education Endowment Foundation*. Available at: https://larrycuban.files. wordpress.com/2013/12/the_impact_of_digital_technologies_on_learning_full_report_2012.pdf.

Luckin, R., Bligh, B., Manches, A., Ainsworth, S., Crook, C. and Noss, R. (2012) *Decoding Learning: The Proof, Promise and Potential of Digital Education* (London: Nesta). Available at: www.nesta.org.uk/publications/decoding-learning.

Ofsted (2011) *ICT in Schools 2008–2011: An Evaluation of Information and Communication Technology in Schools in England 2008–2011* (December). Ref: 110134. Available at: www.gov. uk/government/uploads/system/uploads/attachment_data/file/181223/110134.pdf.

Scottish Government (2015) *Literature Review on the Impact of Digital Technology on Learning and Teaching* (November). Available at: http://dera.ioe.ac.uk/24843/1/00489224.pdf.

Cloud computing:

Department for Education (2017) *Cloud Computing Services: Guidance for School Leaders, School Staff and Governing Bodies* (January). Ref: DFE-00157-2016. Available at: www.gov.uk/ government/publications/cloud-computing-how-schools-can-move-services-to-the-cloud.

ICT leasing agreements:

Department for Education (2017) *Leasing and Subscription Services for School Equipment: Guidance for School Leaders, School Staff and Governing Bodies* (January). Ref: DFE-00042-2017. Available at: www.gov.uk/government/publications/school-procurement-buying-a-multi-functional-device-mfd.

One IT Services and Solutions (2015) *Printing Lease and Management Software Advice for Schools.* Available at: www.oneitss.org.uk/wp-content/uploads/2015/10/Printing-Advice-for-Schools_R2-1.pdf.

To access further research and publications for ICT and technology visit:

British Educational Suppliers Association: www.besa.org.uk/insights/?category=research (Note: this is a subscription service.)

National Foundation for Educational Research: www.nfer.ac.uk/publications-research (Note: you can filter by subject to look specifically at the resources that relate to ICT.)

Chapter 7

School libraries and author visits

Despite the many benefits that a school library can bring, there is no statutory require-ment for schools to have a library. As well as supporting the curriculum, a good library can encourage students to complete their homework, read for pleasure, foster a love and appreciation for books and inspire them to become lifelong readers.

A school library can also provide a hub for learning, reading and collaboration, and sym-bolise a school's commitment to promoting independent learning and reading. Not least, a library can be a very welcoming and attractive space within the school environment.

However, many school libraries are facing cuts or closure, or are being replaced by ICT suites. Schools may be happy to know, therefore, that there is support on offer in areas such as:

■ Building a new school library.

■ Giving your existing library a makeover.

■ Increasing the space in your existing library.

■ Purchasing new books or resources.

■ Buying furniture.

■ Buying new ICT equipment.

■ Training a school librarian.

■ Purchasing a licence for a library management system.

■ Promoting the library and running literary events.

■ Running author-related events, including attracting authors to visit the school.

To ensure the success of your library fundraising project, there are a number of issues that you will need to consider. If you plan to create a new library, for instance, then first you will need to identify how your school would like to use the library and who will use it. For example:

■ Will it be used for class visits, independent reading, group interventions, story time, group study, one-to-one reading, homework sessions, author visits, reading games or surfing the internet?

■ What student year groups and classes will use it?

■ What are the needs of your students (e.g. SEND students or students with EAL)?

Once you have assembled this information, you can then start to ask:

- What types of resources will you need and how many (e.g. fiction books, non-fiction books, foreign language books, braille books, large print books, audiobooks, sensory books, magazines, comics, language CDs and DVDs)?
- Will you need any ICT resources (e.g. computers with internet access, library management software, photocopiers, scanners)?
- How will you decorate the room? Will you invite the children to suggest a theme for the room (e.g. jungle, enchanted forest, outer space)? Try to create an exciting entrance so the children have a positive first impression of the room and feel they are being transported into a magical world!
- What furniture and props will you need (e.g. bookshelves, tables, chairs, desk for the librarian, rugs for the children to sit on)?
- How will the room be organised? Do you need a separate area for Key Stage 1 students and an area with a more grown-up feel for older students, for example? Will you have a dedicated computer area?
- What services will you offer? Will you employ a librarian and will they sell stationery or offer other services?

You will also need to think about how you are going to organise your books and label your shelves. Will you use a formal library classification system (e.g. Dewey, Library of Congress)? Or will you categorise books by year groups and subject areas? Will you have a teacher section and a reference section? Will you separate fiction and non-fiction? Remember that it's useful to shelve books lower down for younger children to make it more accessible to them and to place books for teachers higher up.

Library management is another issue you will need to consider. Will you use an electronic system for checking books in and out? Will teachers manage this process for each class? Who will supervise the library before and after school and at lunchtime? Will you schedule weekly class visits to encourage students to use the library on a regular basis?

You will also need to think about:

- What space you have available.
- Whether there is anything you have that you can reuse for this project (e.g. books, computers, furniture).
- How you would like the room to be decorated.
- What cleaning, repairs and maintenance will need to be done.
- What training you will offer users and librarians.

- How you will promote the library on an ongoing basis.
- Any ongoing costs (e.g. salary, events, books).

You might like to call upon the expertise of a library designer or supplier to help you plan and install your library. Many offer a free design service, helping you to make the best use of the available space and even suggesting ideas you may not have considered. Suppliers' websites often include case studies, news updates, resources and other useful information. Some companies also provide catalogues and brochures on request, which can be useful for sharing ideas with staff. You can find a list of school library suppliers at the British Educational Suppliers Association website: www.besa.org.uk/supplier.

If you would like to introduce library resources to support SEND students, then take a look at the guidance offered by the Royal National Institute of Blind People: www.rnib.org.uk/services-we-offer-advice-professionals-education-professionals/education-resources.

Don't forget that image sites like Pinterest can provide lots of thrifty ideas for your school library scheme. Simply enter keywords such as 'school library, design, display, makeover' and you can access lots of creative ideas from all around the world. Some schools have even converted old double-decker buses to house their school libraries! Pinterest can also be used as a collaboration tool for capturing and sharing ideas with other people. Simply create a group board and then invite colleagues to add to it, pooling your ideas as you go along.

If you need new furniture for your school library, then aim to buy from a company that will dispose of your old furniture in a sustainable and environmentally friendly way. For example, Zoot Educational Furniture gives schools (and other educational institutions) the opportunity to buy new and used (discounted) furniture and equipment: www.zooteducationalfurniture.co.uk.

You may also want to consider employing a librarian to manage your library. You could recruit student librarians or adult volunteers: as well as giving them useful experience it can be great for their CV. You could advertise opportunities internally via your school newsletter or externally. You could also post volunteer opportunities on the Do-it website: https://do-it.org. This useful platform is free to use and reaches 250,000 people every month.

Don't forget that school volunteers will need an enhanced DBS (Disclosure and Barring Service) check if they are volunteering more than once a week or on four days within a 30-day period. As long as the volunteer does not directly benefit from the position there is no charge for the DBS check, although there is a small administrative fee. For more information visit: www.gov.uk/government/organisations/disclosure-and-barring-service.

If you are considering recruiting a professional librarian, then the following websites may be helpful:

- To find more out about the job, including duties, salary expectations, qualifications and so on, see the *TES*'s advice on becoming a school librarian: www.tes.com/articles/becoming-a-school-librarian.

- If you are also a member of the National Literacy Trust, then check out their e-learning Foyle Primary School Library Course at: https://literacytrust.org.uk/programmes/love-our-libraries.

Stay tuned in to what is happening as part of National Libraries Week in October. There are lots of initiatives your school could get involved with: www.librariesweek.org.uk.

Whatever the nature of your project, consult your school library policy as this will set out the school's vision, aims and objectives. If you need help writing a policy, then contact your local Schools Library Service. They can offer a range of help, from recommending suppliers to informing you about any funding opportunities available. They may even know of opportunities to share the costs of employing a librarian with other schools. You can find the details for your local Schools Library Service at: www.sla.org.uk/branches.

Here are some other useful websites to help you create the perfect school library:

Designing Libraries

www.designinglibraries.org.uk
This website provides resources to help with planning and designing your library. It offers a searchable database of new and refurbished libraries in the UK, plus there are case studies, links to suppliers and additional resources.

Primary School Library Guidelines

http://primaryschoollibraryguidelines.org.uk
Here you will find a wealth of information to help you design your library space, plan your budget, write school librarian job descriptions, purchase books, develop policies and more.

School Library Association

www.sla.org.uk
The SLA provide a wealth of information and resources, including publications, book reviews, training information, details of library awards, guidelines, case studies and more. There is also a blog to help schools stay up-to-date.

Schools can also contact their local public library for help, some of which run free general workshops for schools.

There may be a number of things you need to make your project a reality, so perhaps you could invite members of the local community to offer their support.

▩ Would parents and teachers be willing to donate books or help with tasks such as repairing or colour-coding books?

▩ Can your students suggest ideas, paint a mural for your library wall or volunteer as student librarians?

▩ Would local booksellers and other businesses be prepared to support your project by donating products, skills or funding? You could even create a sponsorship proposal where, in return for their support, you agree to name your library after them. You could then invite them to open the library at a grand launch event!

To raise money for your library project you could organise a book-related fundraising activity. Not only can this be lots of fun, but many grant-giving trusts like to support organisations that take the initiative to fundraise for themselves. Here are 10 ideas to get you started:

1. Hold a second-hand book sale. You could sell off any unwanted books and invite students, parents and staff to donate books for your sale too. Maybe you could also sell bookmarks and refreshments at the event.

2. Arrange a sponsored readathon. Not only can this put the fun into fundraising, but it can also encourage students to read more!

3. Hold a family reading breakfast. Invite parents and carers to join their child for breakfast and share and discuss stories.

4. Organise a book-to-film movie night. Pick a famous film based on a book and enjoy a movie night in your school library. You could charge an entry fee and generate an income from selling popcorn and drinks.

5. Host a book fair in the school library. Lots of children's and young adult publishers offer this service, bringing in books that the students can buy. Maybe you could hold these once a term and even get students involved in running them.

6. Have a book-themed dressing-up day. Invite students to come to school dressed up as their favourite literary character and charge them a set fee or invite them to make a donation. Not only do students love coming to school in non-uniform, but it can also raise awareness of literature. For maximum impact you could hold it on World Book Day.

7. Host a story evening. Invite the children to come back into school in their pyjamas, read bedtime stories and enjoy milk, hot chocolate and snacks. You could charge an entry fee and maybe even run a competition for the best-dressed teddy bear!

8. Invite a book-selling company into school. Find a mobile book company who can bring their books and organise a sale for students and parents. You can generate income by earning a sales commission.

9. Host a book swap party. Ask students, parents and staff to bring in a book to swap. Any leftover books can be donated to your library.

10. Organise a raffle or auction. Contact local authors to see if they are willing to donate signed copies of their books to support your project.

Schools can also raise money through the following methods:

The Book People's School Fundraising Scheme

www.thebookpeople.co.uk/departments/schools/school-fundraising/about

Schools can earn around 10% commission (and other rewards) on any sales they help to generate for the Book People. When your supporters shop online, they simply enter a unique fundraising code at the checkout to register the sale to your school. Schools can also request a catalogue, which can be useful for teachers.

Read For My School

http://uk.readformyschool.com

This organisation helps schools to fundraise by running online reading challenges. Schools can access a range of support including webinars and other useful resources to make their fundraiser a success. It is free and easy to set up an account. The organisers take a small service fee based on the donations received.

You could also produce your own school book to sell. Not only can this be a good fundraiser, but it can also promote reading and writing – and help you to meet the requirements of the national curriculum. It is a great way to get students actively involved in your project, and it can be very satisfying for students (and their families) when they see their own work published in a book.

Here are some book publishing schemes for fundraisers:

The Cookbook Initiative

www.thecookbookinitiative.com

Schools, PTAs and other fundraisers can create their very own professional cookbook through The Cookbook Initiative. Simply register online and receive a free starter pack to help you raise awareness and invite students and parents to submit recipes and photos (a minimum of 30 recipes is required). The school can then proofread the recipes, personalise the front page, write a foreword and add sponsors' details. There is no upfront payment required and you only pay on ordering. Prices vary between £4.90 and £6.10 a book, depending on the quantity ordered, plus there is a £15 delivery fee. So if, for example, you ordered 200 books at £4.90 each and sold them for the recommended retail price of £8.50 each, you would raise £705 for your school!

Scholastic's We Are Writers

https://writers.scholastic.co.uk

This scheme offers children the opportunity to see their writing in a book that is co-published with Scholastic. Any school within the UK can sign up and create their own online book. Schools receive a sample book, and then students and their families can buy their own copies. The books are priced at around £5.99, although schools can sell these at a higher price to raise money. Schools also receive Scholastic Rewards for every book sold.

If you are looking for a simple way to refresh your book collection, you could set up a book exchange area in your library and invite students to bring in books from home to swap. You could also set up a scheme to swap books with other schools. This is a resourceful option because both schools and students benefit.

If you have any books that you no longer need and can't sell, don't forget that these can't be recycled with the usual waste paper (because of the glue used to bind them). However, schools may be able to recycle their books using a local recycling scheme. For example, Cash 4 Clothes, which operates in the north-east of England, collects books from schools (which receive 5p per kilo). Find out more at: http://cash4clothinguk.co.uk.

To source books and other resources for your school library, you could also post a message on local Facebook groups or one of the many giveaway websites, such as Freecycle: http://uk.freecycle.org. Items on Freecycle are free and it is a great way to save perfectly good items from going to landfill.

Some suppliers also sell pre-owned books which can be a low-cost way of updating your library. Suppliers of second-hand books include:

Better World Books Limited: https://cares.betterworldbooks.co.uk/category/book-donations

Book Junction: www.book-junction.co.uk

Some bookstores (and even publishers) are willing to donate books which can be used to build up your school library collection or passed on as raffle prizes. It is always worth contacting local book companies and inviting them to support your cause.

Schools can also earn free books by hosting a book fair. Schools can either organise their own book fair by partnering with a local book supplier, or register to take part in an existing book fair scheme. When choosing a company, check what books, resources and display materials they can provide and whether or not staff will be on hand to help out. You should also compare what commission rates and titles are on offer. Most book fair companies offer schools a commission on every book sold, which can be spent on books from their back catalogue.

Here are some book fair schemes:

The Book People Book Fair

www.thebookpeople.co.uk/departments/schools/book-fairs/home

As well as running a School Fundraising Scheme, the Book People can also supply your school with over 150 books to run your own book fair. Simply pick a date and they will send you an organiser's pack. They will then arrange for the delivery and collection of the books (these can be for children or adults). Schools can earn up to 25% commission to spend on books.

Scholastic Book Fair

https://bookfairs.scholastic.co.uk

Scholastic provide schools with everything they need to host a book fair, from free resources to over 200 books. Every book sold at your school can help you to earn free books for your school.

Usborne Book Fair

https://usborne.com/books-for-schools

If you host an Usborne book fair, the company offers up to 60% of the total value of your order in extra free books.

Usborne also run a scheme called the Usborne Community Book Pledge, through which they fundraise for new books on your behalf. With your school's permission, an Usborne organiser can contact local businesses to invite them to make a small donation to help you buy Usborne books for your school. It is really easy to arrange and the organisers take care of everything from pledge letters and posters to collecting donations and delivering books to school. All schools have to do is contact them to set this up. For more details visit: https://usborne.com/books-for-schools/how-it-works/fundraising-for-books.

Did you know that you can fundraise for your school while also fundraising for another cause? Through the Read for Good scheme, schools can raise money for children in hospital while earning free book vouchers for themselves. Students take part in a sponsored readathon, with the sponsor money used to fund books and storyteller visits for your local children's hospital. Schools also receive book vouchers (worth 20% of the amount raised) to be spent at Scholastic Book Clubs. Schools can order a free kit online. Find out more at: http://readforgood.org.

Students can also enter competitions to win prizes for themselves and their school. Here are some competitions which students may like to enter:

BBC's 500 Words competition

www.bbc.co.uk/programmes/p00rfvk1

This competition is aimed at children in the UK aged 5–13 years who have written a story in 500 words or less. The children win prizes for themselves and 500 books for their school library.

National Book Tokens Competitions

www.nationalbooktokens.com/schools

This competition offers one lucky winner the chance to win £5,000 of book tokens for their school (enough to buy 100 books for their library!). The winner also gets £100 of National Book Tokens to spend on themselves.

Also see what competitions are listed on World Book Day's Competitions page at: www. worldbookday.com/play-and-win/competitions.

Students can also receive free books through the following book gifting programmes:

National Literacy Trust Young Readers Programme

https://literacytrust.org.uk/programmes/young-readers-programme

The National Literacy Trust gives books to children in disadvantaged areas. Through a series of fun events, they get the opportunity to choose new books which they can take home and keep.

Scottish Book Trust Bookbug Programme

http://scottishbooktrust.com/bookbug

The Scottish Book Trust awards four free book bags to every child in Scotland from birth to Primary 1.

E-books are usually cheaper to buy than print books, so if you would like to develop a virtual library collection there are lots of digital books that schools can access. Here are some websites offering free e-books:

Amazon: www.amazon.co.uk (for Kindle)

Kids World: www.kidsworldfun.com/ebooks.php

Oxford Owl: www.oxfordowl.co.uk/for-home/find-a-book/library-page

Schools can also listen to free audiobooks at:

Storynory: www.storynory.com

Schools can find a range of other free online resources to help develop a library and organise reading activities. You can find lesson plans, reading notes, activities, story packs and more at:

National Literacy Trust: https://literacytrust.org.uk/free-resources

Oxford University Press: https://global.oup.com/education/children/more/librarians/?region=uk

TES: www.tes.com/teaching-resources/blog/english-love-your-library (there is a small charge for some of the recommended resources)

For a list of volunteer readers schemes and other support, please see the information about English/literacy projects in Chapter 16 (pages 163–164).

If you would like to introduce a computerised library management system, then your first point of contact should be your local School Library Service. They should be able to advise on the best systems and may have information on deals which schools can access. Not only can school library software help to reduce the amount of time staff spend on administration, but it can also help you track your physical library resources. Many suppliers of educational software are willing to give free demonstrations, if requested.

Once your library project is up and running there are numerous awards for which schools can be entered. Not only is it nice to win an award, but some give away prizes too!

Here are some awards and competitions that recognise school book fairs, libraries and librarians:

Book Fair Takeover School of the Year Award
https://bookfairs.scholastic.co.uk/takeover/competition
Scholastic encourages schools to hand over the reins of the book fair to the students by arranging a Book Fair Takeover. They offer an award for the best student involvement. This competition is open to children and young people aged 18 years and under.

Pupil Library Assistant of the Year Award
www.libpupilaward.co.uk
This award recognises the contribution made by students who work in their school library. The winner receives a prize for themselves and for their school.

School Library Association Inspiration Award
www.sla.org.uk/inspiration-award
This award is given to the school library space that shows the most inspiration, innovation, creativity and resourcefulness in its design and use. It is ideal for schools that have refurbished their library or built a brand new one. The award runs every two years and winners are presented with a financial prize.

School Library Association School Librarian of the Year Award
www.sla.org.uk/school-librarian-of-the-year-award
This award is open to both primary and secondary schools. It is a fantastic way to raise awareness of the excellent work your school has done.

Author visits

It can be a rewarding and enjoyable experience to invite a writer, poet, illustrator or storyteller to visit your school to meet the students, promote reading and increase their literary knowledge. Before you organise an author visit, you will need to decide on its purpose. Do you want to inspire the children to read by inviting in a well-known author or local poet? Is there a particular book you would like your literary visitor to discuss? Do you need them to link the visit to areas of the national curriculum?

Whoever is on your wish-list, allow plenty of time to arrange the visit – try to plan six to twelve months in advance as many authors get booked up early. Popular authors are also in demand around World Book Day and National Book Week, so take this into account when organising the visit.

To find an author, you could search online and contact them via their website or social media channels, or get in touch with them via their publisher and/or literary agent (if they have one). To find authors in your area, you could ask your local bookstore or library for help. It could also be worth asking around, as perhaps a member of your school community may have connections with a local author.

Here are some organisations that can help to put you in contact with writers, poets, illustrators and storytellers:

Contact an Author: www.contactanauthor.co.uk

Edinburgh International Book Festival school outreach programme: https://learning.edbookfest.co.uk/schools/outreach

National Association of Writers in Education: www.nawe.co.uk/professional-directory.html

Poetry Society: https://poetrysociety.org.uk/education/poets-in-schools

Scottish Book Trust: www.scottishbooktrust.com/learning/live-literature-programme/apply-for-author-visits

Windows Project: www.windowsproject.co.uk/school-bookings

You can also arrange an author visit through agencies such as:

Apples and Snakes: https://applesandsnakes.org/book-a-poet

Authors Aloud UK: https://authorsalouduk.co.uk

Speaking of Books: www.speakingofbooks.studysupport.info

Many authors charge a fee to visit, and if you have any additional requirements – for example, if you would like them to provide posters to promote the event or to be available for photographs on the day – then there may be extra costs.

You can also find free downloadable teaching resources (including lesson plans, posters and activities) online. See for example:

Beatrix Potter: www.peterrabbit.com/adults

David Walliams: www.worldofdavidwalliams.com/schoolzone

Michael Morpurgo: www.michaelmorpurgo.com

Roald Dahl: www.roalddahl.com/create-and-learn

To cover the costs of the author visit you could:

- Apply a per-student charge to cover the fees (if appropriate for your school).
- Contact other schools in the local area to find out if they would also like a visit as there may be an opportunity to reduce costs – for example, some authors are willing to offer multiple school discounts. You could also contact local book clubs, community centres or libraries.
- Instead of an actual visit, you could request a virtual visit with the author using a free voice and video tool such as Skype.

If you are happy to have a virtual visit, then take a look at the Virtual Authors website: www.virtualauthors.co.uk. It offers an online directory of children's authors and illustrators who are prepared to offer Skype sessions to UK schools. Some authors are willing to offer chats of 15–20 minutes for free.

You will need to agree in advance what the author will do during the visit – for example:

- Read the children a book.
- Run a writing or drama workshop.
- Participate in a Q&A session.
- Sign copies of their books.
- Be available for photographs.

If you intend to photograph or record the event or invite the press, then be sure to seek approval from the author first.

If you would like to offer students the opportunity to purchase the author's books, then you will need to decide whether or not to sell these in advance or on the day of the visit. You will also need to make a decision about where to source the books – for example, will the author bring along copies to sell or will you contact the publisher, a local bookstore or a wholesaler? Most suppliers are prepared to give schools a discount, especially if you are purchasing a large quantity, so don't be afraid to ask. Some authors are also happy to donate some free books to the school, provided a certain order threshold is met.

In order to help the author prepare, it can be useful to inform them about any special needs or behavioural issues the students may have. It is advisable for a member of staff to be available on the day of the visit to accompany the author, supervise the students and manage the book sales.

To ensure the visit is a success, it is a good idea to prepare students in advance by ensuring they are familiar with the author and their work. You could:

- Encourage the students to learn about the author by visiting their website (if they have one).
- Provide books for the students to read.
- Encourage the students to create a display in the school library to raise awareness about the author and their work.

Don't forget to send a letter home too, so that parents/carers are also aware of the visit and any opportunities to buy books.

For help planning your author visit, take a look at Education Scotland and the Scottish Book Trust's report on evaluating author events.[1]

Funding opportunities

When it comes to funding your school library plans, literacy project or author visit, there are various grants available. Here are the details of charitable trusts and other organisations which might be able to offer funding:

Better World Books Limited
https://cares.betterworldbooks.co.uk/grants/literacy-grants-for-libraries
Grants are usually worth up to £10,000.

BookTrust
G8 Battersea Studios, 80 Silverthorne Road, Battersea, London SW8 3HE
www.booktrust.org.uk/what-we-do
query@booktrust.org.uk
0207 801 8800
BookTrust is the UK's largest children's reading charity and is supported by Waterstones book company. The trust offers free books, resources and support to promote the love of reading. They have lots of programmes for schools to help encourage children to read. These include: Time to Read, Letterbox Club, Story Hunters and Ant Club for primary school children, and Buzz Books and Beyond

---

1 Education Scotland and Scottish Book Trust, *Author Events Evaluation: Draft Report* (June 2012). Available at: www.scottishbooktrust.com/learning/teachers-librarians/schools-events-programme/events-impact-research.

Booked Up for Year 7 and 8 students. They also offer free library packs for any secondary school or education provider in England with Year 7 students. Special schools can also claim a free pack, plus they can participate in the Spark Programme. The library packs are funded by the Arts Council and given on a first-come-first-served basis.

BookTrust Cymru and BookTrust Northern Ireland are national programmes for children in Wales and Northern Ireland.

Foyle School Library Scheme

Rugby Chambers, 2 Rugby Street, London WC1N 3QU

www.foylefoundation.org.uk

sls@foylefoundation.org.uk

0207 430 9119

The Foyle Foundation runs the Foyle School Library Scheme which offers grants of £1,000–£10,000.

Moto in the Community Trust: Community Schools

Moto Hospitality Limited, Toddington Service Area, Junction 12, M1 Southbound, Toddington, Bedfordshire LU5 6HR

https://moto-way.com/moto-in-the-community/community-schools

motocharity@moto-way.co.uk

01525 878500

Some Moto service stations have adopted a local school. Schools within a 15 mile radius of a site can also apply for charity grant, which on average makes awards of £1,000.

Penguin Random House UK

www.penguinrandomhouse.co.uk/creative-responsibility/community

The publisher Penguin Random House UK donates books to local primary schools to help them restock their libraries, although they only support schools local to each of their sites (in London, Colchester and Grantham). They also run an employee volunteering scheme, where staff are invited to take two paid work days a year to volunteer for a cause of their choice, and they support employees who are fundraising for good causes by offering to match-fund anything they raise (up to £100 per employee per year).

School Library Improvement Fund

Scottish Library and Information Council, Suite 5.5, Turnberry House, 175 West George Street, Glasgow G2 2LB

https://scottishlibraries.org/funding/school-library-improvement-fund

0141 202 2999

State schools in Scotland can apply for funding to enhance their existing school library (not to create a new one). There is no minimum or maximum amount for bids, but projects must be completed within 12 months.

Siobhan Dowd Trust

c/o 6b Lee Terrace, London SE3 9TZ

http://siobhandowdtrust.com/get-involved

director@siobhandowdtrust.com

This charity supports initiatives which bring children and books together. They run competitions and grant programmes and invite schools to apply for funds.

WHSmith

https://blog.whsmith.co.uk/community-grants-application

WHSmith offers community grants to schools, pre-schools, charities and other community groups. There are two application rounds each year. Grants are offered up to £500, which are funded from the proceeds of their carrier bag sales. Applying is really easy – just complete the application form on their website.

Further reading

Finch, D. (2015) Why All Pupils Deserve a Real School Library, *CILIP* (23 February). Available at: https://archive.cilip.org.uk/blog/why-all-pupils-deserve-real-school-library.

Library Association (2000) *The Primary School Library Guidelines.* Available at: https://librarynext.files.wordpress.com/2008/05/primary.pdf.

Oddone, K. (2017) *School Libraries and Teacher Librarians: Linking to Learning, Literacy and Levelling Up*. Available at: www.linkinglearning.com.au/wp-content/uploads/2017/04/school_libraries.pdf.

Ofsted (2006) *Good School Libraries: Making a Difference to Learning* (March). Ref: HMI 2624. Available at https://images.scholastic.co.uk/assets/a/0f/1c/ofsted-good-school-libraries-1619219.pdf.

Softlink (2017) *The Ongoing Importance of School Libraries*. Available at: www.softlinkint.com/downloads/The_Ongoing_Importance_of_School_Libraries.pdf.

Softlink (2018) *The 2017 Softlink UK School Library Survey Report.* Available at: www.softlinkint.com/downloads/2017_Softlink_UK_School_Library_Survey_Report.pdf.

Streatfield, D., Shaper, S. and Rae-Scott, S. (2010) *School Libraries in the UK: A Worthwhile Past, a Difficult Present and a Transformed Future?* (London: School Libraries Group of CILIP). Available at: https://archive.cilip.org.uk/sites/default/files/media/document/2018-06/slgsurvey-full-school-libraries-report-2010.pdf.

Teravainen, A. and Clark, C. (2017) *School Libraries: A Literature Review of Current Provision and Evidence of Impact* (London: National Literacy Trust). Available at: https://literacytrust.org.uk/research-services/research-reports/school-libraries-literature-review-current-provision-and-evidence-impact-2017.

Chapter 8

School trips, residentials and other opportunities

The cost of school outings, educational visits, day trips, residentials (including trips abroad) and other activities that take place beyond the school grounds can vary from a few pounds to thousands of pounds. The good news is that there are a number of grants available to help schools meet these costs, as well as competitions, resources and other initiatives to help you design the perfect school trip.

Before you begin, you will need to find out what members of staff you will need to work with to organise your trip. This may include the head teacher, school business manager, administrator or class teacher. Most schools have an educational visits coordinator (EVC), who will have received the appropriate training to oversee school trips, so if you are fundraising on behalf of a school, you will need to consult this key person.

If you are the EVC or wish to discover more about the role, then you can learn more from the Outdoor Educational Advisers' Panel at: https://oeapng.info/evc. Make sure you follow essential procedures set out in your school trip policy and work within local authority guidelines. If you are planning a repeat visit, then it is useful to obtain copies of any previous planning documents and trip evaluations to help you plan the best possible experience.

Why not also involve the students and their parents/carers when devising a trip? Perhaps you could run some ideas by your student council or organise a survey to ask which venues parents would recommend, how much they would be willing to pay for a trip, how many trips the students would like each year, whether parents would volunteer to be helpers on the day and so on. You could capture information from these questionnaires to use as part of your funding bid to potential grant-makers, as many like to see evidence of beneficiary involvement. You can find an example of a primary school survey and create your own at SurveyMonkey: www.surveymonkey.co.uk/r/f7mrnf3.

Design your trip

It is important to decide on your learning objectives and desired outcomes, and to weigh up the educational value for attendees. Who is the trip for? What do you want them to gain? What subject areas will the trip cover? How will it support classroom-based learning? Do you want to provide hands-on experiences?

Off-site visits can give students the opportunity to learn in stimulating environments that bring learning to life and enable them to connect what they have learned in the classroom with the real world. They can offer powerful and life-changing experiences, helping to inspire students and ignite a new-found passion for a subject. They can also help young people to gain a deeper understanding and appreciation of the world we live in, giving them opportunities to test ideas, put theories into practice and develop investigative skills. Trips can also be very enjoyable and rewarding experiences, offering students a sense of adventure outside the classroom.

You may find the following research and case studies useful, as they highlight the value of learning outside the classroom:

Council for Learning Outside the Classroom: www.lotc.org.uk/category/research

Learning Away: https://learningaway.org.uk/casestudies

School Travel Forum: www.schooltravelforum.com/teachers-toolkit#research

There are also the more practical matters of how many students the trip will be offered to and their backgrounds and needs. For example, will the trip be aimed at Key Stage 1 children or Year 10 business studies students?

Many funders like to be given details about the beneficiaries of a grant and the difference the activity will make to them, so it is a good idea to include as much information as possible about the students who will participate (just be sure to anonymise any sensitive information). For example, for disadvantaged children living in poverty, the trip may offer an opportunity to see or visit something they would not ordinarily experience, so the grant may be key to helping them access this. For SEND students, the trip may offer key visual or sensory experiences which it is not possible to deliver in a traditional classroom setting. Make sure you describe as many benefits as possible to the potential funder.

You will also need to establish what dates and times you can go on the trip. Do you plan to go during the school day, in the evening, at the weekend or during school holidays? What time of year will you go? When choosing your dates, don't forget to consider any off-peak ticket prices that may be available.

If you are struggling for numbers, perhaps you could consider joining up with another subject group, year group or even school. The more students there are on a trip, the lower the cost per person.

Planning tips

- Check that the dates you are planning don't clash with anything else already scheduled in the school calendar.

- Give yourself plenty of time to plan. Educational travel experts NST recommend that schools organise their trips 6–24 months in advance: www.NSTgroup.co.uk. With advance planning, you have more time to consider all the details and better opportunities to prepare students to help them get the most out of the visit, and you can give parents more time to budget, save money or pay in instalments. If you book in advance you can often take advantage of 'early bird' savings too.

- If you are planning an event in September then don't forget about the Heritage Open Days, when National Trust properties and other historic venues offer free admission for one day only. You can find out the details at: www.heritageopendays. org.uk.

- If you are organising an event in October or November, then it may be worth knowing about the Museums at Night festival, where many museums, galleries, libraries and heritage sites across the UK open their doors after hours to present their treasures in unexpected ways. You can learn more and search events by region at: www.museumsatnight.org.uk.

- It might also be worth investigating whether your local museum runs a programme of events for schools. Many will offer workshops or self-guided tours that are linked to areas of the curriculum.

While you are in the planning phase, it's worth remembering that there are lots of travel partners out there who can help to plan your adventure:

- Outdoor education advisors can be a great source of advice and guidance for outdoor learning, off-site visits and learning outside the classroom. They can also offer support regarding health and safety best practice. You can find a local advisor via the Outdoor Education Advisers Panel at: www.outdooreducationadvisers.co.uk/about-us/find-an-adviser.

- School tour operators specialise in creating trips and residentials and can be real gems of information, helping your trip to run smoothly from start to finish. You can usually search for existing packages on their website or contact them to discuss a bespoke package. You can find an accredited tour operator by visiting the School Travel Forum (a non-profit trade association promoting school travel) at: www. schooltravelforum.com/search.

There are various benefits to using a tour operator which specialises in educational travel:

- You can find out what trips other schools have been on and potentially gain tips from other teachers who have been there, done that.

- You can benefit from their expertise and first-hand knowledge – they may even suggest ideas you had not considered.

- Some tour operators can arrange for a member of staff to accompany you on your trip, giving you added peace of mind.

- Some can offer ground representatives, offering you support in a foreign country and enabling you to benefit from their local knowledge.

- Some tour operators will use a price guarantee to offer you the most competitive deals. You may also be able to access preferential rates for a range of attractions, from museums to restaurants. Many can also give you advice on how to make your budget go further.

- Many tour operators can offer back-up support, such as a 24-hour emergency phone line. If you get stranded abroad due to bad weather, for example, the tour operator should be able to help you organise alternative accommodation, transport and meals, and get back safely.

- Tour operators can also offer a range of other support, such as itineraries, payment collection, organising insurance and so on.

You will need to agree any additional requirements with the trip provider: will they offer a tour guide? Will they run any workshops? Will they provide itineraries or guides? Can they provide lockers for your group to store personal possessions in during your visit, and, if so, do you need to pre-book them? Whoever you plan to partner with, involve them during the early stages of your planning to benefit from their knowledge and resources. Make sure you know exactly what is and is not included before signing a contract.

Don't forget to ask your provider or tour operator if they have any case studies or reports that you can use as part of your funding application. These can all help to reinforce the value of the school trip in the eyes of potential funders.

Research venues

When deciding on your destination, explore possible venues and activities and then establish a shortlist based on your criteria. For example, do you have a maximum travel distance? What areas of the curriculum does the attraction support? Is it suitable for your age group? If you have any wheelchair users in your group, you will also need to confirm that there is adequate access and appropriate facilities. Many venues have a dedicated education officer to help schools plan trips, so be sure to contact them early on.

There are various online directories to help you find suitable events, attractions and venues and make the best of your time away. These include theatres, museums, exhibitions, castles, art galleries, concerts, farms, places of worship, overseas residentials, ski trips and more. Depending on which directory you use, you can often search by curriculum subject, activity, region, key stage, opening times, type of trip and/or keyword.

Plan My School Trip: www.planmyschooltrip.co.uk

School Travel Organiser: www.schooltravelorganiser.com/Directory

UK School Trips: www.ukschooltrips.co.uk/directory

You can also search for providers on the following websites:

- Adventuremark is a non-statutory safety scheme which recognises providers that meet certain standards with regard to managing the potential risks involved with adventure activities. Access a list of approved providers at: www.adventuremark.co.uk.

- The AHOEC Gold Standard is a quality scheme which recognises high-quality and safe providers of outdoor experiences. Discover gold standard providers at: https://ahoec.org/map.

- The British Activity Providers Association lists details of a wide range of accredited centres designed to inspire, motivate and educate school and youth groups from primary to secondary school age. Discover more at: www.thebapa.org.uk/centre-category/school-youth-groups.

- Cornucopia is an online database offering details of over 6,000 collections in the UK's museums, art galleries, archives and libraries. Access the database at: http://cornucopia.orangeleaf.com.

- The Health and Safety Executive website enables users to search providers who are registered with the Licensing Authority. Find a licence holder at: www.aals.org.uk/aals/provider_search.php.

- The Learning Outside the Classroom (LOtC) quality badge is a national award given to providers who meet certain standards. To find out more about these standards and to search for a quality badge holder visit: http://lotcqualitybadge.org.uk/search.

- The Young Explorers' Trust provides details of organisations that they have independently audited. Find approved providers at: www.theyet.org/evaluations/approved-providers.

Working farms offer a range of stimulating and engaging learning opportunities, from hands-on experiences for early years children to practical demonstrations for older students. If you would like to arrange a farm visit, there are lots of organisations that can help:

- Countryside Classroom helps schools to connect with farmers and learn about the natural environment: www.countrysideclassroom.org.uk.

- Food for Life has compiled a farm finder which you can use to search for your nearest farm: www.foodforlife.org.uk/schools/what-can-you-do/visit-a-farm.

- Visit My Farm is an information hub that connects schools with farms that host school visits: www.visitmyfarm.org/teachers.

- If you would like to take your students to a farm in Scotland, then have a look at the Royal Highland Education Trust to help your school create a link with a local farmer: www.rhet.org/teachers/visit-a-farm.

Depending on the type of activity you are looking for, you can also contact the relevant national governing body, such as the British Caving Association or British Canoe Union. These organisations can provide more information about your chosen activity and details of any clubs, courses or training opportunities. You can access a useful list at: https://ahoec.org/links.

If you are aiming to organise a low-cost residential, there are various organisations that can help:

- Pitchup allows users to find details and reviews of over 2,400 camp sites in the UK, Europe and the Americas. Discover more at: www.pitchup.com.

- Schools can stay at Scout Activity Centres, which are great if you are planning an outside adventure. Learn more at: www.scoutadventures.org.uk/schools-and-youth.

Schools may also like to explore opportunities to stay in youth hostel accommodation. Youth hostels can give you a base for self-led adventure and most providers are willing to create a tailored package based on your individual needs. There are hundreds of youth hostel venues across the UK, so whether you plan on visiting an old Norman castle or taking a trip to the seaside, there are a wide range of opportunities available. You can find a list of youth hostel venues by visiting the following websites.

Hostelbookers (for youth hostels across the world): www.hostelbookers.com

Independent Hostels UK (for youth hostels in England, Scotland and Wales): https://independenthostels.co.uk

Irish Youth Hostel Association (for youth hostels in Ireland): https://anoige.ie

VisitScotland (for youth hostels in Scotland): www.visitscotland.com/accommodation/hostels

Youth Hostel Association (for youth hostels in England and Wales): https://groups.yha.org.uk. The Youth Hostel Association have over 80 venues which have been accredited with the LOtC Quality Badge.

When discussing opportunities with venue providers, it can be worth enquiring about any financial support they may offer. Charities like the Outward Bound Trust and Youth Hostel Association, for example, offer grants to help disadvantaged students take part in the activities they provide, which they would otherwise be unable to access. For further details please see:

Outward Bound Trust

Hackthorpe Hall, Hackthorpe, Penrith, Cumbria CA10 2HX

www.outwardbound.org.uk/education-homepage

enquiries@outwardbound.org.uk

01931 740 000

The Trust can offer financial support to help fund up to 40% of the costs of an Outward Bound residential experience. The bursaries are open to UK residents in education, if they are from a low income family or have low educational attainment, if they are from a minority ethnic background or speak English as an additional language, if they have special educational needs or if they are at risk of reoffending. To apply, schools must complete a simple online application.

Youth Hostel Association (YHA)

YHA Communities, YHA (England & Wales), Trevelyan House, Dimple Road, Matlock DE4 3YH

https://groups.yha.org.uk/school-trips/apply-support

breaks@yha.org.uk

01629 592723

The YHA's Educational Breaks Programme aims to help groups which include students who are living in severe poverty, have additional challenges or are eligible for the pupil premium. They can provide groups or schools with one break per year. Please visit their website for details of application deadlines and other programmes.

To help lower the cost of a residential trip, you could also request to partner with another school (perhaps you can camp on school grounds). Don't forget to check out the accommodation and facilities available to hire across the UK on the SchoolHire website: https://schoolhire.co.uk.

Lots of companies are willing to host school trips, so why not contact a local business and ask to visit their site? Site visits can provide a great opportunity to teach students about science and the environment, and can also be linked to personal, social, health and economic (PSHE) education topics.

Organise activities

Planning is essential to make the most of your time away, so aim to structure your activities carefully and set realistic timings. Check admission times and pre-book any activities to make sure your adventures run smoothly. It's important to get written confirmation of all bookings.

Local tourist information centres can be a great source of information about local attractions and events. You can find a list of tourist information centres on the Britain Express website at: www.britainexpress.com/TIC.

TripAdvisor is another useful resource for travel reviews and information. There is also a forum where you can post questions. Visit: www.tripadvisor.co.uk.

Depending on the nature of your adventure, you may like to align it with the National Outdoor Learning Award. This is a free award which helps to capture the personal development outcomes of participants during a residential or regular outdoor learning experience. Further details are available at: www.outdoor-learning.org/Good-Practice/Good-Practice/National-Outdoor-Learning-Award.

There are other schemes with which you could align your trip, but please be aware that there may be costs involved in taking part (contact the organisers for full details).

The Duke of Edinburgh's Award is a youth programme which was founded in 1956 by Prince Philip. It challenges young people (aged 14–24 years) in the areas of volunteering, physical activities, life skills and expeditions. It encourages them to gain new experiences outside of the classroom, thereby helping them to discover their place in the world and become responsible citizens. Find out more at: www.dofe.org.

The John Muir Award is an award scheme which helps people to connect with nature and wild places. It can offer a framework for learning outdoors and it contributes to the requirements of the national curriculum. It is open to everyone. For more information visit: www.johnmuirtrust.org/john-muir-award/schools-and-colleges.

If you are planning a day trip or overnight residential, you will need to make arrangements for breaks and meals. For example, will you take any breaks, and, if so, when? How long will each break last? Where will you make the stopover? Will you need to book a lunch room or seating area? Will the venue provide lunch or will the students need to bring a packed lunch? You will also need to consider students on free school meals, as these will usually need to be ordered in advance.

If you are planning a residential, will you opt for an all-inclusive package, where the venue provides the food, or if you will you opt for self-catering instead? Either way, you will need to consider menu choices, food hygiene, washing up rotas and so on.

Travel arrangements

Travel arrangements will be a key part of your planning. Will you be travelling by coach, train, boat and/or plane? Do you have access to a minibus that will be adequate for your needs? Can you share transport with another school? Does your school already use a transport company that may be able to offer you preferential rates? Do you have any specific transport requirements (e.g. does your transport need to accommodate wheel-chair users)?

As well as taking into account all of these considerations, you will need to decide on pick-up and drop-off points and any stopping-off points for comfort breaks and refreshments along the way. You will also need to consider any implications that might arise from travelling through the night and put in place strategies to deal with travel sickness.

When selecting your mode of transport, remember that it is usually cheaper to travel by public transport than it is to hire a commercial vehicle. For example, most train companies offer discounts for group bookings of 10 or more people, so contact your local train operator for prices. You can find more information about group travel discounts and a list of train operating companies at National Rail Enquiries: www.nationalrail.co.uk/times_fares/46506.aspx.

For information about two-for-one offers when travelling by train, visit the Days Out Guide website at: www.daysoutguide.co.uk.

Some venues and travel companies can help you to arrange transport. They may also be able to offer better rates with transport companies with whom they have links, so it's always worth asking if they can help.

You could try contacting your local council to see if they have any travel passes available. These can allow small groups to travel for free on public transport within a given area, which can be great for local trips.

For a list of UK school transport providers visit:

Britain Express: www.britainexpress.com/great_british_sites/tour-ops.htm

UK School Trips: www.ukschooltrips.co.uk/directory/transport-providers.html

You can also find a list of school minibus and coach operators with BUSK Benchmark accreditation at: www.busk-uk.co.uk/busk-benchmark.

Overseas visits

If you are planning an overseas trip, make sure you allow plenty of time to organise this. Should you be visiting somewhere off the beaten track, then it can be a good idea to consult the Foreign and Commonwealth Office in the planning stages of your trip: www. gov.uk/foreign-travel-advice.

You will also need to make any necessary arrangements for passports and visas. Depending on which country are visiting, you can usually get collective passports (for groups of 5–50 children who are all British nationals and under the age of 18). A collective passport costs £39 and applications take about six weeks. Find out more at: www.gov.uk/collective-group-passports. Alternatively, you will need to make sure that each student has a valid passport.

You may also want to:

▨ Contact your local GP for advice regarding inoculations.

▨ Research, and make arrangements for adequate travel insurance.

▨ Read information about visiting Europe after Brexit. See: www.gov.uk/visit-europe-brexit.

▨ Locate the details of the relevant British Embassy, High Commission or Consulate. See: www.gov.uk/world/embassies.

Other planning considerations

Once you have designed your trip or residential, you will also want to:

▨ Organise worksheets, maps and guide notes for staff and students. Ask your venue if they can help.

▨ Create a register of all group members, including students, teachers and helpers.

▨ Ensure that staff understand their roles and responsibilities and are aware of any students who may need extra supervision.

▨ Keep other members of staff in the loop about your trip, especially if students are likely to miss other classes because they are out for the day.

▨ Carry out risk assessments for transport, accommodation and any activities you are undertaking. For health and safety guidance, consult your EVC, local authority or outdoor education advisor. You can also find the Health and Safety Executive's advice on school trips at: www.hse.gov.uk/services/education/school-trips.htm.

▨ Make a list of everything you need to take (e.g. identity badges, first aid kit, mobile phone, sick bags, registers, spare coins). If you need to buy any equipment, such as camping gear, why not contact other schools, as you may be able to share equipment to help lower costs.

■ Plan follow-up activities for the students, such as writing field trip reports, or completing feedback forms or trip evaluations (this information can help you to measure your own outcomes and plan future events). Many funders like grant recipients to report back to them about the outcome of the trip and what difference their grant has made, so be prepared to demonstrate the impact of their support. Capture any quotes from the students and then select someone to write a brief report based on their shared experiences.

How many helpers will you need on the trip? For this, you will need to think about staff-to-student ratios, so consult your school policy and/or local authority guidelines to determine the recommended number. You will also need to consider the needs of your students and the nature of the trip. Once you have decided how many helpers you need, what will their roles and responsibilities be? For example, how many first aiders will you need and who will be responsible for the first aid kit? Some venues and tour operators are able to offer guides or chaperones, so find out what support is available (and what costs are involved).

To help reduce staffing costs you could appeal for volunteer helpers. However, you will need to consider DBS checks, safeguarding arrangements and any training they may need (refer to your school policies or senior leadership team for advice). If you need to arrange DBS checks, then allow plenty of time for these to come through.

Once the details of the trip have been agreed and approved by the head teacher, you will need to publicise the trip to students and parents/carers, and establish the ground rules and expectations.

■ Draft a letter to be sent home providing details about the trip and its purpose.

■ Let the students know where and when they should meet and what to do if they get lost.

■ Confirm whether or not they need to be in school uniform and any other dress codes.

■ Provide advice on whether they will need to take a packed lunch, money or any equipment.

■ Be clear about what standard of behaviour is expected and set out any procedures for dealing with misbehaviour.

■ Ask for key information from parents, such as any specific requirements (e.g. dietary, allergies, illnesses), emergency contact details and medical information.

■ Collect permission slips and deposits. Make sure you allow plenty of time to chase up any outstanding forms or monies. Give a final date for payment.

- Advise parents of their responsibilities, such as collecting their child on return.

- For overseas residentials, you will need to check the validity of passports and obtain a doctor's note for any medication the students will be taking with them. You will also need to make arrangements for travel insurance and healthcare cover.

- Announce the dates of any parent meetings to discuss plans for the trip.

- Prepare the students to help them get the most out of the journey, such as encouraging them to research the venue(s).

If you need help to administer your trip, then check out eeZeeTrip: www.eezeetrip.co.uk. It is an award-winning web and mobile platform which helps schools to communicate with parents, collect consent forms and receive money for trips and so on. Please note that there is a charge for this service.

Financial planning

Depending on the type of trip you are organising, you may need to take into account the following costs:

- Travel fees (including parking costs and toll road fees).
- Venue entry fees (i.e. usually per student or per group).
- Workshop fees.
- Accommodation fees.
- Food, drink and other consumables.
- Equipment purchases or hire.
- Costs linked with pre-visits to carry out risk assessments.
- Staff wages, DBS checks and any relevant training connected to the event.
- Tour operator fees.
- Contingency funds (e.g. in case a student loses their money).
- Costs for attending planning events (such as travel shows and seminars).
- Insurance fees.

Make sure you get VAT receipts for everything. It is useful to separate the trip's receipts from other school funds.

Most travel insurance policies provide coverage for things like lost luggage, accidents, cancellation, travel delays and medical emergencies. It may be sensible to apply for a group travel insurance policy, as these are usually cheaper than purchasing individual policies for each group member. Don't forget to check whether costs associated with parents are covered too (in case they need to come and collect their child early). You can access government guidance for foreign travel insurance at: www.gov.uk/guidance/foreign-travel-insurance.

Funding opportunities

There are various ways in which schools can pay for or subsidise the cost of a school trip:

- Some schools use their own funds to reduce the amount that parents have to contribute, while other schools organise fundraising activities instead (e.g. bake sales and raffles).
- Pupil premium funding is used by many schools to subsidise or pay for educational trips and residential visits for disadvantaged students.
- It is possible to ask wealthier parents if they would be prepared to make a donation as well as paying for their own child's trip.
- A partnership of schools in Merseyside offers parents a 'match funding' savings scheme. If parents pay early, they pay less overall as their contribution is supplemented by school funds. For more information visit: http://learningaway.org.uk/how-to/affordability.
- Although schools cannot charge for activities that take place during the school day (apart from some music tuition), it is possible to request voluntary contributions from parents and carers. Always refer to your own school's charging policy too.
- You can also appeal to local businesses for help in sponsoring your trip.

For more information on charging for trips, please see:

Child Law Advice: https://childlawadvice.org.uk/information-pages/charging-for-school-activities

Department for Education: www.gov.uk/government/publications/charging-for-school-activities

There are a range of other strategies you could use to help lower your trip costs:

- Don't be afraid to haggle about prices, especially if you are travelling with a large group. Some organisations offer schools discounted entry prices, free coach and minibus parking, free pre-visit tickets for teachers, free resources to help schools plan their visit, school return offers, lunch offers and even educational experts to help them get the best out of their visit. For example, Warner Bros. Studio Tours London (www.wbstudiotour.co.uk) offers schools a free one-hour lesson, a free green-screen experience, free teacher places and free teacher pre-visit tickets.
- Think about how far you want to travel: staying local can help to reduce costs.

▨ Consider the length of your school trip: the longer it is, the more expensive it will be.

▨ If you visit a place regularly, try to build a long-term partnership and negotiate on prices. Many organisations welcome repeat business.

▨ Many venues operate an off-peak ticket pricing strategy, so check out any offers.

▨ Some venues, such as the London Eye (www.londoneye.com) and Sea Life centres (www.visitsealife.com), offer free tickets for teachers. Don't be afraid to ask!

▨ Some venues can offer bursaries and grants, so find out what is available.

▨ Consider linking up with other schools to share transport costs. You can often negotiate lower entry fees if your group size is bigger.

▨ Using volunteers (e.g. governors, parents, members of the local community, older students) can help to reduce staffing costs.

Across the UK, many venues offer free entry for schools – just book in advance and confirm the details with them prior to your trip. Here are just some of the places you can visit:

▨ Many museums in London are free to visit (only charging for certain exhibitions), including the British Museum, Natural History Museum, Science Museum, Somerset House, Tate Modern and Victoria and Albert Museum. Check out their websites for details.

▨ The National Portrait Gallery in London provides some free taught sessions for schools. Please note that there may be an admission charge for some temporary exhibitions. For more information visit: www.npg.org.uk/visit/booking/schools-and-colleges.php.

▨ Schools can enjoy free self-guided visits and workshops at the National Army Museum in London. The workshops are fully linked to the national curriculum and cover subjects such as history, citizenship, geography and STEM. For full details visit: www.nam.ac.uk/schools.

▨ Schools can visit the Houses of Parliament for free, take a tour of the historic building and access a range of workshops. There is even transport subsidy available to eligible schools. Take a look at: www.parliament.uk/education/visit-parliament-with-your-school.

▨ The Supreme Court in London offers free structured visits for school groups. These involve an interactive introductory talk, time in the educational exhibition area and the opportunity to observe an appeal hearing (depending on the court schedule and space in the public seating areas). Due to high demand it is advised that visits are booked at least 10 weeks in advance. To book a visit, simply fill out their online booking form at: www.supremecourt.uk/visits-for-schools-colleges-and-universities.html.

▨ Chester Zoo is keen to inspire a generation of conservationists. They are offering up to 42,000 free entry places for school pupils between November and February. Schools must pre-book their visit, and terms and conditions apply. Please see their website for more information: www.chesterzoo.org/education/all-you-need-to-know/prices-and-payments.

▣ Have you ever fancied taking students to Jodrell Bank Discovery Centre in Macclesfield? Here students can see the world-famous Lovell telescope, explore interactive galleries, speak to expert staff and experience curriculum-linked workshops around astronomy and science. Each year, the Centre offers discounted entry for 15 eligible secondary schools which qualifies them for up to 30 free places for Key Stage 3 and 4 students. Plus, if your school takes 45 or more students, they may qualify for an additional £100 bursary which can help towards travel costs. The Centre also offers a free day of science outreach to eligible schools. For further details visit: www.jodrellbank.net/learn/schools/wp.

▣ Schools can visit the WWF Living Planet Centre in Woking for free. Students can learn about wildlife, oceans, freshwater, forests and other WWF projects around the world. Schools can also access free WWF workshops, although there is a suggested donation. For more information visit: www.wwf.org.uk/get-involved/schools/visit-us.

▣ Primary schools can enjoy a free visit to Warbutons in Bolton via their National School Visitor Programme. Pupils get the opportunity to learn about making bread, food hygiene and healthy eating. Discover more at: www.warburtons.co.uk/corporate/sustainability/community/school-visitors.

▣ Essex Wildlife Trust offers free visits for primary schools to Abbotts Hall Farm in Colchester. This visit can mean a whole day out for your class, incorporating orienteering, a debate about organic farming, and making, cooking and eating flatbreads from wheat grains. Find out more at: www.essexwt.org.uk/discover-learn/school-trips.

▣ Teachers and students can enjoy a free self-led tour of the Firstsite art gallery in Colchester. For more information visit: http://firstsite.uk/learning/schools-and-groups.

▣ Schools can enjoy free educational visits to Royal Horticultural Society (RHS) gardens in Yorkshire, Devon, Essex and Surrey (although they recommend a suggested donation of £3 per child). These visits give students the opportunity to get involved in practical horticulture, art and science, and bring the curriculum to life in an inspiring garden setting. Education officers based at each site are experienced in leading school groups. Learn more at: www.rhs.org.uk/education-learning/gardening-children-schools/school-visits.

▣ English Heritage has over 400 sites across England and offer free school-led visits (just make sure you book at least seven days in advance). Read their terms and conditions and discover more at: www.english-heritage.org.uk/learn/school-visits.

▣ CADW offers free self-led education visits to historic sites in Wales. For a list of locations visit: https://cadw.gov.wales/learn/education/education-visits.

- If you would like to take students on a science visit to a planetarium, then check out We the Curious Science Centre in Bristol. Local schools may be eligible to access their Funded School Visits Programme. Learn more at: www.wethecurious.org/education/what-we-offer.

- National Museums Scotland offers free admission to all four of their museums for pre-booked school groups. This includes the National Museum of Scotland, National Museum of Flight, National War Museum and National Museum of Rural Life. Find out more at: www.nms.ac.uk/about-us/schools-programme/school-visits.

- Historic Environment Scotland offers schools free self-led visits to their properties. There are over 300 historic sites to choose from, enabling students to explore Scotland's heritage and history. Visits must be booked at least 10 working days in advance. Visit: www.historicenvironment.scot/learn/education-visits/free-education-visits.

- Schools, nurseries and educational/community groups can enjoy a free visit to Jupiter Artland sculpture park and art gallery near Edinburgh. Access more details at: www.jupiterartland.org/learning/school-and-universities.

- Primary and secondary school groups can visit the Northern Ireland War Memorial to find out what life was like during the Second World War. Students can watch a presentation, visit the museum, try on war uniforms and enjoy a variety of hands-on learning activities. Visits are free and there is a travel grant of up to £100 per group. Find out more at: www.niwarmemorial.org/education-outreach.

- For the past six years, educational institutions have been eligible to apply to the Landmark Trust's 50 for Free scheme, which offers free short breaks in a wide range of historic buildings across England, Scotland and Wales. For details visit: www.landmarktrust.org.uk/news-and-events.

- Keep your eyes open for special centenary events – for example, in 2019 there were national commemorations of the centenary of the Great War.

To find a wider list of free things to do in the UK, please visit:

Discover Northern Ireland: https://discovernorthernireland.com

Visit England: www.visitengland.com/things-to-do/free#

Visit Scotland: www.visitscotland.com/see-do/attractions/free

Visit Wales: www.visitwales.com/things-to-do

You can find details of free museums and art galleries across the UK via the Money Saving Expert website at: www.moneysavingexpert.com/deals/free-museums-and-art-galleries.

There are also many free festivals in the UK. You can search region by region and discover more at: www.moneysavingexpert.com/deals/free-uk-festivals.

Did you know that students who have won a Blue Peter Badge can gain free entry to over 200 attractions across the UK, including theme parks, zoos and castles? To apply, children (aged 6–15 years) simply send in a letter, poem, picture or story, along with a message of at least 50 words explaining which Blue Peter badge they are applying for and why they deserve to win one. For details visit: www.bbc.co.uk/cbbc/joinin/about-blue-peter-badges.

Variety, the Children's Charity, offers free day trips to disadvantaged children through their Great Days Out scheme. Young people (aged 3–18 years) get the opportunity to visit a zoo, seaside, circus, theme park or other major attraction. So far the scheme has helped 2 million young people. To register, your school or organisation must cater for children with special needs or be located in a deprived area and have a special needs unit. For further information visit: www.variety.org.uk.

Further support

■ If you would like to learn more about low-cost models and access a range of case studies and resources, then take a look at the Learning Away website: https://learningaway.org.uk/how-to/affordability.

■ You can also find examples of low-price trips at Plan My School Trip: www.planmyschooltrip.co.uk/school-trip-costs.php.

■ Stay up-to-date with current offers that might help to reduce the price of your school trips at: www.ukschooltrips.co.uk/offers.html.

There are also lots of free resources to help you develop your trip:

■ To announce school trips and payment deadlines to parents and guardians, you can access a range of letter templates at: www.scholasticatravel.com/2013/07/01/field-trip-letter-to-parents.

■ To obtain a copy of the Department for Education's parents' and guardians' consent form for school trips and other activities visit: www.gov.uk/government/publications/consent-for-school-trips-and-other-off-site-activities.

■ For a model trip risk assessment template and budget planning spreadsheet, check out the free resources offered on the Learning Away website: https://learningaway.org.uk/free-resources/lower-cost-models/6-resource-library.

■ The Outdoor Education Advisers' Panel (OEAP) provides advice about writing trip policies, as well as a range of checklists, templates for self-evaluation forms, information about risk assessments, trip checklists and a whole lot more at: https://oeapng.info/downloads/all-documents.

■ The *TES* provides a collection of resources to help you plan your off-site experience at: www.tes.com/articles/tes-collection-educational-visits-general-information.

There are also many blogs, magazines and case studies online which give tips and advice on planning your educational trip. Here are some which may be of interest to you:

Learning Away: http://learningaway.org.uk

Outdoor Education Advisers' Panel (news page): https://oeapng.info/news

Travelbound (educational trips blog): www.travelbound.co.uk/blog

You can request a free copy of the *School Travel Organiser* magazine, when you register your details, at: www.schooltravelorganiser.com/register.

If you want to apply for a grant or enter a competition to win a free school trip, here are some schemes that you may find interesting. Don't forget to contact the local town council (or local councillors) in the area you are intending to visit to see if they have any pots of money you can access – you are bringing in extra business to the area, after all!

Field Studies Council (FSC) Kids Fund

FSC Head Office, Preston Montford, Montford Bridge, Shrewsbury, Shropshire SY4 1HW

www.field-studies-council.org/about/fsc-kids-fund.aspx

enquiries@field-studies-council.org

01743 852100

This environmental education charity accepts applications from schools and disadvantaged groups: young people aged 4–18 years (or up to 25 for those with special needs). The fund pays for up to 80% of course fees to attend a non-curriculum day or residential course at an FSC Learning Location, including equipment, tuition and waterproof hire costs. Food and accommodation are included for residential courses. One free staff/adult place is provided for every 12 young people. There are three funding rounds each year and the deadlines to apply are 1 March, 1 June and 1 November. Applicants who can raise at least 20% of the cost themselves, and who can show that the course is part of a longer term plan for the group (as opposed to a one-off trip), have a better chance of succeeding. Discover more and apply via their website.

Georgia Williams Trust

PR House, Hortonwood 30, Telford, Shropshire TF1 7ET

https://thegeorgiawilliamstrust.co.uk

georgiawilliamstrust@outlook.com

01952 257608

Grants of up to £250 are available to individuals and local organisations in Telford and Wrekin. In the past they have funded school projects.

Happy Days Children's Charity

Clody House, 90–100 Collingdon Street, Luton LU1 1RX

www.happydayscharity.org/applications

enquiries@happydayscharity.org

01582 755999

Grants are available to help fund day trips and activity holidays for groups of children with additional needs.

Henry Smith Charity Holiday Grants

6th Floor, 65 Leadenhall Street, London EC3A 2AD

www.henrysmithcharity.org.uk

0207 264 4970

One-off grants, from £500 to £2,500, are available. These are only available to support children with disabilities or those living in the most deprived areas of the UK.

Jack Petchey Foundation Educational Visits Grant

Dockmaster's House, 1 Hertsmere Road, London E14 8JJ

www.jackpetcheyfoundation.org.uk/educational-visits

mail@jackpetcheyfoundation.org.uk

0208 252 8000

Grants are offered to facilitate trips (to a maximum of £10 per head) for schools participating in their Achievement Award Scheme.

Merlin's Magic Wand

Link House, 25 West Street, Poole BH15 1LD

www.merlinsmagicwand.org

01202 440082

Merlin's Magic Wand is a charitable organisation providing attraction tickets and travel grants to enable seriously ill, disabled or disadvantaged children aged 2–18 years to enjoy a day out at a Merlin attraction. Applications must be made by parents, guardians, schools or councils. Decisions are usually given within eight weeks.

Newcomen Collett Foundation

66 Newcomen Street, London SE1 1YT

www.newcomencollett.org.uk/organisations.html

grantoffice@newcomencollett.org.uk

0207 407 2967

The Newcomen Collett Foundation makes grants to schools, organisations and other groups for extra-curricular activities, such as school trips, after-school clubs and holiday clubs.

School Journey Association

Units 2/3, 16 Porteus Place, London SW4 0AS

www.sjatours.org/info/financial-assistance

office@sjatours.org

0208 675 6636

The School Journey Association is a registered charity which can offer grants of up to 50% of school trip costs. The grant is designed to help individual children from disadvantaged backgrounds participate in a school journey that is organised by the Association.

School Travel Awards

www.schooltravelorganiser.com/awards

If you are particularly proud of a school trip you have arranged or would like to recognise a teacher or trip organiser, then check out the School Travel Awards. Schools can enter the awards for My Best School Trip and School Trip Champion. Not only will your school gain recognition, but also a trophy and a financial reward (of approximately £1,500) to put towards a future school trip.

You Me Community – Free Days Out for Schools Vouchers

www.youmecommunity.co.uk/freedaysoutforschools.html

Schools and youth organisations can apply for this scheme to help meet the costs of coach hire. If you are accepted onto the scheme, simply encourage members of your community to shop locally and collect as many vouchers as possible within a 28-day period. At the end of this time your school will receive a reward based on the number of vouchers collected. You can earn a maximum of £500 to help part or fully finance coach hire with an accredited BUSK coach company.

Further reading

Department for Education (2018a) *Charging for School Activities: Departmental Advice for Governing Bodies, School Leaders, School Staff and Local Authorities* (May). Ref: DFE-00244-2013. Available at: www.gov.uk/government/publications/charging-for-school-activities.

Department for Education (2018b) Health and Safety: Responsibilities and Duties for Schools. Available at: www.gov.uk/government/publications/health-and-safety-advice-for-schools/responsibilities-and-duties-for-schools.

Education Endowment Foundation (2019) *Outdoor Adventure Learning.* Available at: https://educationendowmentfoundation.org.uk/evidence-summaries/teaching-learning-toolkit/outdoor-adventure-learning.

Nathan, A. (2012) School Trips: Effective Learning Outside the Classroom, *Teach Secondary* (19 December). Available at: www.teachsecondary.com/SEN/view/school-trips-effective-learning-outside-the-classroom.

Ofsted (2008) *Learning Outside the Classroom: How Far Should You Go?* Ref: 070219. Available at: https://dera.ioe.ac.uk/9253.

Ofsted (2012) *The Pupil Premium: How Schools Are Using the Pupil Premium Funding to Raise Achievement for Disadvantaged Pupils.* Ref: 120197. Available at: https://assets.publishing.

service.gov.uk/government/uploads/system/uploads/attachment_data/file/413222/The_Pupil_Premium.pdf.

Peacock, A. (2006) *Changing Minds: The Lasting Impact of School Trips*. Available at: www.peecworks.org/PEEC/PEEC_Research/0179ABED-001D0211.0/Peacock%202006%20field%20trip%20effects.pdf.

QA Research (2008) *'Out of School Trips' Report: A National Report* (March). Available at: www.tourismhelp.co.uk/objview.asp?object_id=429.

Royal Society for the Prevention of Accidents (2013) *Planning and Leading Visits and Adventurous Activities: Guidance for Schools and Colleges Teaching Children and Young People from 5 to 18 Years*. Available at: www.rospa.com/rospaweb/docs/advice-services/school-college-safety/school-visits-guide.pdf.

School Travel Forum (2012) *The Benefits of Outdoor Learning*. Available at: www.schooltravelforum.com/media/1330/the_benefits_of_outdoor_learning.pdf.

Chapter 9
School playgrounds

If you need to be persuaded that playgrounds are of huge benefit to children, then here are some reasons why a creative play space is important to your school:

■ They challenge children and help to improve fitness levels, balance, coordination and motor skills.

■ They encourage children to be physically active and motivate them to burn off excess energy. Not only do they promote health and well-being but they also help to tackle childhood obesity.

■ They can extend children's learning environment. Learning doesn't have to stop just because you've left the classroom – it can be an ongoing process.

■ They can help children learn to manage risks and to know their limits in a fun and safe space.

■ They encourage children to spend time outdoors, where they can enjoy fresh air and generate vitamin D from sunlight. This can boost their mood and help them to return to the classroom with a positive mental attitude.

■ They foster social interaction through games and learning to share and take turns.

■ They are great fun and help children to relax.

There is funding available to help schools and other educational establishments to improve play and exercise provision. However, if you have been tasked with creating a new school playground, then it can be difficult to know where to begin. Here are some tips to help you plan your project.

A good place to start is by identifying your end goals. Perhaps your aim is to:

■ Encourage the children to be more active at playtimes.

■ Expand the exercise opportunities available to students outside.

■ Introduce a new outdoor learning area that can be used all year round.

■ Develop play opportunities that can support the school curriculum.

Consult with key people to understand what they would like from the new playground. For example:

■ Communicate with the children or engage the student council. Find out what they would like in their playground, welcome their ideas and encourage them to draw pictures. Think about how you would like the playground to be seen through their eyes.

▨ Talk to senior leaders, governors, teachers, lunchtime supervisors and other members of staff: what is their vision for the playground? How would teachers like to use the playground? In what ways do staff feel the playground is currently lacking?

▨ Speak with your school's SEND coordinator (if you have one). Find out how the playground can support children with special educational needs and disabilities. If you identify their needs early on, you can build this into your design.

▨ Find out how parents and carers feel about your existing playground. You could involve the PTA, call a general meeting or send out a survey. What do they feel are the strengths and weaknesses? Are there any play opportunities they feel children are missing out on?

Next, you need to identify who will use the play equipment and their needs and abilities. How many children will use the equipment at any one time? What key stage(s) are they? Some equipment may be suitable for children within a particular age range, while other equipment might be perfect for groups of a certain size, so take this into account when developing your plans.

It is a good idea to observe how the children are using your existing playground. Are there any pieces of equipment you would like to keep? If there is a particular piece of apparatus that the children use often then it may be sensible to save some money by reusing it.

If audits or inspection reports have been carried out on your playground, have any problems been identified – for example, does rainwater collect in a certain area? If so, bear this in mind when designing your new playground.

Research what other play facilities are available in the local area, including what apparatus other schools have installed. If you would like to create a unique playground that stands out, then don't install a pirate ship, for example, if a school around the corner already has one!

If you are designing a playground from scratch, think carefully about the right location. Consider the natural landscape and try to get maximum benefit out of the area you have available – for example, why pay extra to flatten a hill if you can cleverly install a slide there?

When considering the location of your playground, don't forget to think about access. Do you want it to be fairly close to the school so the children can reach it easily, or will you need to create a new path to help them get to it safely?

Do you want to divide the play area into different zones? Perhaps you would like a sports area, a gym area or an adventure play area, for example. Do you want a quiet nature area for children to escape to if they are uncomfortable with noise?

Once you have gathered the relevant information, you can start to write a wish list of the features and apparatus you would like to include. There is a whole range of play equipment available, from traditional swings and seesaws to adventure trails and climbing systems, so aim to identify those that match your school's needs and offer the best value.

When you have identified the equipment you need, you can then start to plot where everything will go, taking into account the direction and angle of the sun at different times of year (e.g. slides should never face into the sun), how much space you need around each piece of apparatus in order to comply with safety requirements and whether you will have defined play zones.

When designing your play area, think about how children will experience it and try to create an element of adventure and discovery, so that when they finish with one piece of play equipment, there is another one waiting to entice them.

When planning the project, you may like to contact school playground suppliers, as most offer a free consultation service and can do a free site visit and survey. They can often provide scaled plans, 3D images and sometimes even a 3D video walkthrough. They can also offer useful tips on getting the best value for money and advise on the best materials and products. Not only can you benefit from their specialist knowledge and experience, but they can also provide guidance on health and safety, planning permission and best practice.

When looking for suppliers:

- Choose one that is experienced at working with schools and understands the national curriculum.
- Ensure that any quotation provides a full itemised breakdown of costs, so you can be confident that there are no hidden extras.
- Ask for written confirmation of all the arrangements, including when work will begin, when you can expect it to be finished and the length of the guarantee.
- Find out what aftercare support they offer. Do they offer a maintenance package? Can they perform annual inspections? Can they help to train your school maintenance team to carry out any minor repairs?

Whichever playground company you decide to go with, it is a good idea to carry out some due diligence to satisfy yourself about the quality of their work. Here are some ways in which you could check the credentials of a supplier:

- Ask for evidence of any previous work they have completed and make sure this is recent. Ask for references and request a school visit to check out the work they have done yourself.

- Find out how long they have been established and carry out a credit check to ensure they are financially stable.

- Ask for details about who will be completing the work. Will the company be doing all the work themselves or will they be subcontracting out some elements?

- Find out about the training and qualifications of their design and installation team. Make sure they are trained in all aspects of design and safety.

- Think about safeguarding arrangements. Do all their staff have the necessary DBS certificates?

- If they say they are members of a trade association, ask to see their membership certificate and check that they are listed on the relevant trade association website.

- Ask whether they have won any awards for their work.

- Check that they have appropriate insurance cover (i.e. public liability, product liability and professional indemnity) and ask for copies of any relevant certificates.

- Ensure that the equipment and surfacing conforms to British and European safety standards (i.e. BS EN 1176).

- Always seek legal advice before signing any contracts. This can avoid any embarrassing or costly mistakes.

How much your playground costs will depend on its size and design. The key expenses to consider are the equipment, delivery, installation, surfacing/markings, annual maintenance costs and inspections. If you find the estimated costs are building up, then you may like to explore ways to bring these down:

- Could you build up your playground slowly by buying individual pieces of equipment when you can afford them to help spread the cost over time?

- Ask your supplier about any 'budget friendly' equipment they may have.

- Explore hiring or leasing arrangements rather than purchasing equipment outright.

- Work with what you have. Why spend a fortune removing old asphalt or concrete surfaces, for example, if you can incorporate these into your design?

Find out if your supplier can offer any help towards the cost of your play equipment. They may be able to point you in the direction of grants or provide a funding guide. For example:

- Playdale Playgrounds have published a useful funding guide for the UK. You can request a free copy at: www.playdale.co.uk/playground-equipment-funding.
- Playscheme have a team of expert bid writers: www.play-scheme.co.uk/about/we-help-with-funding.

Even if you intend to refurbish your school playground over time, there may still be grants available. The Greggs Foundation, for example, administers a Local Community Projects Fund which offers grants of up to £2,000 which schools can apply for every calendar year. For details visit: www.greggsfoundation.org.uk/grants.

To reduce the risk of accidents, and to make sure you get the best from your investment, it is important to complete regular inspections to ensure the equipment is in good order. The Royal Society for the Prevention of Accidents (RoSPA) offers lots of relevant advice and information at: www.rospa.com/play-safety/advice.

Here are some further tips to help you develop your school playground and increase your chances of securing funding:

- Try to make the new playground as inviting as possible. Remember that the more creative and imaginative the playground is, the more likely it is to secure funding.
- Funders will be more likely to support you if you make the play area as inclusive as possible.
- As well as outlining how it will benefit your school, let the funders know how your project can improve the local environment. For example, will it transform an area of wasteland into a more wildlife-friendly space?
- Consider including photographs of your current playground (or the area you intend to develop) to give the funder a visual idea of the challenges your school is currently facing.
- Make sure you communicate the benefits of the playground to help the grant-maker understand the difference their funding will make.

Funding opportunities

Kompan Matched Funding Offer
21 Roebuck Way Knowlhill, Milton Keynes MK5 8H
www.kompan.co.uk
internalsales@kompan.com

01908 201002

Kompan run regular competitions offering up to 25% match funding. To qualify, schools must be based in England or Wales and contribute a minimum of £10,000 to the playground project. Keep an eye on the news section of their website for details of future offers.

Lord's Taverners

90 Chancery Lane, London WC2A 1EU

www.lordstaverners.org

foundation@lordstaverners.org

0207 025 0000

Lord's Taverners runs an Outdoor Play Space programme. Grants are generally awarded up to 80% (of the net cost) to a maximum level of £25,000 to help purchase outdoor playground and gym equipment. Applications are only accepted from schools that cater for young people under the age of 25 who have a physical, sensory or learning disability. They do not support schools that cater for socially disadvantaged children or mainstream schools for children with behavioural problems.

Further reading

Department for Education and Skills (2006) *Schools for the Future: Designing School Playgrounds*. Available at: www.gov.uk/government/publications/school-grounds-and-outdoor-space.

English Outdoor Council (2015) *High Quality Outdoor Learning*. Available at: www.outdoor-learning.org/Good-Practice/Good-Practice/High-Quality-Outdoor-Learning.

Learning Through Landscapes (2014) *The Good School Playground Guide: Developing School Playgrounds to Support the Curriculum and Nurture Happy, Healthy Children*. Available at: www.ltl.org.uk/product-tag/good-school-playground-guide.

Ofsted (2008) *Learning Outside the Classroom: How Far Should You Go?* (October). Ref: 070219. Available at: www.lotc.org.uk/wp-content/uploads/2010/12/Ofsted-Report-Oct-2008.pdf.

Public Health England (2015) *What Works in Schools and Colleges to Increase Physical Activity? A Resource for Head Teachers, College Principals, Staff Working in Education Settings, Directors of Public Health, County Sports Partnerships and Wider Partners*. Available at: www.gov.uk/government/publications/what-works-in-schools-to-increase-physical-activity-briefing.

Chapter 10

Environmental projects

We live in a world where forests are being cut down or burnt, natural habitats are being destroyed, animals are being overhunted, fossil fuels are being exhausted, millions of people are dying each year from diseases caused by water pollution, oceans are becoming warmer, droughts and floods are happening more frequently and the disasters keep coming. There are lots of campaigns, schemes, competitions, outreach programmes and other initiatives to help schools become more sustainable and to educate students about biodiversity loss and the climate crisis.

Perhaps you want to:

- Build a shelter or den.
- Run forest school sessions.
- Install a weather station.
- Run recycling workshops.
- Create an outdoor classroom.
- Purchase outdoor tools or equipment.
- Install PV solar panels on your school roof.
- Invite a nature expert into school to deliver talks.
- Create a school market garden or sensory garden.
- Take students on a field trip to learn about conservation.
- Replace single-use plastics with more eco-friendly alternatives.

Fundraising for a conservation project

There are lots of opportunities, tools and resources available to help schools plan and deliver projects relating to conservation and the environment. Depending on the nature of your project and the support you need, there are numerous organisations that are willing to support schools. For example, there are individual charities for frogs, bees, birds, butterflies, trees, clean air, clean oceans, recycling, zoos, botanical gardens, conservation groups and so on. Some organisations can provide educational speakers to deliver talks at your school, while others run award schemes or challenges. Some groups allow students to visit their site for free.

Here are some examples of the help on offer:

Chester Zoo

Moston Road, Upton-by-Chester, Chester CH2 1EU

www.chesterzoo.org/schools/outreach

01244 380280

Schools within 60 minutes of Chester Zoo can request a free visit from their Safari Ranger team who can deliver a one-off workshop. They have a choice of curriculum-linked workshops for each year group from Reception upwards, each lasting 40–60 minutes. The workshops teach students about various topics, such as animals, habitats, life processes, rainforests, evolution and conservation. This service was initiated in 2010 and aims to inspire a generation of conservationists. Chester Zoo can also offer free entry to schoolchildren between November and February.

Greenpeace UK

Canonbury Villas, London N1 2PN

www.greenpeace.org.uk/volunteering/greenpeace-speakers

0207 865 8100

Greenpeace is an environmental organisation with a mission to defend the natural world and help promote peace. They have a network of 'Greenspeakers' across the UK, who are trained, passionate volunteers who can give talks and presentations about the work of the organisation and specific campaigns in areas such as the oceans, forests, air pollution, toxic chemicals and the climate crisis.

Royal Society for the Protection of Birds (RSPB)

The Lodge, Potton Road, Sandy, Bedfordshire SG19 2DL

www.rspb.org.uk/fun-and-learning/for-teachers

01767 680551

The RSPB is working in partnership with Aldi to offer free outreach visits to schools in various cities across Britain. Trained educators can visit your school or early years setting to deliver sessions which encourage students to explore the school grounds for mini-beasts, nature and habitats. Schools can also take part in the RSPB Wild Challenge, which provides a framework for learning. This free award scheme encourages children to connect with and learn about nature through a series of fun and engaging activities. Submissions are accepted from all ages and abilities. It is mainly designed for primary school children in mainstream education, although it can be adapted for home educators, pupils with special educational needs and early years children. The RSPB also provides a range of resources and activities to help schools complete the challenge.

WaterAid

47–49 Durham Street, London SE11 5JD

www.wateraid.org/uk/get-involved/teaching/challenge-water

challengewater@wateraid.org

0207 793 4500

WaterAid is an international charity with the mission to change the lives of people across 28 countries around the world. They run a number of challenges to educate students about water, sanitation, hygiene and basic human rights. Schools can sign up to Challenge: Water, which is perfect for Key Stage 3 and 4 students. WaterAid representatives come into your school for four one-hour sessions which help students to understand water and sanitation problems. Students are put into teams and then take on three exciting competitive challenges. The programme is free, it is closely linked to the national curriculum and provides opportunities for students to develop STEM skills. Teams are supported by industry experts, STEM ambassadors and WaterAid. All students have the chance to achieve a CREST award, giving them national recognition and accreditation for their efforts. While WaterAid can provide schools with sessions and resources, in return schools are encouraged to help raise money for WaterAid.

Wildfowl and Wetlands Trust (WWT)

Slimbridge, Gloucestershire GL2 7BT

www.wwt.org.uk

enquiries@wwt.org.uk

01453 891900

The WWT is the UK's leading wetland conservation charity which operates nine centres across England, Wales, Scotland and Northern Ireland. They provide guided and self-guided learning sessions chiefly aimed at early years to Key Stage 3 children. The hands-on sessions are led by experienced staff, with the aim of promoting learning through exploration and discovery. Please note that there is a charge for these sessions.

The Wildlife Trusts

The Kiln, Mather Road, Newark NG24 1WT

www.wildlifetrusts.org/learning

enquiry@wildlifetrusts.org

01636 677711

The Wildlife Trusts manage 2,300 nature reserves across the UK, the Isle of Man and Alderney. These include heathlands, meadows, ancient woodlands, islands, beaches, moorland and mountains. Most of these reserves (around 98%) are free to visit. Schools can also contact their local Wildlife Trust to see what support they offer schools. For example, they can provide a range of useful resources and may be able to offer guided tours to nature reserves or help to improve school grounds for wildlife. To find a reserve near you or to find the details of your local Wildlife Trust, please visit their website.

World Wide Fund for Nature (WWF)

The Living Planet Centre, Rufford House, Brewery Road, Woking GU21 4LL

www.wwf.org.uk/get-involved/schools

schools@wwf.org.uk

01483 426444

The WWF is an independent conservation organisation which aims to encourage people to take a responsible approach to saving the planet. Schools can enter various awards to receive recognition for their efforts, including the Green Ambassador Awards and the *TES* Sustainable Schools Award.

Young People's Trust for the Environment (YPTE)

Yeovil Innovation Centre, Barracks Close, Copse Road, Yeovil BA22 8RN

http://ypte.org.uk/content/free-school-talks

info@ypte.org.uk

01935 315025

YPTE is a charity which aims to encourage young people's understanding of the environment and the need for sustainability. They offer free school talks for schools within 30 miles of their office in Somerset. Talks can cover a whole range of environmental issues – such as sustainable living, recycling and waste, alternative energies, water and food, British animals, mini-beasts, endangered animals, rainforests, climate change and more – and can be tailored to suit different age groups and abilities.

You can find a list of wildlife conservation groups around the UK via the Tree Surgeon website at: https://treesurgeon.org.uk/wildlife-conservation-groups.

As well as seeking support from conservation charities, schools can also contact other organisations and businesses for help. For example, many energy companies run free programmes to help educate students about the energy they provide. Here are some examples of how energy companies can help schools:

Anglian Water

Lancaster House, Lancaster Way, Ermine Business Park, Huntingdon, Cambridgeshire PE29 6XU

www.anglianwater.co.uk/in-the-community/schools

education@anglianwater.co.uk

Anglian Water operates in the east of England. Their education team are happy to visit schools and deliver free fun and interactive sessions on topics such as water efficiency, pollution, climate change and sustainability. These sessions can encompass all key stages up to A level. The education team are qualified, experienced teachers with current DBS checks. Depending on where you live, there is also the opportunity to visit them at one of their water recycling centres.

Eon Energy

Westwood Way, Westwood Business Park, Coventry CV4 8LG

www.eonenergy.com/about-us/community-matters.html

EUKCommunityRelationsTeam@eon-uk.com

Eon works with schools, charities, local groups and councils in some of the UK's poorest areas. They run a STEM programme called Energise Anything which is designed to engage young people aged 5–18 years. They provide a range of free resources, offer career inspiration and run a number of workshops to help students learn about energy.

Northern Ireland Water

Westland House, 40 Old Westland Road, Belfast BT14 6TE

www.niwater.com/resources-for-schools

waterline@niwater.com

03457 440088

Northern Ireland Water runs an annual schools competition called Every Drop Counts, aimed at primary schools in the country. There are various categories including one for special needs schools. The deadline to enter by is usually in May and winners are invited to an awards ceremony in Belfast, which usually takes place in June. Winning schools receive £250 for first place, £150 for second place and £100 for third place. Students also win 'goody bags' for themselves. They also run a classroom visits programme, educating students about their water processes, and invite schools to visit their sites. They also have a Water Bus – a double-decker bus transformed into a mobile education unit – which can visit schools. All their educational programmes are free.

Shell UK

Shell Centre, London SE1 7NA

https://www.shell.co.uk/sustainability/society/supporting-stem.html

shellschoolsteam@hopscotchconsulting.co.uk

0207 934 1234

The oil and gas company Shell runs the Bright Ideas Challenge to encourage students to use their creativity, problem-solving, teamwork and STEM skills to devise innovative solutions that could power the cities of the future. All regional winners and finalists win cash prizes, plus a funded VIP experience at Make the Future Live festival in London.

Southern Water

Southern House, Yeoman Road, Worthing, West Sussex BN13 3NX

www.southernwater.co.uk/education

Southern Water provides water and wastewater services in Kent, Sussex, Hampshire and the Isle of White. They give free talks to students in Key Stage 2 to help them learn about what is involved in the supply of fresh, clean water and how wastewater is treated before it is returned back into the environment. The company has also developed a range of free resources to support learning about water in schools, including education packs and four children's books. More recently they have launched Water-Saving Mission to help primary schools save water, energy and money.

Thames Water

Clearwater Court, Vastern Road, Reading RG1 8DB

https://corporate.thameswater.co.uk/About-us/Community

school.bookings@thameswater.co.uk

Thames Water supplies water and manages water waste in Greater London, Luton, the Thames Valley, Surrey, Gloucestershire, Wiltshire, Kent and other areas of the UK. If your school is situated in the Thames Water region, then check out their Community Speaker Programme, which enables passionate speakers to come and deliver a talk in your school for free. Their volunteers educate students about water conservation, the water cycle and sewage. Schools can also visit a Thames Water education centre for free, where students will be given an engaging tour of wastewater works, then participate in an interactive session in their well-equipped classroom. Not only can this provide a fun and memorable day out for students, but it can also teach them about water and link it to the national curriculum.

You can find out what other opportunities water companies are offering by visiting the Eco-Schools website at: www.eco-schools.org.uk/get-involved/lea-support.

When planning your environmental project, you may like to align it with other award schemes, such as the Duke of Edinburgh's Award and the John Muir Award. Not only can these schemes give you a framework to work towards, but they can also give your school and students recognition when great things are achieved.

Here are some other awards that schools can enter:

Better Energy School Awards

https://betterenergyschoolawards.org.uk

The Better Energy School Awards aim to encourage environmental education for young people aged 5–11 years. The awards are open to all primary schools in England, Wales and Scotland. To enter, schools must submit details of an environmental project they have carried out, such as work in the school grounds, sensory gardens, wildlife areas or recycling schemes. The overall UK champion receives £5,000, plus there are over 50 other cash prizes.

Community Education Awards – Green Schools Sustainability Award

www.communityeducationawards.co.uk

The Community Education Awards run numerous environmental awards, including the Green Schools Sustainability Award. This recognises projects that lower a school's carbon footprint, promote renewable energy and encourage sustainability. It is open to all schools and pupil referral units.

Eco-Schools National Awards

https://eco-schools.org.uk

Eco-Schools is a free award scheme which was launched in 1994. It aims to help students expand their skills, raise environmental awareness and improve the school environment. Over 18,000 schools are registered and it engages millions of children across 64 countries. Schools can achieve the Bronze, Silver and Green Flag Award. Eco-Schools also provide a range of useful tools and resources to help schools achieve awards.

Nursery World Awards – Enabling Environments Award

www.nurseryworldawards.com

The Nursery World Awards have a category called the Enabling Environments Award. This is open to early years settings and recognises learning environments such as outdoor learning spaces and forest school areas.

TES Schools Awards – Sustainable Schools Award

www.tesawards.co.uk

TES Schools Awards has a Sustainable Schools Award category which recognises schools which take a whole-school approach to sustainability. It is keen to recognise projects which encourage students to develop key skills and put their ideas into action.

You could also check out what is going on during environmental awareness days and weeks. There are usually there are lots of events, competitions and a whole lot more that schools can get involved in. Here are some campaigns your school could be part of:

- January – Big Schools' Birdwatch: www.rspb.org.uk/fun-and-learning/for-teachers/schools-birdwatch
- March – International Day of Forests: www.un.org/en/events/forestsday
- June – Butterfly Education and Awareness Day: www.afbeducation.org/butterfly-conservation/butterfly-education-and-awareness-day
- June – National Insect Week (biennial): www.nationalinsectweek.co.uk
- June – World Environment Day: http://worldenvironmentday.global
- November – National Tree Week: www.treecouncil.org.uk/Take-Part/National-Tree-Week

Have you heard of the Bright Green Future charity? It runs a free training programme for 14–17-year-olds who are interested in the environment, energy and the climate crisis. It is part of a Big Lottery funded project called Our Bright Future. It is aimed at empowering young people to lead progressive change in their communities and local environment. For details and to download an application form visit: www.bright-green-future.org.uk.

Teachers from state schools can also attend the SEEd (Sustainability and Environmental Education) National Sustainable Schools Conference for free. The purpose of the conference is to support educators to embed sustainability into their campus, curriculum and community. It takes place every year in London. See: https://se-ed.co.uk/edu.

Fundraising for a forest school

If you would like to teach students about nature and sustainability – and promote learning outside the traditional classroom – you might like to set up a forest school area. Here are some tips, ideas and tools to give you an insight into what might be involved.

If you want to create a new forest school area, it is advisable to contact your local authority first to ask for help. They may be able to recommend suitable sites and possibly subsidise the cost of visits. There are also forest school organisations of which schools can become (paid) members. Forest School Wales, for example, is a charitable organisation offering support, training and even preferential insurance rates to members to help them run their forest school. For more information visit: www.forestschoolwales.org.uk.

When creating a new forest school or area, you will need to identify the ages and needs of the children who will use it. Do they have any special educational needs and/or disabilities? How many children will use it at any one time?

Forest schools must be led by appropriately qualified leaders who have forest school qualifications and first aid certificates, so you will need to appoint a suitable person to run your forest school. You could bring in a forest school leader from outside the school; however, in the long run it is usually more sustainable to upskill and train an existing teacher or member of staff. For details of accredited forest school courses, please see: www.forestschooltraining.co.uk.

You will need to work out how many adult helpers you need to run your forest school. There is usually one forest school leader plus one helper, although this will depend on staff-to-student ratios, the needs of your students and the nature of your activities. If you are employing a helper or volunteer, make sure you consider DBS checks and safeguarding training.

Most importantly, you will need to identify a suitable location for your forest school. Ideally this will be on your school premises, although this won't be possible for all schools. If this is the case, are there opportunities to collaborate with other local schools and share a site? You can find details of local forest school areas by visiting:

Forest School Association: www.forestschoolassociation.org/find-a-forest-school-provider

Forest School Wales: www.forestschoolwales.org.uk/accessing-forest-school/yg-ar-draws-cymrufs-across-wales

You can also search for local woods to visit for free on the Woodland Trust website: www.woodlandtrust.org.uk/visiting-woods/map.

To identify a suitable forest school area on your own site, observe the natural landscape and try to make the best use of your resources – for example, do you have playing fields, copses, grassed areas or a pond that you can incorporate? Look at the trees, plants and other ecosystems your grounds offer – are there any areas already attracting birds, butterflies, amphibians and other wildlife? Don't forget that even old logs can attract all sorts of interesting creatures!

If you plan on growing plants and produce, then you will need to consider how well-drained the soil is, how much sunlight the area receives (and how it will change with the seasons) and whether you have a nearby water supply.

How often would you like your forest school to take place – for example, will it run weekly throughout the school year or for two solid weeks during the summer term? It is usually a good idea to create opportunities for children to use your forest school on a regular basis to help them connect with nature and the seasons. If you plan to use the area all year round, will you need to install a shelter? Think about seating arrangements too – is the area big enough to accommodate your group size?

Another factor to consider is the accessibility of the area: is it far from the school building? Is the route safe? Can the children walk to it easily? Is there already an existing pathway or would you need to construct a new one? Try to make the route as interesting and fun as possible – could the children observe wildlife, play I spy, tell stories or follow a fun trail along the way?

Don't forget the boundaries too. It is usually a good idea to reserve an area just for your forest school and to section it off by growing plants and trees or cleverly positioning planters.

You will also need to think about health and safety issues and perform any necessary risk assessments. Forest school leaders should also do a daily risk assessment on forest school areas to identify any new risks and put in place strategies to deal with them. You will need to establish comprehensive policies on matters such as clothing, toileting, safety and emergency procedures.

If you are struggling to find a suitable site, don't forget that even concrete areas can be transformed into a forest school using planters, containers, raised beds and clever design. Why not contact a landscape architect to help you develop your ideas? You can find a directory of approved outdoor designers, landscapers, suppliers and training providers on the British Association of Landscape Industries website: www.bali.org.uk/members/directory.

Identify what learning opportunities you would like to provide for the children: what activities do you intend to offer? What do you hope to achieve by running the sessions? Here are some activities you might like to offer:

- Hunting for mini-beasts.
- Creating nature artwork.
- Climbing trees.
- Growing vegetables.
- Playing nature games.
- Using tools.
- Building dens.
- Investigating wildlife.
- Building fires and cooking food.

Don't forget to allow time for the children to freely explore and play too!

To give your project structure, why not take part in the School Enterprise Challenge? The programme is designed to help teachers and students work together to plan and launch a profitable business which also has a positive social and environmental impact, such as recycling waste material to create jewellery or setting up a school garden to sell produce. Not only does the challenge encourage schools to generate income, but they can also access a range of free resources and be in with chance of winning a share of US$50,000 worth of prizes. For details see: www.schoolenterprisechallenge.org.

If you need resources to help you plan your forest school project, here are five websites where you can get access to free lesson plans, risk assessments and more:

Early Learning HQ: www.earlylearninghq.org.uk/lesson-plans-activity-ideas/forest-school-outdoors

Forest Schooled: www.forestschooled.com/resources

Forestry Commission England: www.forestryengland.uk/learning-resources

Twinkl: www.twinkl.co.uk/resource/forest-school-activities

Woodland Trust: www.woodlandtrust.org.uk/get-involved/schools/curriculum-linked-resources

To stay up-to-date with the wider world, why not join the 'I Love Forest School' Facebook group (if your school has a Facebook page)? You can get involved with discussions, post questions and share ideas at: www.facebook.com/groups/124568654451/about.

When it comes to costing your forest school, you will need to take into account the following expenses:

- Design and installation costs – for example, will you use the services of a landscape architect? Will you purchase bird tables, butterfly houses, plants, benches, shelters, fire pits, hammocks and so on?

- Equipment or tools such as firelighters, fire blankets, gloves, cooking equipment, walkie-talkies, whistles and first aid equipment.

- Any materials you need to run your activities, such as craft glue, rope, clay, wood, compasses, tools and so on.

- Drinks and snacks.

- Outdoor clothing for children and staff, such as waterproof suits, wellies, hats, gloves and scarfs.

- Salaries and training costs.

- Insurance premiums. You should discuss your forest school plans with your existing insurance provider as they may be able to update/upgrade your existing policy to reflect the nature of your activities. If you need to take out a new policy, then find out if any forest school organisations you are affiliated with offer discount insurance schemes.

If you need any help or advice when designing your forest school, check out Learning Through Landscapes. This UK charity is dedicated to enhancing outdoor learning and play for children. They offer free membership of their online community, but if you pay a nominal fee you can access a directory of suppliers, lesson plans, publications, training opportunities, member discounts and more. For details visit: www.ltl.org.uk.

Once you have planned your project and identified what funds you need, you can then begin fundraising. Here are five ways you could raise money for an outdoor project:

1. Organise a vegetable, fruit and plant sale. You could ask parents for donations or even contact local garden centres. You could take cuttings from any plants your school may already have and sell these on once they have rooted.

2. Hold a farmers' market event in your school hall or playground. You could raise money by charging each stallholder a fee. (For more on this see Chapter 14).

3. Organise a school fair. You could have a guess the weight of the pumpkin competition and garden-themed lucky dips! If you have an existing school garden, you could give tours and allow visitors to sample produce in exchange for a fee or donation.

4. Arrange a school treasure hunt. You could organise teams and give participants a list of plant-themed items to find that are hidden around your school grounds. You could charge an entry fee per team and offer a prize to the winning team.

5. Host a garden tea party. You could get the children to make sandwiches and cakes or organise a barbeque and charge an entry fee for students and their families. Young children could bring teddy bears and you could organise team games, such as rounders. If you feel really adventurous, you could allow families to camp for the night on your school grounds and charge per pitch.

As well as organising fundraising events, schools can also raise money through taking part in recycling schemes. For example:

TerraCycle Recycling Programme
Sabichi House, 5 Wadsworth Rd, Perivale, Middlesex UB6 7JD
www.terracycle.co.uk/en-GB/brigades
customersupport@terracycle.co.uk
0800 0470 984

TerraCycle offers free recycling programmes for items that cannot be recycled curbside, such as branded air fresheners, personal care products and biscuit wrappers. Educational establishments across England, Wales, Scotland and Northern Ireland simply register online, set up a public drop-off location and send these items off to be recycled. Schools then earn points based on the amount of waste collected, which can be redeemed as charitable gifts or donations. The recycling programmes are funded by brands, manufacturers and retailers around the world – please see their website for full information.

If there are specific items you need to make your garden school project happen, such as plants and tools, then you can register your interest with the following schemes:

- The Woodland Trust is giving away hundreds of thousands of free trees to schools. The aim is to make sure that everyone in the UK has the opportunity to plant a tree. To learn more and apply for a free tree pack visit: www.woodlandtrust.org.uk/freetrees.

- Schools and colleges throughout the UK can receive free trees through the Tree Appeal. The idea is to help schools make the most of their grounds by planting trees. Find out what trees are available and make an application at: www.treeappeal.com/Schools.html.

- The Earth Restoration Service runs two programmes: the School Tree Nursery Programme, (your school receives free tree saplings and essentially becomes a tree nursery until the young trees are ready to be planted out in your school grounds or in the local community) and the Flutter Flowers Programme (schools are matched with a sponsor who provides funding for wild flowers to plant at the school). Discover more at: www.earthrestorationservice.org/schools.

- UK primary schools can receive free flower bulbs by registering to take part in the Bulbs4Kids Golden Flower Bulb Competition. Each school can receive one kit only. To take part in the competition, schools simply send in photos of their flower-growing activities. The school with the most beautiful garden wins! Sign up at: http://uk.bulbs4kids.com.

- Schools can request a free potato-growing kit from Grow Your Own Potatoes. This project was set up to teach primary school children about potatoes and how they fit into a healthy balanced diet. Schools can also access lesson plans and worksheets. Schools can enter a competition once the potatoes have been harvested – and prizes are awarded. For more information visit: http://growyourownpotatoes.org.uk.

- Schools and community groups can receive free tools through the Tools Shed project, which is run by the Conservation Foundation in partnership with HM Prisons. These tools are repaired by prisoners and then given away to schools. Find out more at: www.conservationfoundation.co.uk/tools.

- UK primary schools can borrow a free microscope activity kit from the Royal Microscopic Society (RMS). The kit can be borrowed for an entire term and contains enough microscopes and resources for a whole class of children. The kit is ideal for use in the classroom, but students can also use them on a bug hunt or to explore ponds. RMS organises the delivery and collection of the kits; the only condition is that schools complete a feedback form at the end. For details visit: www.rms.org.uk/discover-engage/microscope-activity-kits.html.

Schools can also find details of lots of free garden goodies that are being given away at the Latest Free Stuff website: www.latestfreestuff.co.uk/free-garden-stuff. Bear in mind that companies give away freebies in the hope of acquiring new customers, so be careful about who you give your contact details to (or tick the opt-out box for receiving future emails).

Here are details of other schemes that schools can get involved with:

- Educational establishments can receive free products and materials from B&Q's Community Re-use scheme. The scheme donates unsellable (non-electrical) items for the benefit of the local community and environment. Nurseries, school, colleges and other community groups can apply – simply contact your local store. For further details see: www.diy.com/corporate/community/waste-donation.

▓ Community RePaint is a UK-wide scheme, run by Resource Futures and sponsored by Dulux, which aims to reuse leftover paint by donating it to communities, charities and individuals in need. Find out more at: https://communityrepaint.org.uk.

▓ If you would like to recruit a volunteer to help improve your outdoor space, then check out the Conservation Volunteers charity. They have a network of conservation volunteers who are keen to build stronger communities. There is an annual membership fee of £38 to join; however, as well as connecting you with potential volunteers, the organisation provides many other benefits, such as discounted insurance rates, negotiated discounts from a range of suppliers of tools, trees, seeds and equipment, plus support and advice with funding. For further details visit: www.tcv.org.uk.

▓ Schools can take part in the Give It a Grow programme, which encourages people to grow organic food. Schools can register, make a pledge and access lots of free online resources at: http://giveitagrow.gardenorganic.org.uk.

▓ Schools can join the RHS School Garden Campaign and receive support to develop a sustainable garden to enhance young people's learning. For more information visit: https://schoolgardening.rhs.org.uk/about-us.

You can also contact local garden centres and nurseries to invite support for your project – perhaps they would be willing to donate a raffle prize or provide hand tools or seeds? Here are examples of how some of the larger garden centres may be able to help:

Dobbies Garden Centres

www.dobbies.com/content/about-dobbies/dobbies-in-the-community.html
community@dobbies.com
Dobbies is the UK's largest garden retailer (they have 67 stores across England, Scotland and Northern Ireland). They are passionate about helping the local communities around their stores to enjoy spending time outdoors and get growing. They launched the Helping Your Community Grow campaign in 2010, which is managed by local stores and offers plants, gardening equipment, support and help (but not cash donations). Projects have to be located within 20 miles of a store.

Wyevale Garden Centres

www.wyevalegardencentres.co.uk
wyevalegardencentres@fourrain.com
0344 272 3000
Wyevale Garden Centres is one of the largest garden retailers in the UK, with over 43 garden centres. As part of their Gardens for Good community programme they are committed to supporting local charities, good causes and schools. All of their stores have a budget available to help these groups. Contact your local garden centre for details.

Think about your project themes and what wider grants may be available. For example, if one of your aims is to encourage students to write poems inspired by nature, then look out for literacy grants too.

When writing your grant application, you will want to communicate the benefits of your forest school project. Here are some examples:

- It can offer a naturally stimulating environment where children can observe, investigate, explore and use their senses.
- It can help children to become aware of their surroundings and the natural world in which they live, helping them to develop a curiosity, love and respect for nature – thereby inspiring the next generation of environmental stewards.
- Open-air learning encourages children to spend regular time outdoors, which can help to reduce stress, improve mental health and boost vitamin D intake.
- It can offer an outdoor environment which is 'wild', yet safe and controlled.
- Children can acquire skills for the outdoors and learn to identify and manage risks (especially if the space is used all year round).
- It can help children to connect classroom theories with reality. It also allows them to develop teamwork and social skills.
- Teachers can observe children outside of the classroom.

Fundraising for renewable energy projects

More and more schools are raising funds to introduce renewable energy systems, such as solar panels, wind turbines, heat pumps and biomass boilers. For example, PV solar panels convert sunshine into electricity; they last around 25 years and produce energy that is clean and green. Not only can they help schools to save money on their electricity bills, but there is also the potential to generate an income. Students also benefit as they can see how renewable energy is generated, and they can help schools to work towards the Eco-School National Awards. They demonstrate 'green leadership', they can inspire other schools to operate more sustainably and, on a larger scale, they can help the country to reduce its carbon emissions.

You can access a carbon footprint calculator (developed by the WWF) at: http://footprint.wwf.org.uk.

You can also check out useful links and resources at: https://1010uk.org/solar-schools/what-next.

If you are considering installing solar technology in your school, then a good place to start is to contact your local authority. They may be able to offer support, advice or funding, recommend contractors or help in other ways. Schools can also request a free consultation with a renewable energy provider, who can help to analyse your current energy bills, survey your school site and determine your roof capacity and solar potential. They should be able to recommend the best solutions, provide current industry advice and tell you about any financial support available.

You can find a list of renewable energy suppliers at the Solar Trade Association's website: www.solar-trade.org.uk/member-list.

There are price comparison websites which can provide free quotes for solar panels and renewable energy installations. For details visit:

Compare My Solar: www.comparemysolar.co.uk/solar-panel-prices

Renewable Energy Hub: www.renewableenergyhub.co.uk/search-installers

You can also find renewable energy providers at energy and sustainability exhibitions, where there are usually opportunities to take part in seminars and advice clinics. To find details about sustainability events near you visit: www.eventbrite.co.uk/d/united-kingdom/sustainability-events.

When it comes to shopping for solar power technology, you will need to select the right solution for your school. Solar panels are usually cheaper and more efficient than solar tiles, although they are less attractive and less discreet. There are various manufacturers of both solar panels and solar tiles, so make sure you compare the price, efficiency, value for money and product warranty of each option. Aside from the cost of the solar panels/tiles, you will need additional items such as mounting frames and cables. Schools may also benefit from purchasing a solar battery storage system to store surplus energy.

To determine which solar energy system is right for you, it is useful to assess your school's current energy consumption per day (in kilowatt hours). For a quick insight into how much energy your school is generating, visit the Solar for Schools website: www.solarfor-schools.co.uk. Simply enter your school name and address into their search box feature and you can instantly access a 'solar profile' of your school. It analyses your current electricity usage and calculates how much you could save in both carbon emissions and money over a 25-year period if you installed a solar energy system. It takes less than 10 seconds to do and can return some really useful information.

You will also need to assess what roof space you have available to accommodate solar panels. If you have a small roof, for example, higher efficiency solar panels may be a better option. Although they are more expensive, they produce more energy per panel than the less efficient panels. Don't forget to barter, especially if you are looking to install solar panels across multiple sites.

To get maximum benefit from your solar panels you will need to install them in the best possible place. Ideally you will have a large south-facing roof which is angled towards the sun; the stronger the sunshine, the more electricity is produced (but don't forget that solar panels may still generate some electricity even on cloudy days). If you don't have suitable roof space, solar panels can be mounted on the ground. Solar panels tilted at an angle benefit from being cleaned by natural rainfall; if they are installed on the ground, their efficiency may be compromised by any debris that builds up.

You will also need to think about how you will maintain your renewable energy equipment, so be sure to discuss maintenance plans with your supplier and be aware of any ongoing cost commitments before you sign up. You should also put in place strategies to monitor your equipment: will you be able to access real-time data about your carbon savings? Will you be given a display unit for your school reception area?

Although solar energy systems can be costly to install, once they are in place they can generate free, clean electricity for years to come. This can be used on site and thus cut the costs of school electricity bills. As energy prices continue to rise, schools can relax in the knowledge they will not be affected by this. The money schools save on their energy bills can then be spent on teaching and learning.

If you are struggling to find the capital for this project, schools can explore other options such as a power purchase agreement (PPA). A PPA means that an energy provider (or third-party asset investor) agrees to fund the installation and maintenance costs; in return, the school agrees to purchase electricity from them at an agreed rate which is cheaper than the original supplier. The benefits to the school are that there are no upfront costs or ongoing fees and they can enjoy lower energy costs over a fixed period. The downsides are that the price also includes the cost of professional services provided by the energy provider and that schools can save more money over the long term by owning the PV system outright. Make sure you choose the best option for your school.

The charity Solar for Schools helps schools to connect with investors and installers who fund the installation costs and then sell electricity at a pre-agreed rate to the school. Once all of the costs have been deducted, they then share any profits with the school. For more details visit: www.solarforschools.co.uk. Be sure to research schemes thoroughly and find out what other funding models are available before signing any contracts.

State-maintained and grant-aided schools can apply for an interest-free loan to help make energy-saving improvements (including insulation and LED lighting) through the Salix Energy Efficiency Loan Scheme (SEELS) which is funded by the Department for Education. For details visit: www.salixfinance.co.uk/loans/schools-loans.

If you would like to apply for a grant to help fund your solar panels, you could also explore:

- Grants offered by your existing gas and electricity supplier.
- Grants offered by local service stations.

- Grants offered by local landfill sites.
- General capital grants.
- Environmental grants.
- STEM-related grants.

Don't forget that crowdfunding is another way to raise money for environmental projects. You can see an example of a school fundraising for solar panels on the Crowdfunder website: www.crowdfunder.co.uk/the-wight-school-solar-panel-project.

Funding opportunities

Here are details of grants and other support which your school may like to explore:

3Mgives

3M Centre, Cain Road, Bracknell RG12 8HT
www.3m.co.uk/3M/en_GB/gives-uk
innovation.uk@mmm.com
08705 360036

3M is a science-based technology company that is committed to improving lives and doing business in the right way. Employees are entitled to take one work day per year to participate in a 3Mgives volunteering project associated with STEM education and/or sustainable living. Rather than making financial donations, 3M offer volunteers' skills instead. They also run a community programme, partnering with schools close to their major UK sites. STEM Ambassadors work with schools to show that scientists and engineers don't spend all their lives wearing white coats working in laboratories! They demonstrate that a wide range of interesting and rewarding careers are open to people with STEM qualifications. 3M also runs the 3M Young Innovators Challenge for schools. See their website for details.

Ernest Cook Trust

The Estate Office, Fairford Park, Fairford, Gloucestershire GL7 4JH
http://ernestcooktrust.org.uk/grants
admin@ernestcooktrust.org.uk
01285 712492

At the time of writing, the Trust were reviewing their funding priorities and designing new grant-giving schemes in line with their overall mission of learning from the land. Check their website for up-to-date details.

Esmée Fairbairn Foundation

Kings Place, 90 York Way, London N1 9AG
https://esmeefairbairn.org.uk

info@esmeefairbairn.org.uk

0207 812 3700

One of the Foundation's funding priorities is to connect people with nature and environmental issues. They support work which inspires people to connect with nature and encourages them to take action to make a difference.

Local Schools Nature Grants Scheme

www.ltl.org.uk/naturegrants

Grants are available up to the value of £500 in products or training from the company. They do not award cash grants.

Marks & Spencer's Energy Fund

www.mandsenergyfund.com

hello@mandsenergyfund.com

The M&S Community Energy Fund offers community groups the chance to win a slice of £300,000 in grants.

Naturesave Trust

South Devon House, Babbage Road, Totnes TQ9 5JA

www.naturesave.co.uk/naturesave-trust

mail@naturesave.co.uk

01803 864390

The Trust is administered by Naturesave Insurance which allocates a percentage of premiums to spend on community, environmental and sustainability projects. Small grants are usually awarded under £3,000; however, they can also consider funding larger projects.

Nineveh Charitable Trust

8 Mill Lane, Saffron Walden, Essex CB10 2AS

www.ninevehtrust.org.uk/how-to-apply

Schools within the UK can apply to the Nineveh Charitable Trust fund. Projects must relate to the health, welfare and education of the general public. In the past the Trust has helped to fund a school sensory garden, forest school programmes, gardening equipment and an after-school club.

Further reading

Forest school projects:

ESP Play (2017) How to Create a Forest School Style Environment in Your Playground (29 August). Available at: www.espplay.co.uk/how-to-create-a-forest-school-style-environment-in-your-playground.

Harris, F. (2018) Outdoor Learning Spaces: The Case of Forest School, *Area*, 50: 222–231. Available at: www.forestschooltraining.co.uk/_webedit/uploaded-files/All%20Files/Research%20 papers/Harris-2018-Area.pdf.

O'Brien, L. and Murray, R. (2007) Forest School and Its Impacts On Young People: Case Studies In Britain, *Urban Forestry & Urban Greening*, 6: 249–265. Available at: www.outdoorrecreationni. com/wp-content/uploads/2015/11/Forest-School-and-its-impacts-on-young-children_OBrien_ Murray-2007.pdf.

Woodland Trust and Forestry Commission Scotland (2015) *Outdoor Learning Pack for Primary School Teachers*. Available at: www.woodlandtrust.org.uk/mediafile/100146207/Getting-outside-the-classroom-learning-pack.pdf.

Sustainability projects:

Carbon Trust (2012) *Schools: Learning to Improve Energy Efficiency* (March). Available at: www. carbontrust.com/media/39232/ctv019_schools.pdf.

Department for Education (2012) *Top Tips for Sustainability in Schools* (February). Ref: DFE-32056-2012. Available at: www.gov.uk/government/publications/top-tips-for-sustainability-in-schools.

Department for Education and Education and Skills Funding Agency (2012) Tips to Reduce Energy and Water Use in Schools. Available at: www.gov.uk/government/publications/top-tips-to-reduce-energy-and-water-use-in-schools.

Department of Energy and Climate Change (2014) *'Power to the Pupils': Solar PV for Schools*. Available at: www.gov.uk/government/publications/power-to-the-pupils-solar-pv-for-schools.

Friends of the Earth (2015) *Get Your School to Run on Sun: How Every School Can Benefit from Solar Power*. Available at: https://friendsoftheearth.uk/sites/default/files/downloads/solar-pack-schools-46837.pdf.

Chapter 11
Walking, cycling and scooting projects

Many schools have walking bus schemes, cycle trains and even scooter clubs, and there is funding and other support available to help make this happen.

Perhaps you are keen to:

▦ Increase the number of students and families walking or cycling to school.

▦ Improve punctuality and attendance.

▦ Promote sustainable ways to travel.

▦ Reduce noise and air pollution around your school.

▦ Encourage students to develop healthy habits and live active lives.

▦ Teach students the Green Cross Code and promote road safety.

▦ Educate students about the local community and increase their geographical awareness.

There are lots of benefits to walking, cycling or scooting to school schemes. They can help to reduce traffic congestion and resolve parking issues, creating a safer environment outside the school gates. They can promote physical exercise and offer opportunities for students to travel together and socialise before the school day begins. They can help to keep students safe on their journey to and from school – and help them to arrive on time for registration! They also promote an environmentally friendly and inexpensive way of travelling.

If you – or your potential funders – still need to be convinced, here are some powerful facts:

▦ '1 in 4 cars on the road during the morning peak are on the school run and over 2,000 schools and nurseries in England and Wales are within 150 metres of a road with illegal levels of air pollution.'[1]

---

1 J. Irvin, chief executive of Living Streets quoted in H. Smith, *Swap the School Run for a School Walk: Our Solution for Active Children, Healthy Air and Safe Streets. A Living Streets Report* (London: Living Streets, 2018), p. 3. Available at: www.livingstreets.org.uk/media/3618/ls_school_run_report_web.pdf.

- 'Three quarters of children live within a 15 minute cycle ride of a secondary school, while more than 90% live within a 15 minute walk or bus journey from a primary school.'[2]

- 'Nearly a third of children aged 2 to 15 are overweight or obese and younger generations are becoming obese at earlier ages and staying obese for longer.'[3]

- 'Only 22% of children aged between 5 and 15 met the physical activity guidelines of being at least moderately active for at least 60 minutes every day (23% of boys, 20% of girls).'[4]

If you would like to access statistics about road safety and accidents from the Department for Transport, then please visit: www.gov.uk/government/collections/road-accidents-and-safety-statistics.

To ensure your scheme is a success, you may also like to contact your local authority's road safety team, as they can offer advice, guidance and information about training. They may even have funding available (from central government), so it can be worth making contact with them in the early stages of your project.

If there is another school in the area which has already set up a travel scheme, why not contact them for advice on how best to organise your own scheme? If the school is nearby and the students take similar routes to school, perhaps there could be an opportunity to create a joint travel scheme.

Find out if your school has a school travel plan as this can be useful when developing your project. If you need additional help or want to find out more, then check out the travel planning information on the Modeshift STARS website: www.modeshiftstars.org/about/travel-planning.

Here are five websites to help you organise and manage a school travel scheme:

Brake
www.brake.org.uk/schools-communities
Brake is a road safety charity which provides lots of teaching resources.

Future Travel
www.futuretravel.org.uk/teacherdownloads
Future Travel provides free curriculum-linked resources to support lessons in Key Stage 3 geography, science and citizenship.

---

2 Department for Transport, *The Cycling and Walking Investment Strategy* (April 2017), p. 9. Available at: www.gov.uk/government/publications/cycling-and-walking-investment-strategy.

3 See www.gov.uk/government/publications/health-matters-obesity-and-the-food-environment/health-matters-obesity-and-the-food-environment--2.

4 See www.gov.uk/government/publications/health-matters-obesity-and-the-food-environment/health-matters-obesity-and-the-food-environment--2.

Letz Go Green

http://letzgogreen.org

Letz Go Green provides educational resources for schools and students, enabling them to learn about sustainable travel.

Living Streets

www.livingstreets.org.uk/walktoschool

Created in 1929, Living Streets is the UK charity for everyday walking. Check out their Walk to School programme.

Sustrans

www.sustrans.org.uk

Sustrans is a registered charity that has been promoting walking and cycling since 1977. Their volunteer Active Travel Champions visit schools and communities to encourage people to travel actively.

When developing ideas for your travel scheme, try to engage students, teachers, parents and governors to gauge who is interested in what type of scheme. Perhaps you could devise a survey to find out things like:

- How students and families are currently travelling to school (e.g. are they arriving by car, bus, bike or on foot?).
- What route(s) people are currently taking to school.
- Who would use a walking bus regularly.
- What difference a new walking bus would make to families.
- Whether there is anything that would discourage students from walking to school.

You will need to plan your routes carefully, including where each one will start, and determine any 'bus stops' along the way. Make sure that any routes (and bus stops) you choose are safe, and try to keep road crossings to a minimum. Contact your local road safety team if you feel that any pathways could be improved. They can usually help with signage, lighting/markings and safety barriers. Can your school make any routes more attractive? Perhaps you could encourage the students to carve wooden sculptures and ask permission from the council to install these along the route!

Try to link your project to areas of the national curriculum. For example, you could encourage the students to look at maps and help plan routes to teach them geography, or invite them to conduct traffic surveys and translate data into graphs and charts to teach numeracy.

If you are planning a new walking bus, then you will need to decide how many days it will run. It is a good idea to start small and build up slowly – perhaps establish just one to begin with which operates for one day a week on a single route to see how well it goes down with the students.

You will need to identify a responsible person to lead your scheme and work out how many escorts will be necessary. You will also need to devise rotas and assign key roles – for each walking bus there is usually a 'driver' and a 'conductor'. Try to recruit positive role models, such as parents, carers, older students and staff members, to accompany the children and supervise them along the route. Make sure that all volunteers have the necessary DBS checks and training.

If you are struggling to find escorts, then you may like to look for outside support. You could ask your local police community support officers for help (they may be able to give a talk on personal safety too). You could also look to charities like Sustrans for volunteers (see page 117 for contact details).

You will also need to think about health and safety. At least one of the escorts should be qualified in first aid and carry a well-stocked first aid kit. You should also draw up rules to ensure that participants act responsibly and know the consequences for unwanted behaviour. It is important to complete a risk assessment for each route; contact your local authority if you need help with this.

Plan how you will promote the scheme and try to get as many students involved as possible. Perhaps the students could design leaflets to promote road safety or enter a competition to publicise your scheme. You could also discuss road safety in your weekly assembly as part of the Healthy Schools agenda.

To keep your project interesting and promote key messages, you may also like to get involved with some of the national awareness days. Here are some key dates with a travel theme:

- March/July/November – Beep Beep Day (for nurseries and schools with children aged 2–7 years): www.brake.org.uk/schools-communities/pre-schools
- May – Happy Shoesday: www.livingstreets.org.uk/what-we-do/projects/happy-shoesday
- May – Walk to School Week: www.livingstreets.org.uk/what-we-do/projects/walk-to-school-week
- June – National Bike Week: http://bikeweek.org.uk
- October – International Walk to School Month: www.livingstreets.org.uk/what-you-can-do/campaigns/international-walk-to-school-month
- November – Road Safety Week: www.roadsafetyweek.org.uk

Here are some challenges that schools can get involved with to encourage sustainable travel:

▨ The Big Peddle challenge usually takes place in the spring for two weeks. To take part, schools record the number of journeys that children make by cycling or scooting to school. The school with the highest number of journeys wins. In 2019, 2,299 schools registered and 746,278 children took part. For more see: https://bigpedal.org.uk.

▨ Schools in Wales can take part in the Big Shift Cymru five-day challenge. It is a free-to-access online challenge: schools simply complete a quick survey about their school, then set individual targets to encourage students to travel to school in an active way. Schools can register a class, year group or even the whole school and participants earn a certificate for taking part. Find out more at: http://bigshiftcymru.sustrans.org.uk.

Your school travel scheme can also help you work towards various awards and accreditations. Modeshift STARS, for example, is a free national award recognising schools that demonstrate excellence in cycling, walking and other forms of sustainable travel. There are bronze, silver and gold awards. If a school achieves a gold award, it is automatically entered into the National STARS School Travel Award which recognises the best schools in the country. It is free for schools in England (outside London). For details see: www.modeshiftstars.org/education. Schools based in London should look out for Transport for London's STARS accreditation scheme: https://stars.tfl.gov.uk.

If you are launching a new cycle or scooter scheme, then you will need to review the area your school reserves for bikes and scooters to ensure there is adequate provision. It is important to provide a secure area, not only to keep them safe and protected from the elements but also to encourage more people to cycle and scoot to school. If you need to develop an area of your car park, there are various cycle stands, shelters and other structures available. Contact manufacturers which offer a range of products and who can advise on the best solution for your school. Find out whether you need planning permission, especially if the structure you plan to install is close to any boundaries. You will also need to ensure that you have security cameras in place.

Keep an eye out for competitions that help schools to win a bike shelter. These are usually organised by street furniture manufacturers and run in conjunction with awareness events such as National Bike Week (which takes place every June). Also look out for capital grants if you need funding for cycle shelters, storage lockers or new pathways.

Depending on the nature of your project, there may be various costs involved in making it happen. For example, you might need funding for:

▨ High-visibility vests, reflective clothing and helmets.

▨ Waterproof ponchos.

- Whistles.
- Bikes.
- Scooters.
- Cycle shelters.
- Outside lockers.
- Security cameras.
- Insurance.
- Road safety workshops.

You will also need to take into account any costs incurred for promoting your scheme, such as posters, leaflets or cycle maps. If you are trying to incentivise the children to travel by foot or bike by offering prizes for journeys made or distance travelled, then remember that these don't have to cost the earth – they could be as simple as rewarding children with extra play time, house points or certificates. Letz Go Green have created some certificates which you can download for free and hand out to children participating in your scheme (you must register on the website first): http://letzgogreen.org/certificates.

When it comes to insurance, there are various issues you need to consider:

- Find out if your travel scheme can be covered under the local council's insurance. If so, ascertain what the requirements are to ensure that you are fully covered.
- If the scheme is being organised by the school PTA, then it may already be covered under the PTA's existing insurance policies.
- Check what insurance the school already has – for example, children on the walking bus may already be covered under the pupils' personal accident insurance.

Find out what help your local authority can offer, as they can sometimes help out with costs or supply information about grants. They may even be able to loan bikes and scooters to students. Find out if there are any bike libraries in your area from which families may be able to borrow bikes.

If you are considering buying re-conditioned bikes, there are various schemes available for schools. For example, some charities, recycling centres and social enterprise companies receive bike donations which they then service and repair for schoolchildren, refugees and people on a low income. They sell these on at low cost or donate them for free. There are also prison schemes that give inmates opportunities to engage in meaningful work, learn mechanical skills and improve future employability by gaining a qualification in cycle mechanics.

Halfords donates re-conditioned bikes as part of their CSR programme. So far they have donated hundreds of bikes to help disadvantaged people and given new helmets to primary school children in economically challenged parts of the UK. For details see: www. halfordscompany.com/corporate-responsibility/community.

Schools can also be nominated to receive scooters from Scooter Aid. This organisation revamps old, unwanted scooters and then donates them to good causes within the UK. Since 2012 they have helped over 200 charities and good causes. To learn more visit: www.micro-scooters.co.uk/scooteraid-recycle-rehome-relove.

Have you heard of the Big Bike Revival? The project has been running for more than four years and aims to help people to begin or get back into cycling. There are lots of free cycling events across England and Scotland, including free bike check-ups, puncture repair workshops and learn-to-ride sessions. To find an event near you visit: www.cyclinguk.org/bigbikerevival.

When planning your fundraising activities, consider timing events to tie in with any national campaigns taking place. Many donors set aside a budget to support these campaigns, promote key messages and help good causes. For example, if you need high-visibility clothing to keep children safe when travelling to and from school, then look out for giveaways during Road Safety Week. It is organised by the charity Brake and takes place every November. Many businesses support Road Safety Week and give away freebies to promote it – look on Twitter using the hashtags #RoadSafetyWeek, #giveaways and #competitions. Thousands of schools, nurseries, colleges and other organisations take part to promote road safety. To get involved and to find out more visit: www.roadsafetyweek.org.uk.

Specsavers opticians have donated hundreds of hi-vis vests to schools and community organisations, and in the past they have given out free hi-vis vests to children entering their stores during Road Safety Week. To find details of your local store visit: www. specsavers.co.uk/stores.

Local businesses may also be willing to sponsor your scheme, particularly those keen to promote safety. For example, local construction companies usually want to be seen as responsible businesses; if they already purchase safety clothing for their own needs, they might be in a good position to help you too. Local supermarkets, cycle shops or garages might be prepared to pay for some hi-vis clothing if it identifies them as the sponsor and features the company name.

You could also invite local clubs to join you in raising money. Members of a local walking or cycling group might be prepared to complete a sponsored walk or cycling challenge to fundraise for your project.

Is your school signed up to receive Bikeability training? This programme – from the National Standard for Cycle Training (and recognised by the Department for Transport) – offers cycle training to children (in Years 5 to 7) as well as training for adults and families.

Some local authorities offer Bikeability for free or at a reduced price. To find out more visit: https://bikeability.org.uk.

Schools can also sign up to cycle-to-work schemes to help staff save money when buying a new bike. These are employee benefit schemes where staff pay a 'salary sacrifice', usually over a 12-month period. The idea is to help employees spread the cost of buying a new bike; it can also help them to save money as it is a tax-efficient scheme. If your school signs up to a provider like Cyclescheme, for example, staff can save 25–39% of the cost of a new bike and accessories. To learn more about Cyclescheme and to access a savings calculator visit: www.cyclescheme.co.uk/calculator. While this doesn't represent a material saving for the school, staff would be acting as positive role models for the children if they were regularly seen cycling or walking to school.

If you would like to apply for a grant, then check to see if any funds are available from the Department for Transport and other transport agencies. Travel Scotland is currently offering match-funded grants from £5,000 through the Smarter Choices, Smarter Places Open Fund, which is open to schools, colleges and universities. The purpose of the grants is to encourage more walking and cycling in Scotland. For further information visit: www.pathsforall.org.uk/active-travel/smarter-choices-smarter-places/open-fund.

Funding opportunities

Here are some grants which schools may like to explore further:

Active Travel Funding

Rosebery House, 9 Haymarket Terrace, Edinburgh EH12 5EZ
www.sustrans.org.uk/scotland/schools/active-travel-funding-schools
scotland@sustrans.org.uk
0131 346 1384
There are two sources of funding to support active travel to school in Scotland. The Cycle and Scooter Parking Fund provides funding for parking facilities in schools, while the Places for Everyone fund supports walking and cycling infrastructure around schools.

Albert Hunt Trust

Wealth Advisory Services, 440 Strand, London WC2R 0QS
0345 304 2424
The Albert Hunt Trust offers grants to fund projects that improve physical and mental welfare. Previous grants have ranged from £1,000 to £30,000, although most grants are between £1,000 and £2,000. In the past they have donated money to schools for health and well-being projects.

Further reading

Cycling UK (2017) Cycling to School or College. Briefing 7c (November). Available at: www.cyclinguk.org/sites/default/files/document/2017/12/schools-and-colleges_7c_brf.pdf.

Department for Transport (2017) *The Cycling and Walking Investment Strategy* (April). Available at: www.gov.uk/government/publications/cycling-and-walking-investment-strategy.

Letz Go Green (n.d.) *School Travel Campaign Toolkit*. Available at: http://letzgogreen.org/workshops/Toolkit/School-Travel-Campaign-Toolkit.pdf.

Smith, H. (2018) *Swap the School Run for a School Walk: Our Solution for Active Children, Healthy Air and Safe Streets: A Living Streets Report* (London: Living Streets). Available at: www.livingstreets.org.uk/media/3618/ls_school_run_report_web.pdf.

Smith, L., Norgate, S., Cherrett, T., Davies, N., Winstanley, C. and Harding, M. (2015) Walking School Buses as a Form of Active Transportation for Children: A Review of the Evidence, *Journal of School Health*, 85(3): 197–210. Available at: https://onlinelibrary.wiley.com/doi/full/10.1111/josh.12239.

Chapter 12
Music projects

If your school needs to raise money for a music project, there are different options you can take depending on the time you have available to fundraise and the level of funding you need. If you only need a small amount of funding – to buy a few instruments, for example – then it can be worth organising a school fundraiser or kindly asking your PTA for a donation. However, if you need a more substantial amount of funding – perhaps to build a new music centre – then you may also like to crowdfund, explore grants, attract a sponsor or use a combination of these methods.

If you would like to plan a school fundraiser, then there are lots of fun music-themed events you can organise. Here are five ideas to inspire you:

1. *X Factor*-style competition or talent show: You could invite singers, musicians and dancers to perform in front of families and generate money by selling tickets and refreshments.

2. Dance evening: Invite a local dance instructor into school for an evening of line dancing or Irish dancing. Alternatively, you could organise a school disco, themed disco, roller skating disco or even a silent disco. You could sell tickets and provide snacks and drinks.

3. Karaoke evening: Invite students, families, staff and other supporters to get together for a social night to raise money for your cause.

4. Music festival: Host a summer concert on your school grounds and invite local singers and musicians to perform. You could also organise a barbeque and other stalls.

5. Sponsored silence: Challenge members of your school community to stay silent for the day to help raise money.

Another way schools can raise funds is by creating a music CD to sell to parents, families and the local community. You could invite students to sing a new song or even create a whole album. Not only can this help to raise money, but it can also be lots of fun! You could create the CD in school or partner with a company. For example, Recordings 4 Schools can help you to make a professional music CD. Simply view their online calendar and book a date that is convenient. Engineers will travel to your school with their mobile recording studio and then edit and master the recordings onto a CD. They deal with all aspects of copyright clearance and can even design the artwork and packaging. Although there are no upfront recording costs, schools must commit to a minimum order of 50 CDs, so be sure to investigate the costs and read the terms and conditions. Recordings 4 Schools can record at all schools, colleges and universities across the UK. They also run a price match policy – they aim to match or beat the price of a similar service. To find out more (and to listen to audio samples), check out their website: www.recordings4schools.co.uk.

If you would like to leverage support from the local community, then remember that organisations don't always have to provide money or donations to help. If a business can give you access to their customers, by allowing you to fundraise on their premises or attend an event, they can still play a key role in helping you to raise money.

Here are some examples of how different organisations can help you to raise funds for your music project without directly giving themselves:

- Local pubs could organise a charity collection from customers.
- Supermarkets could allow you to bag pack or fundraise in their foyer.
- Shops could help you to sell raffle tickets.
- Some hospitals have a desk to allow charities and good causes to sell crafts and raise money.
- Some local shopping centres allow students to perform and ask for donations from the public.

Try to create lasting relationships with organisations that are prepared to help out, and keep thinking ahead. If you would like your local corner shop to sell raffle tickets on your behalf in the future, then thank them in your school newsletter, credit them on your website and/or send them a handwritten thank-you card. These gestures don't have to cost you a penny but they can make a real difference. Today they may have helped you to raise just £50, but over the months and years their backing can really add up. Always show appreciation for any support given, especially as some will have to make a genuine sacrifice to help. Aim to build up a support network, so the next time you need to fundraise you already have people you can turn to.

There are a number of musicians who are willing to perform in schools or run workshops. Here is some information you may find useful:

CAVATINA Chamber Music Trust

52D Maresfield Gardens, London NW3 5RX
www.cavatina.net/schoolconcerts.html
0203 601 2978
This charity offers free chamber music concerts in state-maintained schools across the country (independent schools are asked to cover half of the performers' fees). Schools will need to pay travel costs but the charity will try to find a local ensemble.

Live Music Now Ltd

www.livemusicnow.org.uk/children_young_people_and_sen

send@livemusicnow.org

0207 014 2829

This charity is dedicated to offering live music experiences to the most disadvantaged people in society. One of their programmes caters for children with special educational needs.

Music for Youth

Music for All, Bailey House, 4–10 Barttelot Road, Horsham, West Sussex RH12 1DQ

www.mfy.org.uk/events/primary-proms

01403 800500

This charity runs the Primary Proms scheme, offering primary school children the opportunity to attend free live music events across the UK. For further details, including a resource pack, see their website.

If you are interested in grants for music projects, there are grants for schools, grants for music partners, grants for individual teachers and even grants for students. The Paul Hamlyn Foundation, for example, has an Arts-based Learning Fund; although schools can't apply for this directly, arts organisations working with schools can. The Foundation also has a grant programme called the Teacher Development Fund, which aims to help primary school teachers deliver arts-based learning opportunities. For further information visit:

Paul Hamlyn Foundation

5–11 Leeke Street, London WC1X 9HY

www.phf.org.uk/funds/access-and-participation-fund

information@phf.org.uk

0207 812 3300

If you identify any music students that need help, then it's useful to know that there are grants (and interest-free loans) to help musicians purchase musical instruments, as well as charities that hire out musical instruments. Grants are also available to help pay for professional music lessons and to cover any performance fees (including travel expenses). In addition, there are opportunities for students to attend music therapy sessions for free.

Nordoff Robbins, for example, is a national music therapy charity which aims to transform the lives of vulnerable people across the UK. They provide free sessions for children of all ages in their centres and units – from one-to-one music therapy to specialised music lessons and shared group sessions. Teachers and parents can make a referral if they think a child would benefit from music therapy. For full details see: www.nordoff-robbins.org.uk.

Funding opportunities

Here are some schemes which teachers can nominate music students for:

Felicity Belfield Music Trust

69 North End, Ditchling, Hassocks, West Sussex BN6 8TE

www.felicitybelfieldmusictrust.co.uk

info@felicitybelfieldmusictrust.co.uk

Teachers can recommend students to the Felicity Belfield Music Trust if they believe 'the student is worthy of a better instrument than they can afford'. The Trust helps students to purchase a new musical instrument (excluding harps and electronic equipment). The instrument is loaned to the student and given back when they reach the age of 25. Students can print off an application form via their website.

National Youth Arts Trust

c/o The Furniture Practice, 31 Pear Tree Street, London EC1V 3AG

www.nationalyouthartstrust.org.uk

admin@nationalyouthartstrust.org.uk

07891 835589

The Trust offers £1,000 bursaries for young people (who have been resident in the UK for at least three years) aged between 7 and 25 years who are eligible for the pupil premium (the senior management team must provide confirmation of this). Bursaries can be used to fund professional musical lessons, both instrumental and singing. As part of the application, schools must act as a referee by providing a letter of recommendation (which is signed, stamped and on letterheaded paper) which testifies to the applicant's passion, talent and commitment to the art form.

If your school would like to apply for a grant to help fund a music project, then here are some organisations you may wish to contact:

Jessie's Fund

15 Priory Street, York YO1 6ET

http://jessiesfund.org.uk

info@jessiesfund.org.uk

Jessie's Fund work with special schools and also support individual children with complex additional needs through the provision of music therapists. The majority of their larger grants are between £2,000 and £4,000.

Music for All

Bailey House, 4–10 Barttelot Road, Horsham, West Sussex RH12 1DQ

www.musicforall.org.uk

01403 800500

Grants of up to £2,500 are available. Music for All are also able to donate musical instruments and tuition.

Restore the Music UK

www.restorethemusicuk.com

info@restorethemusicuk.com

07767 776934

The trust offers grants to schools across London to enable them to buy musical instruments and fund tuition. Primary schools can apply for up to £10,000 and secondary schools up to £20,000.

Roger David Burrows Music Fund

c/o The Burrows Family, 17 Squires Lane, Martlesham Heath, Ipswich, Suffolk IP5 3UG

www.rogerdavidburrows.co.uk

Schools and other educational establishments can apply for £150 to help purchase musical instruments or equipment.

Universal Music UK Sound Foundation

4 Pancras Square, London N1C 4AG

www.emimusicsoundfoundation.com

emimusicsoundfoundation@umusic.com

0203 932 6101

Instrument and equipment awards can provide schools with up to £1,500 to purchase new resources.

Further reading

Music Mark, Arts Council England and National Governors' Association (2016) *Music Education: A Guide for Governors.* Available at: www.musicmark.org.uk/marketplace/a-guide-for-governors-music-education.

Savage, J. (2017) *Funding Music Education in Your School.* Available at: www.ucanplay.org.uk/funding-music-education-in-your-school.

Savage, J. and Barnard, D. (2019) *The State of Play: A Review of Music Education in England 2019* (Manchester: Musicians' Union). Available at: www.musiciansunion.org.uk/StateOfPlay.

Youth Music (2014) *Taking an Outcomes Approach: From Planning to Evaluation.* Available at: https://network.youthmusic.org.uk/sites/default/files/Taking_an_Outcomes_Approach_from_planning_to_evaluation.pdf.

You can also view reports on the Music Mark website at: www.musicmark.org.uk/marketplace/types/reports.

Chapter 13
Extra-curricular clubs

There are many benefits to offering extra activities beyond the formal school day, which could include breakfast clubs, lunchtime clubs, after-school clubs, wrap-around clubs, holiday clubs and playschemes. They can cover areas as diverse as chess and cooking to foreign languages and photography.

There are a range of charitable trusts offering grants to support schools that want to run a club. When applying for grants, you will want to provide the funder with key information about your club:

- Confirm whether you are you planning to pilot an idea, set up a new club, relaunch a club or simply need help to sustain an existing one. Let them know when the club was established (or when it will be launched).

- Give them information about your club and let them know why it is a good idea. For an existing club, your club policy can usually provide a range of useful information such as the aims and objectives, operating hours, capacity rates, administration and booking arrangements, planned activities and safety procedures. You could include a copy of your policy with your application (if requested), as funders often like to see evidence that clubs are run responsibly. Just make sure the policy is up-to-date and has been signed off by your governing body.

- You may also want to include promotional materials (such as brochures, photographs and posters) advertising your club, as these often present information in a visual way. Don't forget to enclose any relevant newspaper articles too. However, try not to overwhelm the funder with too much material and only send them information they are happy to receive.

If you intend to launch a new club or improve an existing one, then why not invite ideas from members of your school community – teachers, students, governors, parents, club staff and so on. You could:

- Hold a meeting to welcome ideas (make sure the minutes are recorded).

- Conduct a survey or questionnaire to uncover current opinions about the club directly from those who attend and the staff who run it. This can provide an independent perspective on your club, which you can use to support your application.

- Work with the school council to get an insight into what the students would like from their club (funders favour projects that engage the beneficiaries). Perhaps the students could help you to make a video appeal (just be sure to get the necessary photograph and video permissions first).

- Create a governor sub-committee to evaluate the club.

- Engage any school–parent groups, such as the parents forum, friends group or PTA. Perhaps you could ask the chair if they will make your club an agenda item for the next meeting.

Here are some useful websites to help you set up a new club or develop an existing one:

- The Out of School Alliance provides a wealth of resources, information packs, templates for club policies, how-to guides, administration forms and so on at: www.outofschoolalliance.co.uk. Please note that there is a charge for their resources.

- Take a look at the Department for Education's research collection at: www.gov.uk/government/collections/extended-schools.

- The charity Family Action has put together a series of resources and case studies from recent projects which have been funded by the Department for Education. See the Learning Exchange – Information for Schools at: www.family-action.org.uk/what-we-do/children-families/schools-education/school-information.

You can also access a range of free resources about school clubs at:

SEDL Archive: www.sedl.org/pubs/free_afterschool_az.html

SparkleBox: www.sparklebox.co.uk/misc/extra-curricular

Teaching Ideas: www.teachingideas.co.uk/subjects/school-club-resources

If you are considering setting up a new club, it can be helpful to research what existing clubs operate in your area. You can find details on childcare outside of school hours, including breakfast clubs, homework clubs and after-school clubs, via your local council at: www.gov.uk/childcare-out-of-school-hours.

The Out of School Alliance also has a directory of out-of-school clubs run by its members, broken down by county: www.outofschoolalliance.co.uk/out-of-school-clubs.

The John Muir Award can be integrated into after-school clubs and other extra-curricular activities. The award gives schools a framework for learning outdoors and contributes to the requirements of the national curriculum. You can learn more about the benefits and access case studies from participating schools and colleges at: www.johnmuirtrust.org/john-muir-award/schools-and-colleges.

To develop your application, you will need to let the funder know why you need the grant:

▨ Grant-makers like to learn about the people who will benefit from the grant, so try to give them as much information as possible about why your club has been established and what it hopes to achieve. You could describe your club demographics – for example, are you operating in a deprived area and would like to give students from low-income families the opportunity to access activities that their circumstances may usually prevent them from accessing? Are parents struggling to pay club fees due to unemployment or redundancy? Is a year group underperforming in a certain subject and your club has been set up to help raise attainment?

▨ Refer to the club register to identify attendance rates. Are you struggling to maintain student numbers? Do numbers fluctuate throughout the term, presenting you with the problem of having to provide staff for maximum capacity even though only a few students are attending? Do you have a waiting list and wish to extend provision to offer it to even more students?

▨ Tell the potential funder about any other challenges the club is facing: is your club struggling to meet operating costs? Are you concerned about its sustainability? Are club facilities or resources outdated? Has the club received any negative feedback or complaints which you need help to act on? Describe the problems, the solutions you propose and the benefits you aim to bring.

▨ Don't forget to describe the outcome of any audits, surveys or meetings you have carried out, as this can all be used as evidence.

▨ You may also like to let the funder know what the club is doing well: what benefits does it offer? Is it run by passionate teachers? Is it helping students to improve academically? Do students find it fun and enjoyable? Are club members winning medals or awards? Are parents invited to watch performances? Perhaps look through your recent Ofsted report to capture any relevant quotes.

With any grant application, you will need to be clear about how much money you are asking for and what it is needed for. Make sure you describe exactly how much funding is necessary every week in order to break even.

Here are some expenses you may want to include:

▨ Costs for materials, ingredients and equipment.

▨ Staffing costs, including salaries, training fees, volunteer expenses and DBS checks.

▨ Expenses associated with special visitors (such as educational speakers visiting the school).

▨ Operating costs.

- Any hire costs.
- Costs for running competitions, workshops and challenges.
- Costs associated with external providers.
- Marketing and promotional expenses.
- Costs associated with any administrative software.
- Contingency funds.

If you need to purchase materials for your club, take a look at the suppliers directory produced by the Out of School Alliance, where you can find details for a range of suppliers, from arts and crafts materials to books and stationery: www.outofschoolalliance.co.uk/suppliers. Don't forget to check out their product reviews too, as these describe some 'must-have' items for clubs: www.outofschoolalliance.co.uk/product-reviews. Also take a look at the PTA+ suppliers directory at: www.pta.co.uk/suppliers.aspx.

You will need to arrange appropriate insurance cover for your club. The easiest way to do this is to upgrade your existing insurance policy. If you are a member of the Out of School Alliance, then members can get 15% off with Morton Michel Insurance. Discover more at: www.outofschoolalliance.co.uk/insurance.

If you use an external provider to manage your extended activities, then you should first consult any providers your school already works with. For example, could your sports provider run activities during the school holidays or your breakfast club provider host an after-school club?

If your club staff need further training, you can find a list of training providers at: www.outofschoolalliance.co.uk/training-providers.

As well as applying for grants, schools can deploy a range of other strategies to help cover the costs of out-of-school clubs:

- Will you charge each student a club entry fee? If you opt for a fee, will you charge per visit or per term? Under governmental guidance, after-school provision is classified as an 'optional extra', so schools can charge for this but they can't use it as a money-making enterprise (i.e. charges for providing materials, books, instruments or equipment must not exceed costs).[1]

- Will you offer concessions or free places? If so, will you offer it to everyone or just a select few? Will you offer a free place to siblings? Some schools choose to subsidise costs (e.g. using pupil premium funding) as they feel that charging for clubs may

---

1 See Department for Education, *Charging for School Activities: Departmental Advice for Governing Bodies, School Leaders, School Staff and Local Authorities* (May 2018). Ref: DFE-00244-2013. Available at: www.gov.uk/government/publications/charging-for-school-activities.

prohibit some children from attending. Some also ask for voluntary contributions from parents.

▨ Will you fundraise to cover the costs? If so, how? For example, some schools encourage students to grow fruit and vegetables which are then sold to parents to help raise money for a breakfast club. Other schools approach local companies to invite them to sponsor the club. Don't forget to ask your local council for details on any relevant grants too.

If your club is running a deficit, then be sure to tell the funder about this. Let them know that although your school receives government funding, there are still lots of things that your budget doesn't allow for, such as additional books, teaching aids, play equipment and extra-curricular activities.

Here are some tips to help lower your club costs:

▨ Try to reduce staffing costs by inviting parents or students to help run the club. If you plan to do this, you will need to consider arrangements for safeguarding, DBS checks, training and so on.

▨ Aim to partner with a voluntary organisation to help deliver the club. For example, you could explore opportunities with your local Council for Voluntary Service. You can find their details at: www.navca.org.uk.

▨ If you are a state-maintained school in England, then it's worth knowing about Into Film Club, which offers access to thousands of free films for school clubs. See: www. intofilm.org/clubs.

▨ Code Club UK has a nationwide network of volunteers and educators who run free coding clubs for young people aged 9–13 years. For details visit: www.codeclub. org.uk.

▨ If you are in the Bristol area, why not request a free Brunel Badge Loan Box, provided by the Brunel Institute? The box contains exciting activities for 6–14-year-olds, which are perfect for after-school clubs, holiday clubs and other educational clubs. You can see the range of boxes on offer and access further information at: www.ssgreatbritain.org/brunel-institute/learning/loan-boxes. Museums around the country offer similar educational initiatives, so find out what is on offer near you.

If you are successful in securing a grant, you will need to report back to the funder to describe the difference this has made. You should aim to:

▨ Confirm how the grant has been spent and the impact it has had on students.

▨ Summarise attendance trends. If attendance has increased, provide the numbers to demonstrate how many students attended the club before and how many attend it now. Are numbers still increasing? Also consider the total number of students in the school and what proportion now attend the club. Has it reached maximum capacity?

▨ Describe what people are saying about the club by surveying students, parents and staff and capturing any relevant quotes. Do students enjoy the club and look forward to arriving?

▨ Has the grant enabled you to carry out any activities which you wouldn't have been able to do otherwise?

▨ How has the club contributed to the wider school's success? If your school has experienced the threat of closure, for example, then let them know if your club has played a role in helping to turn this around.

▨ If you have opened up your club to neighbouring schools or the wider community, then tell your funder about the impact of their grant.

Breakfast clubs

There are many reasons to offer a breakfast club. A report by the Food Foundation reveals that 'The number of children experiencing symptoms of food insecurity, or whose family income is evidently insufficient to afford a healthy diet amounts to between 2.5 and 4 million; between 20% and 30% of all children in the UK.'[2]

This is shocking information, considering the fact that the UK is one of the top ten richest countries in the world. Many children are missing out on essential vitamins and minerals: left to fend for themselves, they end up snacking on junk food rather than eating a nutritious breakfast or just skip breakfast altogether. The physical effects of malnutrition include fatigue, dizziness, poor growth and diminished cognitive function, including poor memory and attention and lower IQ.

Kellogg's has explored the effects of hunger and discovered that children who do not get enough to eat can become isolated, withdrawn or aggressive.[3] They can struggle to build and maintain friendships, and their concentration and behaviour can be affected. Hunger is therefore a barrier to learning which, in turn, can affect a child's academic performance. Save the Children has reported that 'chronically malnourished children are nearly 20% less literate',[4] while a 2008 study by the School Food Trust revealed how Key Stage 2 results were improved by the presence of a breakfast club.[5]

---

2 Food Foundation, *Children's Future Food Inquiry: Final Report* (2019), p. 5. Available at: https://foodfoundation. org.uk/publication/childrens-future-food-inquiry-final-report.

3 Kellogg's, *No Food for Thought*, p. 16.

4 Save the Children, *Results for Children 2013 Annual Review* (2013), p. 15. Available at: www.savethechildren.org/ content/dam/usa/reports/annual-report/annual-report/sc-2013-annualreport.pdf.

5 School Food Trust, *Findings: The Impact of Primary School Breakfast Clubs in Deprived Areas of London* (Sheffield: School Food Trust, 2008).

Teachers have also reported that it can be a real struggle to teach students who are hungry, as they can become easily distracted and misbehave, so many teachers end up taking in extra food for them. This is not a long-term solution for tackling hunger. By providing breakfast clubs, schools can ensure that students get the nutrition they need and encourage good dietary habits by helping them to eat breakfast on a regular basis. A good breakfast can help students to start the day in a positive and alert frame of mind. It can also help with attendance and punctuality, as it encourages students to arrive before the start of the formal school day.

As well as providing breakfast, many clubs also offer a variety of activities – from singing sessions and exercises classes to arts and crafts activities and reading sessions. Not only can a breakfast club be enjoyable, but these activities can also be very stimulating and can even support a student's education. Young people enjoy the socialising benefits of breakfast club and love catching up with friends before school starts.

Aside from students and teachers, parents also appreciate the low-cost childcare element of breakfast clubs. According to Kellogg's, breakfast clubs can save parents £35.20 per week in childcare costs (a total saving of £26.4 million for working parents across the UK each week).[6]

If you are planning to run, or currently operate, a breakfast club, then it's worth knowing that there are various funding schemes for which your club could be eligible, including the Greggs Foundation, Kellogg's Breakfast Clubs and Magic Breakfast. These schemes can offer start-up grants, training support, food donations and employee volunteers.

The Magic Breakfast Club Scheme is a partnership run by Magic Breakfast and Family Action. These two charities are currently working together to deliver the Department for Education's National School Breakfast Programme: the government plans to invest up to £26 million (from the soft drinks industry levy) in over 1,770 schools in disadvantaged areas of England. You can find details about these schemes at the end of the chapter. Please be aware that there may be waiting lists for new clubs to receive support from these funders, so be sure to contact them as early as possible and factor this time frame into your plan. (At the time of writing, the scheme did not have enough funding to accept new schools, although they were encouraging expressions of interest which would be kept on file.)

As well as applying to specific breakfast club schemes, there are also general grants you could apply for, depending on what additional activities you offer. For example, if you also offer singing sessions at your breakfast club then you could explore music grants, or if you run story-time sessions, you could seek out literary grants.

---

6 Kellogg's, *School Breakfast Clubs: A Lifeline for Working Parents* (2014), p. 2. Available at: www.kelloggs.co.uk/content/dam/europe/kelloggs_gb/pdf/R4_FINAL%20WORKING%20PARENTS%20REPORT.pdf.

There are lots of useful online resources to help run your breakfast club:

- Kellogg's offer a range of free downloadable resources from their website, and they publish an e-newsletter twice a term which is full of inspiration and ideas. Discover more at: www.kelloggs.co.uk/en_GB/what-we-believe/breakfast-club-network.html.

- The Shake Up Your Wake Up website offers free downloadable resources, breakfast ideas, school recipe sheets, activities and games ideas: www.shakeupyourwakeup. com/information-for-schools.

- Twinkl provides a Breakfast Club Activity Pack which contains worksheets, experiments and games: www.twinkl.co.uk/resource/t-c-1181-breakfast-club-activity-pack.

When setting up a new breakfast club, there are various things you will need to consider:

- Access: What hours will the club operate and for how many days of the week? How many students would you like to reach, and what is your maximum capacity? Which students do you feel will benefit most from attending the club? Will you offer it to just Key Stage 1 children, or will it be inclusive to all? Will places be open to other nurseries and schools, or just to students from your own school? Will you invite parents and teachers to the breakfast club (e.g. once a term)? Note: Some schools make it their policy that any students on child protection plans must attend their breakfast club.

- Food: What menu will you offer? Will you offer a variety of choices and cater for all dietary requirements? Will you offer cold options like low-sugar cereals, fruit and yoghurt, or hot choices such as eggs and beans on toast, pancakes or fry-ups? You will also need to consider what drinks to offer (e.g. hot chocolate, water, milk, fruit juice).

- Practicalities: Where will you run breakfast club? Will you hold it in the main school dining room or use a classroom instead? What kitchen facilities do you have access to? How and where will you store the food?

- Activities: What additional activities will you offer alongside breakfast? Will you allow students to go outside? Will you offer obstacle courses, picnic breakfasts, ball games or gardening sessions? If you require students to stay indoors, could you offer balloon badminton, homework sessions, treasure hunts or board games? (Kellogg's likes to give awards to clubs that offer extra activities – these can also make your club more appealing to students too.) You could also encourage younger children to bring their toothbrush to breakfast club and support them to brush their teeth after breakfast.

- Administration: Will you trial the club first before formally launching it? How will students book their place? Will you need to invest in club administration software to manage payment and bookings? If you are charging, will students need to book and pay in advance?

▓ Staffing: Who will supervise it – internal staff or external providers? How many adult helpers will you need? What experience and qualifications do they need (e.g. DBS checks, food hygiene, first aid)? Who will complete the necessary paperwork and administration work related to running the club? Who will coordinate the club? Who will complete the necessary risk assessments? Most breakfast clubs are run by teaching assistants, although teachers, catering staff, parents, PTA members and student volunteers also help out. Another option could be to create a new role for a breakfast club assistant (for a set number of hours per week during term time).

▓ Marketing: How will you advertise and promote the club? Will you publicise it at parent open days, or take a more proactive approach by advertising it on your social media channels?

▓ Finances: How much will it cost to run the club? You will need to consider expenses such as food and drink, equipment and resources, marketing and promotion, club administration software subscription fees, cleaning expenses, staffing expenses (including training fees) and any running costs relevant to your club (e.g. electricity, gas, water, rent). Don't forget to factor in any security arrangements too – perhaps your caretaker will need to arrive earlier to open up and prepare the building.

When it comes to charging for school breakfast clubs, some schools charge per breakfast while others price individual food items separately, so you will need to select the best strategy for your school. Some funding schemes, such as the Greggs Foundation Breakfast Club, only accept applications from primary schools where the breakfast club is free for children to attend. However, some schools prefer to charge students, not only so the club is self-sustaining but also to ensure that the food isn't perceived as a handout.

When developing your plans, it's a good idea to ask parents, students, teachers and other staff members for any suggestions they may have. To help you get started, check out the breakfast club questionnaire templates and resources available on the Healthy Schools London website at: www.london.gov.uk/what-we-do/health/healthy-schools-london/awards/resources/healthy-take-aways/healthy-eating. A range of breakfast club case studies are also available from Magic Breakfast at: www.magicbreakfast.com/case-studies.

Here are some other ways you can engage your students:

▓ Get them involved in planning activities and making decisions about menus, music and so on.

▓ Bounce ideas off your student council.

▓ Invite students to help prepare their own breakfasts. This can teach them key life skills and give them the challenge of picking their own healthy meal.

- Can students grow fruit and vegetables for your breakfast club? Not only can this help students to understand and appreciate where their food comes from, but it also gives them the opportunity to taste their own produce!

- Invite older students to help staff the club. This can introduce them to the world of work and give them a useful experience to include on their CV.

- Get students involved in the national Breakfast Club Week which takes place every year in January. For more details visit: www.shakeupyourwakeup.com/breakfast-week.

For further guidance on setting up and running your breakfast club, contact your local council's Healthy Schools Team.

Once your breakfast club is up and running there is the potential to access food donations from redistribution schemes such as those run by FareShare, City Harvest London and Neighbourly (see Chapter 14 for more details). These three charities donate perfectly good food which cannot be sold through normal channels (because it may have a short shelf-life or the packaging is damaged or incorrectly labelled). Not only can these donations help to reduce your outgoing expenses, but you are also rescuing good food from going to landfill.

If you are currently running a breakfast club and are proud of its success, then why not enter the Kellogg's Breakfast Club Awards? Winners are selected from different regions and each club is given a prize of £1,000, plus an additional £1,000 if they are a grand winner. For further details visit: www.breakfastclubawards.co.uk.

If you are intending to relaunch your breakfast club, or simply need to raise awareness of it, then here are some ideas that could help:

- Update your menu and the activities on offer.

- Run a competition – for example, encourage the students to design a new breakfast club poster to promote it.

- Invite families to join their child for breakfast. This enables them to try out the menu and discover the benefits of the club.

- Offer free taster mornings to attract new starters.

- Provide themed breakfasts such as 'Breakfast fit for a king or queen'. The students will enjoy selecting a new theme for each term.

- Invite students to attend in a superhero costume (as a one-off event!).

- Invite local councillors, police or celebrities to come along and help serve breakfast.

- Develop a breakfast club newsletter (monthly or bi-monthly) to help keep families up-to-date with club news and to promote it regularly.

To apply for a breakfast club grant, you will need to tell the potential funder about any problems your club is facing:

- Are teachers noticing that students are coming into school hungry? Do they feel they have to bring in food for these students? If so, how big is the problem?

- Do you operate in a deprived area? Are you aware of parents who are struggling to afford to provide breakfast for their children?

- Does your club have a waiting list? Is there always a queue of hungry students and parents waiting outside for the breakfast club to open?

- What difference has your club made to students and how has it improved their lives? Have teachers noticed a difference in academic performance? Are students more punctual because they have started attending breakfast club?

- Are your attendance numbers low? Are you struggling to attract the students that need breakfast most? Or is charging for entry limiting the number of attendees?

- Are you worried that students will arrive late during exam week, and so plan to provide free breakfasts to all students sitting exams?

- Are there any compliance issues regarding food standards and hygiene?

- Are you struggling financially? Do you have limited funding, or are you operating in deficit and trying to save your breakfast club from closing?

You will also need to communicate the benefits of your club and offer reasons why the funder should support you. For example:

- Describe your ethos and belief that every child should have a happy, healthy start to the day, regardless of background or financial situation.

- Let them know about your strategy for tackling child hunger and malnutrition through offering breakfast.

- Discuss your plans for raising awareness about the importance of eating a regular healthy breakfast.

- Explain how you plan to offer a safe haven to safeguard students who don't get this at home.

- Let them know how you plan to make your club fun and stimulating. Describe the benefits of any extra activities you offer and mention any opportunities you provide for students to socialise.

- Describe how breakfast club is part of your wider wrap-around care strategy to support families who work or study.

■ Describe how the people who run the club are positive role models and are keen to help students be the best they can be.

■ Send any photographs, posters or images that illustrate your breakfast club (as well as any problems it is facing).

School holiday clubs and playschemes

The school holidays can put a lot of financial strain on low-income families. According to the Trussell Trust, many households are skipping meals and even going days without eating because of financial struggles.[7] Some are also worried about how they are going to keep their child entertained as they cannot afford to take them out during the holidays and resort to staying indoors instead.

School holiday clubs and playschemes can offer a range of benefits:

■ They keep children mentally stimulated and entertained during the school holidays by providing a range of structured and supervised activities alongside recreational and play opportunities.

■ They offer children and young people a safe, happy and healthy environment to play in, so they don't have to feel trapped or isolated at home during the holidays.

■ They give children and their families the opportunity to socialise and interact, as well as allowing children to play and thereby develop social and emotional relationships.

■ They can engage parents by encouraging them to attend the club or to help through volunteering. They can also offer a low-cost childcare solution for working families.

■ In some cases, playschemes also provide meals which can help to combat holiday hunger.

When developing a school holiday club or playscheme, you will need to think about:

■ How many weeks will you operate for? Will you operate Monday to Friday or just for a couple of days? Will you offer morning or afternoon sessions, or a mixture of both? Most holiday sessions run from 10am to 12pm and from 2pm to 4pm. If you are planning to apply for grant aid, then please note that some councils will not fund playschemes that operate in the evening.

■ Where will you operate the playscheme (e.g. school hall or classroom)?

---

7 Trussell Trust, *Financial Insecurity, Food Insecurity, and Disability: The Profile of People Receiving Emergency Food Assistance from the Trussell Trust Foodbank Network in Britain* (June 2017), p. vii. Available at: www.trusselltrust.org/wp-content/uploads/sites/2/2017/07/OU_Report_final_01_08_online2.pdf.

- What activities will you offer? If you provide dance lessons, circus skills, cookery sessions, arts and crafts activities and so on, will you need any extra equipment? Do you also plan to take the children out on day trips?

- Who is your playscheme for? Will it be targeted at a specific age group, or can parents and/or carers attend too? What additional needs do they have, and will they need any specialist support? What is the maximum number of children you can accommodate per session? Is it only for pupils from your own school or can children from neighbouring schools attend too?

- Will you provide breakfast? Do children need to bring their own packed lunch or will you be providing food? Will you offer any breaktime drinks or snacks? Will you provide food only for the children attending? What about their parents/carers/siblings? What food and hygiene certificates will you need?

- Who will staff your playscheme? Will parents be encouraged to help? How many paid staff and volunteers will you need, and what experience and/or qualifications do you require them to have? Will any staff need training? Do volunteers have the necessary DBS checks? You will also need to work out roles and responsibilities – for example, who will take the register? Who will complete the administration tasks? Who will be the first aider?

- Will you be charging children to attend? If so, how much? Could you offer a discount to parents who book early to help you get an idea of numbers and plan accordingly?

- Will you provide transport to and from the venue?

- Do you have the necessary insurance in place for your holiday club? Can you upgrade your existing policy so that it covers you all year round rather than term times only?

- If you plan on opening up your club to the wider community, why not advertise it in your local library or leisure centre? You could also send a press release to local newspapers and magazines. Don't forget to let your local Family Information Service know too, and any other organisations that can make referrals.

- How will you monitor and evaluate the impact of your project to ensure its success? Think about keeping club registers, timetables and details of any activities you put on.

For further help in setting up your holiday club, please see:

Filling the Holiday Gap: www.fillingtheholidaygap.org

Out of School Alliance: www.outofschoolalliance.co.uk/holiday-club-tips

When choosing which dates to run your club, it is useful to check what other events are happening in the local community to avoid any clashes. You can find out what play-schemes are offered in your area (whether run by a school or a private or voluntary organisation) at: www.gov.uk/after-school-holiday-club. It is also worthwhile asking parents directly what dates work best for them.

There are various grants available to help fund activities during the school holidays. In the first instance, contact your local council to see if they are running any schemes – for example, they sometimes offer funding for a set period of time. They may also provide travel passes to enable small groups to travel for free on public transport within a given area, which can be great for day trips.

When applying to your local council for a grant, make sure you let them know how your playscheme will contribute to their strategic plans (they often give preference to playschemes which show this). Local school meals providers may also be able to offer support for your project.

When writing your grant application, don't forget to disclose any additional needs the children attending your playscheme may have (e.g. physical disabilities, learning needs), as this can often impact on funding decisions. There may even be additional funding schemes you can access. You should also tell the potential funder how you have identified the need for this provision – perhaps from a survey of parents/carers. Also tell them about any other problems your playscheme will address – for example, are local families experiencing financial distress, and will your club help to alleviate some of the worry by providing meals and activities for young people?

Your grant application will need to specify any costs that are necessary to run your club. This might include:

- Funds to purchase any games or equipment (e.g. arts and crafts materials).
- Costs associated with taking the children out on day trips.
- Administration costs.
- Expenses for food and drink.
- Costs associated with staff such as wages and any necessary training.
- Volunteer expenses.
- Other overhead costs (e.g. gas, electricity, rent, insurance).

It is extremely important to keep VAT receipts for any purchases you make and a full record of your expenditure.

Funding opportunities

Here is a list of grants and awards for school breakfast clubs, lunchtime clubs, after-school clubs, wrap-around care, holiday clubs and playschemes:

Bristol Youth and Community Action

Royal Oak House, Royal Oak Avenue, Bristol BS1 4GB

http://quartetcf.org.uk/grant-programmes/bycag-holiday-2

applications@quartetcf.org.uk

0117 989 7700

They offer Holiday Activities Grants of up to £2,500 to schools in Bristol and the surrounding area. Express Grants of up to £5,000 are also available all year round.

Central England Co-operative Community Dividend Fund

Central England Co-operative Limited, Central House, Hermes Road, Lichfield, Staffordshire WS13 6RH

www.centralengland.coop/community/our-community-projects

enquiries@centralengland.coop

01543 414140

The Community Dividend Fund can provide grants of up to £5,000 to organisations in Central England, although the average grant is £2,000. Applicants must be members of the Co-operative for six months before applying.

Comic Relief

89 Albert Embankment, London SE1 7TP

www.comicrelief.com/funding/applying-for-funding/guidance

grantsinfo@comicrelief.com

0207 820 2000

Although applications are not accepted from schools, they do accept applications for work in schools. This could be a voluntary sector organisation which runs after-school sessions on school premises or a voluntary sector group working in partnership with a school. Schools could therefore contact a voluntary sector organisation and encourage them to apply for a grant on their behalf. Projects must take place within the UK.

Greggs Breakfast Club

Greggs Foundation, Greggs House, Quorum Business Park, Newcastle Upon Tyne NE12 8BU

www.greggsfoundation.org.uk/breakfast-clubs/how-to-apply

breakfastclubs@greggsfoundation.org.uk

01912 127626

The Greggs Breakfast Club programme can offer product donations and monetary grants. At the time of writing, the Greggs Foundation was actively fundraising to enable it to continue to meet the demand from schools but schools are able to join the waiting list.

Kellogg's Breakfast Club Programme

Forever Manchester, 2nd Floor, 8 Hewitt Street, Manchester M15 4GB

www.kelloggs.co.uk/en_GB/what-we-believe/breakfast-club-network.html

kelloggs@forevermanchester.com

01612 140940

Kellogg's is working with Forever Manchester to provide breakfast club funding to schools in need. Schools are invited to apply for a grant of £1,000.

Kitchen Social Scheme

www.mayorsfundforlondon.org.uk/kitchen-social

info@mayorsfundforlondon.org.uk

0207 983 6539

The Kitchen Social programme offers young people in London a safe place to go during the school holidays where they can socialise and enjoy a free healthy meal. As well as funding, the scheme also provides free training and resources. The programme was launched in 2017 and has already engaged 95 hubs across 23 boroughs.

Magic Breakfast

St Magnus House, 3 Lower Thames Street, London EC3R 6HD

www.magicbreakfast.com

info@magicbreakfast.com

0207 836 5434

Magic Breakfast is an award-winning UK charity providing free and nutritious breakfast foods to primary schools in the greatest need (qualifying schools in England will have at least 35% of students in receipt of pupil premium funding). At the time of writing there was a waiting list but schools can submit an expression of interest.

Newcomen Collett Foundation

66 Newcomen Street, London SE1 1YT

www.newcomencollett.org.uk/organisations.html

grantoffice@newcomencollett.org.uk

0207 407 2967

The Foundation makes grants to schools, organisations and other groups. In total they have £100,000 a year to give in grants.

Woodward Charitable Trust

The Peak, 5 Wilton Road, London SW1V 1AP

http://woodwardcharitabletrust.org.uk/portfolio/how_to_apply

contact@woodwardcharitabletrust.org.uk

0207 410 7026

Children's Summer Playschemes grants are usually in the range of £500 to £1,000. They can only be paid to registered charities, but schools can apply if they nominate a registered charity to accept the donation on their behalf.

Further reading

Out-of-school clubs:

All Party Parliamentary Group on School Food (2015) *Filling the Holiday Gap: Update Report 2015*. Available at: www.fillingtheholidaygap.org/APPG_Holiday_Hunger_Report_2015.pdf.

BBC Children in Need (2010) Holiday Playscheme Review. Available at: www.bbc.co.uk/tv/isite_assets/pudsey/grants/playschemebrief.pdf.

Campbell, M., Watson, N. and Watters, N. (2015) *The Cost of School Holidays: A What Works Scotland Literature Review* (July). Available at: http://whatworksscotland.ac.uk/wp-content/uploads/2015/07/The-cost-of-school-holidays.pdf.

Chanfreau, J., Tanner, E., Callanan, M., Laing, K., Skipp, A. and Todd, L. (2016) *Out of School Activities During Primary School and KS2 Attainment*. UCL Institute for Education Centre for Longitudinal Studies Working paper 2016/1. Available at: www.natcen.ac.uk/media/1135440/CLS-WP-2016-Out-of-school-activities-during-primary-school-and-KS2-attainment.pdf.

Ofsted (2012) *Regulating Provision Made Before and After School or During School Holidays* (December). Ref: 120378. Available at: http://dera.ioe.ac.uk/16248.

Scottish Executive (2003) *School's Out: Framework for the Development of Out-of-School Care*. Available at: www.gov.scot/resource/doc/47032/0023963.pdf.

Breakfast clubs:

Centre for Evaluation and Monitoring and Durham University (2016) *Greggs Breakfast Club Programme 400th School Celebration: A Preliminary Investigation Into the Characteristics of Participating Schools* (December). Available at: www.greggsfoundation.org.uk/sites/default/files/uploads/docs/Durham_Research_Greggs_Breakfast_Club_School_Level_Report.pdf.

Education Endowment Foundation (2016) Breakfast Clubs Found to Boost Primary Pupils' Reading, Writing and Maths (4 November). Available at: https://educationendowmentfoundation.org.uk/news/breakfast-clubs-found-to-boost-primary-pupils-reading-writing-and-maths-res.

Education Endowment Foundation (2017) Magic Breakfast. Available at: https://educationendowmentfoundation.org.uk/projects-and-evaluation/projects/magic-breakfast.

Food Foundation (2019) *Children's Future Food Inquiry: Final Report*. Available at: https:// foodfoundation.org.uk/publication/childrens-future-food-inquiry-final-report.

Food in Schools (2005) *Healthier Breakfast Clubs*. Available at: www.london.gov.uk/what-we-do/ health/healthy-schools-london/awards/sites/default/files/FiS%20Healthier%20Breakfast%20 Clubs.pdf.

Graham, L., Russo, R. and Defeyter, M. (2015) The Advantages and Disadvantages of Breakfast Clubs According to Parents, Children, and School Staff in the North East of England, UK, *Frontiers in Public Health*, 3, Article 156. Available at: www.ncbi.nlm.nih.gov/pmc/articles/PMC4457018.

Graham, N. and Beadle, S. (2017) *Breakfast Clubs Setup and Implementation: Briefing for School Leaders*. Ref: DFE-RR650 (London: Department for Education). Available at: www.gov. uk/government/uploads/system/uploads/attachment_data/file/603947/Evaluation_of_Breakfast_ Clubs_-School_briefing.pdf.

Graham, N., Puts, E. and Beadle, S. (2017) *Evaluation of Breakfast Clubs in Schools with High Levels of Deprivation*. Ref: DFE-RR651 (London: Department for Education). Available at: www. gov.uk/government/uploads/system/uploads/attachment_data/file/603946/Evaluation_of_ Breakfast_Clubs_-_Final_Report.pdf.

Health Promotion Agency for Northern Ireland (2009) *Healthier Breakfast Clubs*. Available at: www.publichealth.hscni.net/sites/default/files/Healthier%20Breakfast%20clubs%2009_10.pdf.

Kellogg's (2014) *School Breakfast Clubs: A Lifeline for Working Parents*. Available at: www. kelloggs.co.uk/content/dam/europe/kelloggs_gb/pdf/R4_FINAL%20WORKING%20PARENTS%20 REPORT.pdf.

Kellogg's (2017) *The Future of School Breakfast Clubs: A Funding Crisis in the UK*. Available at: www.kelloggs.co.uk/content/dam/europe/kelloggs_gb/pdf/Funding+Crisis+- +future+of+school+breakfast+clubs+-+a+funding+crisis+in+the+UK.pdf.

Kenway, P. and Street, C. (2000) *Breakfast Clubs: A 'How to' Guide* (London: New Policy Institute). Available at: www.npi.org.uk/publications/children-and-young-adults/ breakfast-clubs-how-guide.

Save the Children (2013) *Results for Children 2013 Annual Review*. Available at: www. savethechildren.org/content/dam/usa/reports/annual-report/annual-report/sc-2013- annualreport.pdf.

School Food Trust (2008) *Findings: The Impact of Primary School Breakfast Clubs in Deprived Areas of London* (Sheffield: School Food Trust).

Trussell Trust (2017) *Financial Insecurity, Food Insecurity, and Disability: The Profile of People Receiving Emergency Food Assistance from the Trussell Trust Foodbank Network in Britain* (June). Available at: www.trusselltrust.org/wp-content/uploads/sites/2/2017/07/OU_Report_final_01_08_ online2.pdf.

Chapter 14
Food projects

There are lots of businesses, charities and other sources of support available if you are fundraising for a food-related project – perhaps you need help to buy new catering equipment, run a cookery course or support your breakfast club.

Across the UK, many restaurants, family bakeries, food outlets, farms and other organisations offer product donations, grants and free educational programmes. Some organisations welcome visits from schools so students can see where food comes from and gain a valuable insight into how the food industry works. Some run free cookery classes to help students acquire valuable hands-on cooking experience, develop new skills and find out that cooking can be fun! Representatives from some organisations may be willing to come into your school for free to deliver educational talks or run workshops about diet and nutrition. Other organisations are happy to help schools fundraise, either by actively fundraising on their behalf or giving them the opportunity to purchase products at a reduced price.

Here are some examples of the type of help businesses can offer – research your local area to find out what might be available:

Fifteen Cornwall

On the Beach, Watergate Bay, Newquay TF8 4AA
www.fifteencornwall.co.uk/school-group-visits
leanne@cornwallfoodfoundation.org
01637 861000
Fifteen Cornwall welcomes school visits to their beachside restaurant. The aim is to inspire children and give them an opportunity to practise cooking skills, try out different food and learn about the importance of local sourcing. While there is no charge for these visits, donations are welcomed to the Cornwall Food Foundation charity.

Lindt Master Chocolatiers

Top Floor, 4 New Square, Bedfont Lakes, Feltham, Middlesex TW14 8HA
www.lindt.co.uk/help/donations-sponsorships
donationrequests-uk@lindt.com
Schools and other non-profit organisations can request product donations from Lindt Master Chocolatiers. Donation request forms can be downloaded from the above web link and must be completed and returned at least nine weeks before the event. Recipients are selected every month (apart from June, July and August). Priority is given to organisations located in the surrounding area of the headquarters

of Lindt & Sprüngli (UK) Ltd, who are based in Middlesex. Organisations may receive one donation within a 12-month period. Please note that all donations are granted from the head office only and not local Lindt Chocolate Shops.

Pizza Express

www.pizzaexpress.com/kids/school-visits

Pizza Express offers free visits to primary schools. Children can spend a morning at their local restaurant, learning about food, tasting ingredients and making pizza. The aim is to make cooking exciting and enjoyable for children while they are still young. They operate over 490 restaurants in the UK and schools can request a free visit via their website.

Roberts Bakery

Roberts Bakery, Rudheath, Northwich, Cheshire CW9 7RQ

www.robertsbakery.co.uk/community

Roberts Bakery is a family business based in Northwich, selling fresh bread across England and North Wales. Roberts is always looking for new and exciting ways to get involved in the local community, from cooking lessons in schools to donations of baked goods and charitable grants. Please note that they only accept applications from local causes via their website, so apply using their online form. They look over all the requests on the first Monday of every month (so allow four weeks for a response). They also run a scheme for primary schools called the School of Brilliant Bread Baking, providing two-hour sessions in schools to teach children how to bake bread.

Vallebona Panettone Scheme

Vallebona Limited, Unit 14, 55–59 Weir Road, Wimbledon, London SW19 8UG

www.vallebona.co.uk/school-fundraising

charity@vallebona.co.uk

0208 944 5665

Each year Vallebona offers schools a fundraising scheme in the lead-up to Christmas. They sell their Christmas panettones at cost price, so that schools and charities can reap the profit when they resell them at the recommended retail price (offering 60–70% mark-up).

Schools can also request donations from food redistribution organisations such as:

City Harvest London

Unit 22, Acton Park, London W3 7QE

www.cityharvest.org.uk

food@cityharvest.org.uk

0207 041 8491

City Harvest collects nutritious surplus food from restaurants, grocers, manufacturers, wholesalers, hotels and caterers. They then deliver this food to help organisations that provide meals to vulnerable people, including school breakfast clubs and after-school programmes, homeless shelters, soup kitchens, centres for veterans and organisations that assist people with alcohol or drug addictions.

FareShare

Unit 7, Deptford Trading Estate, Blackhorse Road, London SE8 5HY

www.fareshare.org.uk

enquiries@fareshare.org.uk

0207 394 2468

FareShare is a national food redistribution charity working to relieve poverty and reduce food waste. They receive in-date, quality food donations from various suppliers and redistribute these to social causes across the country. Schools may apply for support. They have regional centres across England, Wales, Scotland and Northern Ireland. You can register an interest in receiving food on their website.

Felix Project

Unit 6, Concord Business Centre, Concord Road, London W3 0TJ

http://thefelixproject.org

schools@thefelixproject.org

0203 034 4350

The Felix Project collects fresh, nutritious food that cannot be sold and delivers this surplus food to schools and charities in London so they can provide healthy meals and help the most vulnerable in society.

Neighbourly

DeskLodge House, Redcliffe Way, Bristol BS1 6NL

www.neighbourly.com/aboutsurplus

hello@neighbourly.com

0117 422 0860

Neighbourly connects local stores that have a surplus with charities and projects that put it to good use within the community. As well as running a food redistribution scheme, they also redirect non-food donations including household items, cleaning products, toiletries, kitchen equipment, furniture and more.

OLIO – The Food Sharing Revolution

https://olioex.com

hello@olioex.com

OLIO connects neighbours with each other and with local shops so surplus food and other items can be shared, not thrown away. Download the app to discover offers available near you.

If you would like to arrange a school trip to a farm, kitchen or garden, then check out the trips directory on Countryside Classroom. It offers a list of places schools can visit across

England and Wales, some of which are free. There are also lots of free resources relating to food and farming on their website: www.countrysideclassroom.org.uk.

You could also check out the Country Trust, an educational charity which operates across England and North Wales. They work with primary schools to provide opportunities for disadvantaged young people to visit farms and learn where food comes from. These visits are free but transport costs are not provided. For details please visit: www.countrytrust. org.uk.

You can find details of other food growing organisations that are willing to support schools on the Food Growing Schools London website: www.foodgrowingschools.org/ support/directory.

There is also free training available for teachers. For example, the British Nutrition Foundation is a national charity supporting food and nutrition in schools. They can provide free online training for teachers to offer them information about healthy eating and the curriculum. They also offer free resources and further support. For details visit: www. nutrition.org.uk/foodinschools.

Did you know that various businesses run food-related competitions? For instance, Pink Lady apples run a competition called Write It which encourages young people to write stories on the theme of food. One winner from each of the three age groups (under 10, 11–14 and 15–18) receives some great prizes, plus the winning schools are given a box of Pink Lady apples. Stories must be between 250 and 750 words. You can find out more by visiting: www.pinkladyapples.co.uk/writeit.

There are also lots of events happening across the country to celebrate national awareness days. Here are some food-themed campaigns that you may like to be part of:

- March – Nutrition and Hydration Week: https://nutritionandhydrationweek.co.uk
- May – National Vegetarian Week: www.nationalvegetarianweek.org
- June – British Nutrition Foundation Healthy Eating Week: www.nutrition.org.uk/ healthyliving/hew.html
- June – National Picnic Week: www.nationalpicnicweek.co.uk
- October – World Food Day: www.fao.org/world-food-day
- October – National Baking Week: www.nationalbakingweek.co.uk
- October – Sugar Awareness Week: www.actiononsugar.org/sugar-awareness-week
- November – National School Meals Week: http://thegreatschoollunch.co.uk

There are also food-related awards which schools can win:

Community Education Awards – Healthy Eating Award

www.communityeducationawards.co.uk/categories-and-individual-awards

This award recognises the role that schools play in the promotion of healthy eating, along with the benefits that a balanced diet can have on children's health now and in adulthood. The award is open to all schools including primary, junior and secondary schools, academies and pupil referral units.

Nursery World Awards – Nursery Food Award

www.nurseryworldawards.com

This award is open to early years settings whose food provision promotes children's health and well-being. To apply, send details of your approach to providing healthy meals and snacks, along with how your setting involves children in cooking and learning about food.

TES Awards – Healthy School of the Year Award

https://tesawards.co.uk

This award recognises a teacher or school with clear evidence of promoting a healthy food and physical activity programme or well-being culture for students and staff. The supporting documentation should contain a case study illustrating the whole-school approach to health. Entries should also show where other curricular areas have benefited.

Whatever your food-related project, make sure it complies with your school's food policy. Schools have a responsibility to promote a healthy, well-balanced diet and must comply with a number of regulations relating to food served at breakfast, mid-morning break, after-school clubs and in tuck shops and vending machines. Contact your local Healthy Schools Team if you need any advice.

Is your school encouraging all eligible students (or their families) to register for free school meals? Schools receive pupil premium funding for each eligible student who is signed up, which can bring in valuable funds for the school, so make sure your school is sending out regular reminders and putting strategies in place to improve take-up. Schools can access a model form for free school meals and the pupil premium at: www.gov.uk/government/publications/free-school-meals-and-pupil-premium-registration-form.

Families in England can also apply for free school meals at: www.gov.uk/apply-free-school-meals.

As well as contacting third parties for help, schools can also organise events to raise funds. Have you thought about holding a school farmers' market event in your school hall or playground? You could invite parents, teachers and local businesses to sell home-made produce, and if your school has a garden or orchard you could encourage students to make jams, chutneys and other produce. You could generate an income through any produce you sell, by selling tea and coffee and by charging each stallholder a fee. If you feel that this is an idea you would like to pursue and you need help to set it up, then check out Food for Life's *School Farmers' Market* resource pack, which is available to download for free at: www.foodforlife.org.uk/schoolfarmersmarket.

Did you know that by organising a food-themed event schools can work towards the Food for Life Awards? To learn more visit: www.foodforlife.org.uk/schools/criteria-and-guidance.

Another way schools can raise money is by creating a school recipe book. For example, students could submit their favourite recipes for breakfast, lunch, dinner or snacks. These could be laminated and made into a booklet and sold to members of the school community. Not only can this help to generate money for your school, but students also feel proud when they see their work in a finished book.

Don't forget that schools can also create a professional cookbook through The Cookbook Initiative, as detailed on page 58. As well as raising funds, schools can also use this opportunity to share recipes and promote healthy eating and cooking. Each book is professionally printed, spiral-bound and produced in full colour.

Is your school already fundraising via the website Charitable Bookings? This site features a list of over 8,500 restaurants across the UK and details of over 250,000 hotels across the world. Every time a customer makes an honoured booking via their app, the restaurant donates £1 for each diner in the party to a charity of their choice. Hotels donate £1 for every guest for every night. Many schools are registered with this platform because it's a savvy way to fundraise and achieve unrestricted income for your school. To find out more visit: https://charitablebookings.com.

Funding opportunities

As well the support listed thus far, schools can apply for grants for food-related projects. Here are some funders that you might like to explore further:

Esmée Fairbairn Foundation
Kings Place, 90 York Way, London N1 9AG
https://esmeefairbairn.org.uk
info@esmeefairbairn.org.uk
0207 812 3700
The Foundation offers grants for food and well-being. They are keen to raise awareness of the importance of food and the impact it can have on people's lives. Most grants awarded are under £60,000, although they can support projects over £1,000,000.

Healthy Hearts Grants
Suite 12D, Joseph's Well, Leeds LS3 1AB
https://heartresearch.org.uk/apply-for-grants/healthy-hearts
info@heartresearch.org.uk
0113 234 7474

Heart Research UK have partnered with Subway to offer grants of up to £10,000 for new, innovative projects that benefit the community in some way.

Morrisons Foundation

Hilmore House, Gain Lane, Bradford, West Yorkshire BD3 7DL

www.morrisonsfoundation.com

foundation.enquiries@morrisonsplc.co.uk

0845 611 4449

The Morrisons Foundation supports charities making a positive difference in local communities. Schools with a registered charity arm, such as a PTA, are eligible to apply. Grants are available to fund specific items and there is no maximum amount that can be applied for.

Warburtons

Hereford House, Hereford Street, Bolton BL1 8JB

www.warburtons.co.uk/corporate/sustainability/community

0800 243 684

Warburtons offer small Community Grants worth up to £250 in England, Wales and Scotland. You can submit a grant request via their website. Warburtons bakeries can also offer product donations to support local community activities (fill out their online donation request form at least three weeks before your event).

Further reading

Cabinet Office, Department of Health and Social Care, HM Treasury and Prime Minister's Office (2016) *Childhood Obesity: A Plan for Action*. Available at: www.gov.uk/government/publications/childhood-obesity-a-plan-for-action.

Kellogg's (2014) *No Food for Thought: The Impact of Hunger in UK Classrooms*. Available at: www.kelloggs.co.uk/content/dam/europe/kelloggs_gb/pdf/R1_Kelloggs%20No%20food%20for%20thought.pdf.

Public Health England (2014) *The Link Between Pupil Health and Wellbeing and Attainment: A Briefing for Head Teachers, Governors and Staff in Educational Settings*. Available at: www.gov.uk/government/publications/the-link-between-pupil-health-and-wellbeing-and-attainment.

Public Health England (2017) New Change4Life Campaign Encourages Parents to 'Be Food Smart' [press release] (3 January). Available at: www.gov.uk/government/news/new-change4life-campaign-encourages-parents-to-be-food-smart.

Chapter 15
PE and sports projects

Sporting activities can deliver many benefits to students. Not only is PE an important part of the national curriculum, but NHS guidance recommends that children and young people aged between 5 and 18 years should engage in at least 60 minutes of physical activity a day.[1] This can help to prevent obesity, diabetes, asthma and other illnesses, while also having a positive impact on emotional well-being and social development.

By taking part in regular physical exercises, students also have the opportunity to improve their motor skills, balance, coordination, muscular strength, sporting knowledge and physical literacy. It also helps to improve overall fitness levels and encourages young people to develop healthy lifelong habits. Games can allow students to have fun, helping to boost mood and confidence, combat stress and even improve behaviour. Team exercises can help students learn to cooperate and value each other and give them a sense of belonging. It also helps to develop leadership skills.

You may need help to raise money for your PE or sports project. Perhaps you want to:

- Purchase new sports kits.
- Buy PE equipment.
- Install a new sports hall, tennis court, multi-games area or all-weather pitch.
- Improve your indoor sports provision.
- Invest in staff training and CPD.
- Hire qualified PE coaches to develop physical literacy within your school.
- Increase the number of sports activities you offer.
- Organise a competitive event, such as a sports day or tournament.

Did you know that schools can access various schemes that allow them to purchase new sports items at reduced prices? If you need to buy football shirts, mouth guards, swimming caps, swimming belts and so on, then take a look to see what discounted stock is available to buy from In Kind Direct: www.inkinddirect.org. Note that you will need to register before you can order from them.

---

1 See www.nhs.uk/live-well/exercise/physical-activity-guidelines-children-and-young-people.

If you are fundraising for a large project, then it can be worth requesting donations of specific items instead of fundraising to buy them. For example, if you need to source sports kits or equipment, then here are some programmes you may find interesting:

- If you need sports kits for cricket, football or rugby, then take a look at the Lord's Taverners Sports Kit Recycling Programme. The charity donates surplus kit from manufacturers, clubs and members of the public. Find out more at: www. lordstaverners.org/applications.

- If you are willing to purchase sports equipment second-hand, then take a look at Sportsafe. This organisation works with over 14,000 schools nationwide and supplies all types of sports equipment. They collect equipment that schools no longer need, then clean, service or repair it (and issue a safety certificate). Schools can also donate equipment to this scheme. For details visit: https://sportsafeuk.com/corporate-social-responsibility/schools-recycling-scheme.

- Schools can purchase second-hand sports items from Sports Traider. Launched in 2009, this non-profit organisation has established the first chain of charity shops in the UK that specialise in sports kit and equipment. All the money raised goes back to helping grassroots sports within the communities surrounding their shops. To find out more information (and to find a shop) visit: http://sportstraider.org.uk/shop-finder.

- If your school operates in or near the Borough of Halton (in Cheshire) and you know of a student who needs help to access sports items such as football boots or cricket whites, then check out ReSport UK. This charity project takes used and unused donated sportswear and sports equipment and redistributes it back into the community. Find out more at: https://resportuk.com.

- Don't forget that parents or carers can get help with the cost of school uniforms and PE kits (if they are on certain benefits, for example) through their local council. For details visit: www.gov.uk/help-school-clothing-costs.

Always make sure that any item(s) you purchase second-hand are safe and suitable for your needs. Always visually inspect items, check they are fit for purpose, ask to see safety certificates and find out what warranty they come with. If you need further advice, then contact your local authority.

To reduce your upfront costs, there are also opportunities for schools to hire sports and play equipment. For example:

- Hire Fitness hires gym equipment to secondary schools. You can pay a monthly hire fee or take out a standard lease. For more information visit: www.hirefitness.co.uk/school-gym-equipment-hire.

- Reading Play offers schools and other community groups in the Borough of Reading the opportunity to hire a range of items from sports kit to play equipment. They offer a selection of packages to suit different needs. Find out more at: www. readingplay.co.uk/hire.

Similarly, have you considered renting your local swimming pool to raise money for your project? You could invite members of your school community to enjoy a fun-filled hour in the pool and raise money by charging them an additional entry fee. You can find out the locations of local swimming pools on Pool Finder: www.swimming.org/poolfinder.

There are lots of ways for schools to raise money to fund PE and sports projects, including organising fun events for members of the school community to enjoy. Here are five sports-themed fundraising ideas:

1. Host a sports quiz fundraiser: You could charge an entry fee per team and provide prizes. You can access lots of family sports quiz questions online – for example, www.knowalot.org/sports-kids-quiz.htm.

2. Organise a sponsored sporting event, such as a sponsored walk, fun run or indoor row: You could print off a sponsor form from Twinkl: www.twinkl.co.uk/ resource/t-c-1378-editable-sponsorship-form.

3. Organise an 'It's a Knockout' competition: You could provide a family barbeque and hire inflatables via the Knockout Challenge website: www.itsaknockout.org/ schools-and-youth-knockouts.

4. Arrange a football tournament: You could charge a registration fee and sell refreshments on the day. You could even award certificates and prizes too!

5. Organise an assault course: You could charge an entry fee, sell refreshments and offer prizes.

Schools can also explore opportunities to raise money online. Why not sign up to a fundraising platform like Total Giving to create a fundraising page and appeal for donations? There is no charge to use this service, meaning that schools can keep 100% of the donations received. It takes less than five minutes to create a fundraising page. For details visit: www.totalgiving.co.uk.

Schools could also try to get support from the local community. Perhaps members of a local running club would be willing to complete a sponsored marathon to help raise money for your project, or staff at a local play area might be prepared to host a fundraising event on your behalf. For example, Jump Xtreme run trampoline parks and softball pits in Greater Manchester, Bolton and the West Midlands and they are willing to help schools, PTAs and other organisations to raise money. For further details visit: www. jumpxtreme.co.uk/fundraisers.

You could invite local people to support your project by organising a raffle or auction. You could invite nearby shops, entertainment venues and organisations to contribute prizes. For example, many football clubs will donate signed shirts, footballs and photographs to help charities and organisations with fundraising activities. Many premier league football clubs also have their own charitable foundation, many of which run school programmes, enterprise programmes and football tournaments to help students in neighbouring areas. If your school is near a professional club, find out if they can offer any support! Find a premier league football club at: www.premierleague.com/clubs.

Don't forget to keep an eye on events happening in your local area, as there may be opportunities to raise money. If there is a football match scheduled at a local stadium, for instance, why not ask if you and a team of students can hold a bucket collection on the day?

Did you know that you can partner with an organisation to raise money for your project? For example, Soccer Star Coaching is giving schools the opportunity to raise money through the Soccer Star Challenge. This is a free football fundraiser for primary schools, which aims not only to raise money but also to encourage children to lead healthy, active lifestyles and show them the fun they can have while taking part in sport. The average amount raised can vary from £700 to £4,000+ depending on the size of the school. For more information visit: http://soccerstarcoaching.co.uk/speed-test-challenge.

If you need help buying new PE equipment, then check out Sports for Schools. This company can organise a sponsored event on your behalf and pass on 60% of the total raised. Schools receive this money as a voucher which can be used to purchase PE equipment from one of their approved sports equipment partners. For more information visit: www.sportsforschools.org/funding-for-schools.

Depending on what sporting activity you are fundraising for, you could contact the relevant sporting association and enquire about whether they run any funding programmes. You can find a comprehensive list of UK sporting associations via the Sports Clubs website: www.sports-clubs.net/Sport/Associations.aspx. When researching grants, make sure you target those that are specifically related to PE, education and sports. If you want to promote a certain sport, then try to look for more specialist grants. Think about what your project outcomes are and what it is you would like to achieve. For example, if you are trying to boost outdoor learning or encourage a healthy, active lifestyle, then focus on grants specific to this goal.

If your project includes elements of other curriculum subjects, then consider what wider grants may be available. If you intend to improve student literacy through the power of sport, then check out literacy grants too. The National Literacy Trust run a range of programmes to teach students literacy by engaging them with sports. For details visit: https://literacytrust.org.uk/programmes/sport-and-literacy.

Finally, think about the timing of your project: if you would like to offer sporting activities after school hours or during the holidays, then find out what out-of-school funding may be available.

Funding opportunities

Depending on the nature of your project, here are some examples of grants and other opportunities on offer:

Baily Thomas Charitable Fund

c/o TMF Global Services (UK) Ltd, 960 Capability Green, Luton, Bedfordshire LU1 3PE
www.bailythomas.org.uk
info@bailythomas.org.uk
01582 439225

The Baily Thomas Charitable Fund can provide small grants (£250– £5,000) and large grants (over £10,000) to support people with learning disabilities.

Hockey Youth Trust

176 Orchard Way, Addlestone, Surrey KT15 1LW
www.thehockeyyouthtrust.co.uk
01932 853059

The Trust awards grants to clubs and schools of between £100 and £1,200.

John Lyon's Charity

Griffin Lodge, 45a Cadogan Gardens, London SW3 2TB
http://jlc.london/schools
info@jlc.london
0207 259 1700

Primary, secondary and special schools are eligible to apply to any of the charity's grant funds. However, organisations must operate in their beneficiary area: Barnet, Brent, Camden, Ealing, Hammersmith & Fulham, Harrow, Kensington & Chelsea, Westminster and the City of London.

Les Mills Fund for Children

https://lesmillsfundforchildren.org.uk
info@lesmillsfundforchildren.org.uk
0207 605 7733

The Les Mills Fund for Children makes awards of up to £1,000 to registered charities which aim to improve the education and physical and emotional well-being of children up to the age of 16.

Persimmon Homes Community Champions

Persimmon House, Fulford, York YO19 4FE
www.persimmonhomes.com/charity
contact@persimmonhomes.com
01904 642199

Persimmon offers Community Champions funding, giving away up to £2,000 each month.

Sport England

21 Bloomsbury Street, London WC1B 3HF

www.sportengland.org/funding

funding@sportengland.org

03458 508508

Sport England provides small grants of between £300 and £10,000.

Swansea City AFC Community Trust

Liberty Stadium, Landore, Swansea SA1 2FA

www.swanseacity.com/community-trust

info@scfccommunitytrust.co.uk

01792 616 607

The Trust runs a grant scheme called SwansAid which helps charities and community groups across South West Wales. The fund offers grants of up to £5,000.

Further reading

Department for Education (2013) *Evidence on Physical Education and Sport in Schools* (June). Ref: DFE-00092-2013. Available at: www.gov.uk/government/publications/evidence-on-physical-education-and-sport-in-schools.

Foster, D. (2018) *School Sports in England.* House of Commons Library Briefing Paper No. 6836 (8 June). Available at: https://dera.ioe.ac.uk/31766/1/SN06836_.pdf.

Ofsted (2018) *Obesity, Healthy Eating and Physical Activity in Primary Schools: A Thematic Review into What Actions Schools Are Taking to Reduce Childhood Obesity* (July). Ref: 180017. Available at: www.gov.uk/government/publications/obesity-healthy-eating-and-physical-activity-in-primary-schools.

Sport England (2019) *Active Lives Children and Young People Survey: Attitudes Towards Sport and Physical Activity.* Available at: www.sportengland.org/media/13851/active-lives-children-survey-2017-18-attitudes-report.pdf.

Chapter 16

Other projects

In this chapter I've listed a number of funding sources by theme.

Careers

There are lots of business enterprise, careers and mentoring programmes on offer, so find out about any that are running in your area. Many businesses are keen to build strong links with local community groups and give back to the area they serve. They are also eager to inspire young people to consider a career within their industry, and so may offer work experience programmes, tours of their site, industry speakers and sometimes grants too.

Here are some examples of school career programmes, outreach programmes, enterprise challenges and other business-related funding:

Edge Grant Fund

Edge Foundation, 4 Millbank, Westminster, London SW1P 3JA

www.edge.co.uk/projects

enquiry@edge.co.uk

0207 960 1540

The funding programme operates biennially and offers grants totalling £1 million. Funds can be used to increase teachers' knowledge of different career sectors, help schools to engage with employers and fund career courses, workshops, visits and learning materials.

First Give Programme

JHUB, Haskell House, 152 West End Lane, West Hampstead, London NW6 1SD

www.firstgive.co.uk

info@firstgive.co.uk

0207 443 5169

First Give works in partnership with secondary schools to help young people to give their time, tenacity and talents to improve their local communities. Students have the opportunity to compete for £1,000 of grant money. The programme is heavily subsidised but schools will have to cover part of the costs.

Fiver Challenge

Yeoman House, Sekforde Street, Clerkenwell, London EC1R 0HF

www.fiverchallenge.org.uk
fiverchallenge@y-e.org.uk
07966 048074

Primary schools can take part in the free Fiver Challenge. As part of the four-week programme, children are given £5 to get their business ideas off the ground with the aim of making as much profit as they can. At the end of the challenge the children repay their £5 pledges plus the 50p legacy contribution. The aim of the competition is to teach pupils key skills for lifelong learning while also having fun!

Racing to School

75 High Holborn, London WC1V 6LS
www.racingtoschool.co.uk
info@racingtoschool.co.uk
07798 655427

This education charity delivers free outdoor learning activities for young people at racecourses, studs and trainers' yards across the country. The Education Programme is designed to engage young people at racing-related venues, spark interest in the sport of horseracing and open minds to the many different career opportunities within the industry. The Work Programme is designed to support schools in their careers education provision by raising awareness of the job opportunities racing has to offer. The Riders' Programme encourages young people to consider racing and thoroughbred breeding as a possible career route or leisure activity. The charity also works with young people with special educational needs and particularly aims to engage those from inner-city, rural and deprived areas.

Royal National Lifeboat Institution (RNLI)

West Quay Road, Poole BH15 1HZ
https://rnli.org/youth-education/educational-visits
0300 300 9990

The RNLI saves lives at sea across England, Wales, Scotland and Northern Ireland. They have a team of education volunteers and lifeguards who can come and visit your school for free (or you can meet them at an RNLI beach location). Their interactive presentations cover a range of topics, including sea and beach safety and how lifeboat rescues work, and also give an insight into their charity. Schools can arrange a presentation by completing their online form.

Tycoon Enterprise Competition

Peter Jones Foundation, Palliser House, Palliser Road, London W14 9EQ
www.tycoon.com
tycoon@pjfoundation.org
0207 471 0520

Tycoon Enterprise Competition is spearheaded by Peter Jones CBE, entrepreneur and star of *Dragons' Den*. It aims to encourage the UK's budding entrepreneurs to get involved in business by giving them a start-up loan of between £50 and £1,000 to run a business while at school or college. Schools and further education colleges can take part and register a maximum of five teams.

Virgin Money – Make £5 Grow

Community Hub, Make £5 Grow, Virgin Money, Jubilee House, Gosforth, Newcastle upon Tyne NE3 4PL

http://make-5-grow.co.uk

make5grow@virginmoney.com

0191 279 8001

Make £5 Grow gives young people aged between 9 and 11 years the experience of starting a small business using a £5 loan from Virgin Money. Over 800 primary schools and 60,000 students have participated in the programme. It is free to join, and Virgin Money provides lesson plans, resources and a loan of £5 per student. The school keeps any profit made by the students' small businesses once the loan has been repaid.

Watkin Jones Group

Llandygai Industrial Estate, Bangor, Gwynedd, LL57 4YH

www.watkinjones.com/about-us/community-engagement

info@watkinjones.com

01248 362516

Watkin Jones Group are keen to encourage young people to consider a career within the construction industry. The Group's Community Fund also awards grants of up to £500 to help ideas become reality.

If you would like to contact professionals who are willing to give careers talks, then check out the following websites:

Founders4Schools

www.founders4schools.org.uk

Founders4Schools is a free service for state-maintained and private UK schools and colleges, which connects students (aged 8 years and upwards) with local business leaders. Teachers can use the Founders4Schools website to arrange events at their school, such as career talks, mock interviews and workplace visits.

Inspiring the Future

www.inspiringthefuture.org

Inspiring the Future connects teachers from schools and colleges with thousands of volunteers across the UK from a huge range of jobs – at all levels, from apprentices to CEOs – through a secure online platform. The aim is to show students what exciting and unique careers are possible and how they can achieve them. This is a free service.

Don't forget that there are also educational charities, the police, local fire and ambulance services and other organisations which offer outreach programmes and may be willing to deliver free career talks in schools.

Have you heard of Step into the NHS, which promotes careers in the NHS? There are competitions available for Key Stage 2 and 3 classes and resources aimed at Key Stage 4. Take a look at: www.stepintothenhs.nhs.uk/schools.

There are also organisations and charities which offer school speakers who can come into class or assembly, or speak at awards ceremonies or events, to raise awareness of key issues as well as the work they do. Some speakers offer their services for free (provided travel expenses are met), while others apply a charge.

Here are some examples of organisations that can help you to find free school speakers:

- The British Science Association lists STEM presenters who can visit your school for free during British Science Week: www.britishscienceweek.org/find-a-presenter. If you need financial assistance to book a presenter or to organise an event, they may be able to offer a grant.

- Global Dimensions is a charity-run website which provides details of key speakers on global issues: https://globaldimension.org.uk/classroom/school-speaker-services.

- The Royal Astronomical Society offers a list of scientific speakers who are willing to do outreach work: https://ras.ac.uk/education-and-careers/for-schools-and-teachers/1834-list-of-school-speakers.

- The Speakers for Schools charity can provide a range of speakers (from sports speakers to arts speakers): www.speakers4schools.org.

Literacy and numeracy

If you are seeking support for English or literacy, then (as well as the suggestions outlined in Chapter 7) here are some examples of grants, volunteer reader programmes and other opportunities:

CLiPPA Schools Shadowing Scheme
Centre for Literacy in Primary Education, Webber Street, London SE1 8QW
https://clpe.org.uk/poetryline/clippa
info@clpe.org.uk
0207 401 3382/3
Primary schools across the UK and beyond can take part in the Centre for Literacy in Primary Education's Schools Shadowing Scheme. CLiPPA provides teaching sequences, so that teachers can focus on getting children to read, write and perform

poetry over a three-week period. See their website for further details about how to get involved.

Coram Beanstalk

Coram Campus, 41 Brunswick Square, London WC1N 1AZ

www.beanstalkcharity.org.uk

0845 450 0307

Coram Beanstalk is a national charity that provides one-to-one literacy support to children in England who struggle with their reading ability and confidence.

If you would like students to enter literacy-related competitions (some of which award prizes), then here are some websites where you can find details of competitions:

National Literacy Trust: https://literacytrust.org.uk/competitions

Poetry Society: https://poetrysociety.org.uk/competitions

Young Writers: www.youngwriters.co.uk/competitions

If your project is related to English, maths or science, then check out:

Let Teachers SHINE

Princes Exchange, 2 Princes Square, Leeds LS1 4HQ

www.shinetrust.org.uk

info@shinetrust.org.uk

0113 280 5872

Let Teachers SHINE offers up to £15,000 to teachers who have brilliant ideas to help disadvantaged children succeed in English, maths or science.

Science

There are also lots of charities set up to promote science in schools. Here is a selection of science-related grants which you may like to explore further:

British Society for the History of Science

www.bshs.org.uk

office@bshs.org.uk

The Outreach and Education Committee of the BSHS offers Project Grants of up to £200 to support engagement with the history of science.

Institute of Physics School Grants Scheme

Institute of Physics, 37 Caledonian Road, London N1 9BU

www.iop.org/about/grants

schoolgrants@iop.org

0207 470 4800

Grants of £600 are available to promote the teaching of physics and engineering in schools and colleges based in the UK (for young people aged 5–19 years).

Microbiology Society

Charles Darwin House, 12 Roger Street, London WC1N 2JU

www.microbiologysociety.org

grants@microbiologysociety.org

0207 685 2677

Funds of up to £1,000 are available to support science education. Applicants must be members of the society.

Ogden Trust School Partnerships Programme

Unit 3c, The Phoenix Brewery, 13 Bramley Road, London W10 6SP

www.ogdentrust.com/school-partnerships

office@ogdentrust.com

0208 634 7470

The Trust's School Partnerships Programme offers funding and support to groups of schools that are committed to enhancing physics teaching and learning.

Royal Society Partnership Grants

6–9 Carlton House Terrace, London SW1Y 5AG

https://royalsociety.org/grants-schemes-awards/grants/partnership-grants

education@royalsociety.org

0207 451 2531

The Royal Society offers Partnership Grants worth £3,000 to enable children aged 5–18 years to carry out STEM projects by partnering with a professional working in a STEM industry. There are fixed application windows, so make sure you check the website for up-to-date information.

Society for Applied Microbiology

LABS, 90 High Holborn, London WC1 6LJ

www.sfam.org.uk

communications@sfam.org.uk

0207 685 2596

Members (who have been registered for a minimum of two years) can apply for an Educational Resources Grant of up to £5,000 per annum.

You could also check out the STEM Directory, which helps teachers to search for shows, workshops, debates, challenges, visiting speakers and more. There are details of competitions and challenges to help inspire and engage students. Teachers can also access a range of career development opportunities and resources, plus it's the perfect website to help you find a STEM Ambassador and stay up-to-date with the industry! To find out more visit: www.stem.org.uk/enrichment/stem-directory.

The Royal Astronomical Society runs annual competitions, including the Patrick Moore Medal. This award recognises outstanding primary and secondary school teachers in the fields of astronomy or geophysics. There is no need to be a member of the Society to enter the awards and teachers can even nominate themselves. For more visit: www.ras.org.uk/education-and-careers/education-prizes.

Engineering

If your project is related to engineering, then take a look at the following schemes:

Engineering Education Scheme Wales

www.stemcymru.org.uk

If your educational establishment is based in Wales, then have a look at the Engineering Education Scheme Wales. They run a number of activities and outreach work for students, including the Jaguar School Challenge to challenge primary school children to design and manufacture racing cars.

F1 in Schools

Armytage Road, Brighouse, Yorkshire HD6 1QF

www.f1inschools.co.uk

0207 344 8449

F1 in Schools runs a competition to get young people aged 9–19 years to engage in STEM subjects.

James Dyson Foundation

Tetbury Hill, Malmesbury, Wiltshire SN16 0RP

www.jamesdysonfoundation.co.uk/our-work/engineering-for-schools.html

jamesdysonfoundation@dyson.com

01666 828001

Every year, the Foundation offers grants and a number of Dyson machines for fundraising purposes. They support engineering education projects and organisations in and around Malmesbury, Wiltshire, where their head office is based. It is a simple application process and educational establishments can apply online. The Foundation also offers free resources for schools (such as engineering kits and teacher packs). See the website for details.

Capital projects

If you are looking for help with capital initiatives, running costs or projects relating to your school building, then take a look at the following grants:

Michelin Community Involvement Programme

https://michelindevelopment.co.uk/support-community-organisations-charities

Michelin aims to build relationships with organisations that benefit communities local to their manufacturing operations at Stoke-on-Trent, Dundee and Ballymena. Donations and support are generally awarded for specific activities, not general operating costs (although some operating costs may be allocated for the administration of a project). They can support charities, educational establishments and not-for-profit entities. Highest priority is given to organisations in their core focus areas of education, mobility safety and environment. Application forms can be downloaded from their website.

Rank Foundation

12 Warwick Square, London SW1V 2AA

www.rankfoundation.com

contactus@rankfoundation.com

The Foundation awards Pebble Grants to registered charities (including PTAs and friends groups) which are raising money for projects where the total cost is less than £1 million.

Wolfson Foundation

8 Queen Anne Street, London W1G 9LD

www.wolfson.org.uk

0207 323 5730

The Foundation offers grants of up to £100,000 for capital initiatives, such as new buildings. Match funding is preferred for projects costing over £50,000.

Support for staff

If schools need help with costs relating to staffing, there are both general grants and more specialist grants available. The Geography Association, for example, provides information about funding opportunities for geography teachers: www.geography.org.uk/Funding-opportunities-for-geography-teachers. Check out any associations your teachers are affiliated with and what grants you may be able to access.

If you are looking for funding to support staff with international visits, then take a look at the grants offered by the British Council: https://schoolsonline.britishcouncil.org/partner-school/apply-funding.

You can find information about government funding for grants relating to apprentices at: www.gov.uk/take-on-an-apprentice.

There are also various websites to help schools find free volunteer tutors:

Action Tutoring

The Dock, Tobacco Quay, Wapping Lane, London E1W 2SF

https://actiontutoring.org.uk

hello@actiontutoring.org.uk

0203 872 5894

Action Tutoring is an education charity which supports students from disadvantaged backgrounds. They provide high-quality volunteer tutors to work with primary and secondary school students, increasing their subject knowledge, confidence and study skills. They seek to partner with schools with at least double the national average of pupils eligible for free school meals. Their website also offers a useful range of facts and statistics.

Tutorfair Foundation

Runway East, Lower Ground, 10 Finsbury Square, London EC2A 1AF

https://foundation.tutorfair.com

support@tutorfair.com

0203 322 4748

Tutors can be found in a wide range of locations and for a good variety of subjects, including maths, English, French, Spanish, science and history. The Foundation runs two programmes: the In-School programme (for schools across London) and the On-Demand Application (available to schools across the UK). Both programmes are aimed at schools with a 50% pupil premium take-up, or higher. Schools can register their interest by completing the online application form.

You could also contact an education charity, such as the Access Project, which matches volunteer tutors with GCSE and A level students at their partner schools in London, the Black Country and the East Midlands. Find out more at: www.theaccessproject.org.uk.

There are also competitions for staff which recognise the contribution they make to school life:

- The Jack Petchey Foundation runs the School Leadership Awards, which give young people the opportunity to nominate an inspiring adult to win the Leader Award. Winners receive a certificate and medallion! They are also invited to apply

for a small grant once a year (approximately £750). To find out more visit: www.
jackpetcheyfoundation.org.uk/leader-awards.

▨ The Varkey Foundation runs the Global Teacher Prize which celebrates exceptional
educators. There is a US$1 million award. This competition was won by a teacher
based in North London in 2018. For details visit: www.globalteacherprize.org.

As well as these awards, there are also other awards your school may like to enter to
recognise outstanding teachers, support staff and teams:

▨ The *TES* Schools Awards have various categories to celebrate teachers and support
staff. It is free to enter and open to state and independent schools across the
UK. Schools can enter as many categories as they wish. Find out more at: www.
tesawards.co.uk.

▨ There are numerous categories in the *TES* Independent School Awards, including the
Senior Leadership Team of the Year Award. For details visit: www.isawards.co.uk.

▨ The Community Education Awards have various categories, including awards
for the best teacher, teaching assistant and community champion. See: www.
communityeducationawards.co.uk.

▨ The Nursery World Awards include annual awards for the best Early Years
Teacher and Nursery Practitioner. For details on the various categories see: www.
nurseryworldawards.com.

Here are some grants that may help you to cover staff costs:

BBC Children in Need
Grants, PO Box 649, Salford M5 0LD
www.bbc.co.uk/corporate2/childreninneed
pudseygrants@bbc.co.uk
0345 609 0015
Grants are given for a broad range of projects, including staff training, direct project
costs, minibuses, computers and so on. Applicants can apply to the Small Grants
Programme which can potentially award up to £10,000 for three years. Please note
that grants cannot be spent on services that schools have a statutory responsibility
to provide or to purchase equipment that will be used within curriculum time.

Garfield Weston Foundation
Weston Centre, 10 Grosvenor Street, London W1K 4QY
https://garfieldweston.org
admin@garfieldweston.org
0207 399 6565

The Foundation offers Regular Grants up to £100,000 and Major Grants offering £100,000+. They can help to fund general salaries but they won't fund a specific position or job.

National Lottery Awards for All

1 Plough Place, London EC4A 1DE

www.tnlcommunityfund.org.uk/funding/programmes

general.enquiries@tnlcommunityfund.org.uk

0345 4102030

The Awards for All programme runs in England, Wales, Scotland and Northern Ireland (the contact details listed here are for England – please see the website for all other areas). Grants are given between £300 and £10,000.

If you are looking for grants relating to staff training, then don't forget to enquire whether your training providers offer any help with funding.

If you are seeking financial support to purchase a new school minibus, then as well as contacting BBC Children in Need and the Garfield Weston Foundation (see above), the following grant may be of interest too:

Variety Sunshine Coaches Scheme

Variety House, 93 Bayham Street, London NW1 0AG

www.variety.org.uk

info@variety.org.uk

0207 428 8100

Variety, the Children's Charity runs the Sunshine Coaches scheme which provides schools with their own minibus so young people can go on educational or vocational trips. They mainly support children with disabilities or special needs. Please note that organisations are required to raise funds to access this scheme and a minimum donation is required. Please see their website for details.

Health and well-being

For grants and other programmes relating to health and well-being, here are some examples of the type of help on offer:

▪ Always and Tampax run a puberty education programme called About You. They have teamed up to offer schools free kits to help students embrace puberty with confidence. These are suitable for 11–14-year-olds. Find out more at: www.always.co.uk/en-gb/puberty-education-programme-always-tampax.

▪ Speak Out, Stay Safe is a free schools programme run by the NSPCC. It teaches primary school children aged 5–11 years to speak out if they are worried, either to a trusted adult or to Childline. Their interactive assemblies and workshops are a great way for children to learn about safeguarding in a lively and memorable session. This programme is delivered in England, Wales, Scotland and Northern Ireland. To discover more and request a visit go to: www.nspcc.org.uk/preventing-abuse/our-services/working-with-schools.

- The Global Learning Programme is a free programme for UK schools. It provides an exciting opportunity to develop global citizenship in the classroom and beyond. Schools can join for free and take advantage of resources and CPD training. The programme is available in England, Wales, Scotland and Northern Ireland. You can register and access more information at: http://glp.globaldimension.org.uk/registration.

- Schools in England and Wales who are supporting young carers may be interested in the national Young Carers in Schools Award. Not only can this award help you to achieve best practice within your school, but it can also help you to demonstrate to Ofsted how you are supporting the needs of young carers. Schools can sign up to the free Young Carers in Schools initiative and access a range of free webinars at: https://youngcarersinschools.com.

- Animal welfare organisations – for example, the PDSA and Dogs Trust – can come into your school to deliver free talks and workshops (linked with the national curriculum) on pet care and animal health. For a list of participating organisations see: www.peteducationresources.co.uk/visits-and-events/we-come-to-you.

Did you know that families may be eligible for the Emergency Essentials grant, which provides up to £300 to help families with children in severe poverty to purchase essential items, such as a bed or cooker? Applications must be made by registered referrers who support the family. The grant is offered by Children in Need and administered by Family Fund Business Services. For more information visit: www.bbc.co.uk/programmes/articles/5lZprr4dJ5SmmHwKLfVNtsX/emergency-essentials.

If you are looking for grants related to special educational needs and disabilities, including disadvantaged children, then here are some grants you might like to explore:

Edward Gostling Foundation

The Grants Manager, Suite 1, 61 Thames Street, Windsor, Berkshire SL4 1QW
www.edwardgostlingfoundation.org.uk
info@edwardgostling.org.uk
01753 753900
Formerly known as the Act Foundation, the Foundation provides a Small Grants Programme for applications under £5,000 and a Large Grants Programme for applications over £5,000. Funding is targeted at people living with a mental and/or physical disability or long-term illness, so only special schools are eligible to apply.

Foyle Foundation

2 Rugby Street, London WC1N 3QU

www.foylefoundation.org.uk

info@foylefoundation.org.uk

0207 430 9119

As well as the School Library Scheme (mentioned in Chapter 7), the Foyle Foundation offers learning and arts-based grants, with a particular focus on supporting children with special educational needs.

Lady Allen of Hurtwood Memorial Trust

Chatsworth Cottage, Collington Lane West, Bexhill on Sea TN39 3TA

http://ladyallentrust.org.uk

The Trust aims to encourage and promote the education and welfare of young children and their families, especially those with disabilities and/or deprivations. Grants are awarded annually, usually in the region of £1,000.

School Angel

www.schoolangel.org.uk/grants.html

admin@schoolangel.org.uk

01539 234200

The School Angel grant programme helps individual children with a physical or mental disability or who are experiencing social deprivation. Your school must have been an active member of School Angel for at least six months to be eligible to apply. Schools can register via the website.

St James's Palace Charitable Foundation

St James's Place House, 1 Tetbury Road, Cirencester, Gloucestershire GL7 1FP

www.sjpfoundation.co.uk

The St James's Place Charitable Foundation runs a Small Grants Programme, which is open to registered charities and special needs schools in the UK. Grants are awarded up to £10,000.

Variety Grants

Variety House, 93 Bayham Street, London NW1 0AG

www.variety.org.uk

info@variety.org.uk

0207 428 8100

Variety, the Children's Charity can offer grants of between £100 and £6,000 to support individual children with specific additional needs.

Wooden Spoon

Sentinel House, Ancells Business Park, Harvest Crescent, Fleet, Hampshire GU51 2UZ

https://woodenspoon.org.uk

charity@woodenspoon.org.uk

01252 773720

Wooden Spoon, a children's rugby charity, offers grants to enhance and support the lives of children and young people (under the age of 25) who are disadvantaged physically, mentally or socially. There is no minimum or maximum grant, although projects must have a predicted lifespan of five years (preferably ten).

Part III
Additional Information

EMPLOYEE VOLUNTEERS

NOMINATION SCHEMES

CROWDFUNDING

FUNDRAISING EVENTS

FREE RESOURCES

PRODUCT DONATIONS

COMMISSION SCHEMES

GRANTS

CLUBS

ONEY-SAVING IDEAS

SPONSORSHIP

ATCH FUNDING

HIRE SCHEMES

SPORTS

FREE EDUCATIONAL SPEAKERS

Chapter 17
Fundraising events

Fundraising events, such as summer fetes and themed nights, can be enjoyed by students, staff and members of the local community. They are fun events that people look forward to and that provide an opportunity to relax, socialise and (depending on the occasion) enjoy a range of attractions, entertainment and sometimes food too. While fundraisers can be a good earner for the school, they also give something back to supporters.

These types of events create opportunities for individuals and businesses to actively support your school, whether that is by helping out behind the scenes, donating items for a stall or raffle, or volunteering to help out on the day. Income can be generated by:

- Charging entry prices.
- Charging stallholder fees.
- Commission from third-party sales.
- Earnings from stalls run specifically for the school.
- Money raised from raffles.

Here are 20 examples of family-friendly fundraising events which schools can organise:

1. Fetes.
2. Discos.
3. Themed dinners or tea parties.
4. Fashion shows.
5. Singing contests.
6. Auctions.
7. Art exhibitions.
8. Quiz nights.
9. Sleepovers.
10. Balls.
11. Barbeques.
12. Fancy dress parties.
13. Treasure hunts.
14. Breakfast mornings.

15. Hog roasts.

16. Movie screenings.

17. Karaoke.

18. Games nights.

19. Talent shows.

20. Concerts.

Another way to raise money is by holding a sale in the school hall or playground. For example, you could sell:

▨ Home-made cakes or home-grown flowers donated by students, parents and staff.

▨ Food, artwork or crafts made by the students.

▨ Fruit, vegetables or plants grown on the school allotment.

▨ Jams and chutneys made from home-grown produce.

Schools can also raise money by offering a 'service' in return for a donation or set fee, such as car washing.

Schools can also host a range of competitions and tournaments and generate an income by charging spectators and/or teams an entry fee. Teams or individuals could also get sponsored per goal.

Here are 10 ideas for competitions and tournaments:

1. Sports tournaments (e.g. netball, basketball, dodgeball, football, tennis, rounders).

2. Sports races.

3. Triathlons and relays.

4. 'It's a Knockout' battles.

5. Inflatable games competitions.

6. Boardgame or games console tournaments.

7. Bake-offs.

8. 'Guess the name of the baby' photo competitions.

9. Obstacle courses.

10. Model-building competitions.

Another idea is a sponsored event where individuals or teams are invited to complete a challenge and actively encouraged to seek sponsorship money from their own networks. Participants could set up and promote their own e-giving pages and the school could place a collection box in the reception area. Students, parents, carers, staff, governors, volunteers and other members of the community can all help to raise money for your school. The challenge doesn't have to be too energetic or scary, just something fun which challenges the individuals involved.

The school could organise a general sponsored event for everyone to take part in (such as a sponsored walk) or invite individuals to devise their own independent challenges. Some people prefer to undertake a challenge that has personal meaning to them – perhaps there is something they would like to be motivated to give up for a month or a goal they would like to achieve. If the event is organised for staff teams this can also be a great team-building exercise!

Here are some ideas for sponsored activities:

- Sponsored silence.
- Food challenge.
- Climbing wall challenge.
- Dog walk.
- Readathon.
- Head shave or leg wax.
- Fitness challenge (e.g. walkathon, marathon, swimathon, Zumbathon).
- Juggling, hula-hooping or skipping.

Whatever the event you are planning, try to be creative and make it as interesting as possible. If you can make the idea seem zany and wacky or put a fun twist on a conventional idea, then it is more likely to attract attention and support. People tend to be more enthusiastic about something that is unusual and different – which can be good news for helping to raise awareness about both the cause and the school.

Here are some more unusual examples of fundraising events:

- Instead of organising a traditional fancy dress competition, why not organise a bad taste fancy dress competition instead – where the worst or silliest costume wins?
- Rather than having a traditional running or sports race, why not make this a mud run or colour run instead?
- If participants are reluctant to do a sponsored head shave, then perhaps they could be tempted to grow bizarre facial hair or dye their hair instead.
- Instead of organising a conventional bike race, why not organise a bike race with a difference – where participants have to pedal as slowly as possible in order to win?
- Rather than holding a traditional auction, you could organise a blind auction – where bidders write down their pledges instead and the highest pledge wins. You could run this over the period of a week to accumulate more bids.

Students and families love it when staff get actively involved in fundraisers. If you are organising a fancy dress competition, for example, and staff are reluctant to dress up, try to incentivise them by awarding a prize for the best staff costume. If you have a really intrepid head teacher or member of senior staff, they can be key to raising money for your school. Perhaps they would agree to:

- A 'jailbreak' fundraiser – where they are locked in a classroom (by a mystery person) and only allowed out once enough 'bail money' (or donations) has been raised! They could be given a mobile phone to ring their contacts to request bail money, and members of staff could make appeals on their behalf too. This could be run in conjunction with a trail of clues for supporters to try to work out who locked them in the classroom – with a prize for the first one to crack it!

- A 'wall stuck' fundraiser – where they are literally stuck to a wall with duct tape! Participants are invited to buy (or make a donation for) a length of duct tape which is then used to stick the volunteer to the wall!

- 'Bid for the boss' – if you are organising an auction, perhaps the head teacher would be willing to offer the promise of a lunchtime slot. For example, staff might like the opportunity to share some ideas or perhaps a group of students would like the chance to discuss an issue!

When organising the event, remember that advance planning is key. Here are some tips to help you plan a successful event:

- Try to book people as early as possible to avoid disappointment. For example, if you would like to invite the local fire service to attend your summer fete, then remember that lots of schools request them during the summer term and they get booked up early. If you intend to contact local businesses to ask them to donate raffle prizes, then anticipate that other schools and organisers may be doing the same thing. If you make last-minute requests you are more likely to be turned down, so contact them early!

- Think about the time and day you aim to hold the event. Instead of organising the summer fete on a Saturday, when people will have to come back into school, why not catch them straight after school on a Friday, when they are there anyway?

- Check the school diary for any clashes and find out what local events might be planned on the same day, which you would rather avoid (perhaps another local school is already planning a summer fete that day).

- If you would like to hold your event at the end of term, try to avoid holding it during the final week, when everyone is busy, and instead schedule it for a week or two before. Also aim to pencil in a back-up date in the school diary, just in case the original event has to be rearranged. For example, if you have to cancel your Christmas fair at the last minute because of bad weather, you may find that other activities (such as the nativity play and Christmas disco) take priority and an alternative date can't be found.

- Make sure you have a sensible staff-to-student ratio, and ensure that all your helpers and volunteers are DBS checked. You should also have enough members of staff on board who know the school protocols and can deal with any challenging situations should they arise, as your volunteers may not be sufficiently trained or experienced.

- Try to be resourceful and use what you already have available for the event. For example, if you have access to a bouncy castle, then perhaps you could organise a sponsored bounce – participants could be sponsored for the number of bounces per minute! Or if you would like to organise a sponsored walk, but it isn't practical to leave the school grounds, then why not organise a sponsored walk around the school instead?

- Try to think of additional ways to generate income during the event. If you are organising a competition, for example, then perhaps you could sell drinks and refreshments or organise a raffle. If you are holding a bonfire night event, then you could have a barbeque and invite participants to make a donation towards a firework display.

Always be thankful and appreciative of any donations or support your school receives, no matter how big or small: aim to build strong, lasting relationships with supporters. Rather than focusing on what you can get, try to create mutually beneficial relationships and identify what you can give in return too. For example, if a parent completes a sponsored event and raises money on your school's behalf, bear in mind the time and effort they have taken to do this and don't let their contribution slip by unnoticed. Thank them in person, send them a thank-you card or invite them into a school assembly to recognise and celebrate their achievements. Take a photograph of them presenting their cheque to your school, display it in reception and in your school newsletter or post it on social media (just let them know your intentions first). These ideas don't necessarily have to cost a lot of money, but they are small tokens that can illustrate how appreciative you are, and will make the supporter feel valued for the good work they have done.

Rather than making a direct request for money, there are other ways you can ask for support:

- Invite local businesses to buy something instead. If you are fundraising to build a new classroom, for instance, you could launch a 'buy a brick' campaign, where for a fixed sum people can buy one brick that will go towards the building project (obviously, you can invite them to buy as many bricks as they like). Often, donors appreciate a more tangible way of seeing the difference their money is making.

- Try to give donors something in return to make the experience more positive for them, whether it's advertising a local business within your school or giving the children a sticker in return for their donation.

Every season there are lots of opportunities to raise money, so grab a calendar and plot some ideas in line with key dates:

▨ Choose fundraisers that work in harmony with the seasons – for example, host a candlelit supper in the winter and a family barbeque in the summer.

▨ Organise fundraisers that will catch people in the spirit of a major public event, such as a tea party to celebrate a royal wedding or high-profile sporting event.

▨ Consider any cultural or religious celebrations that you would like to mark in school, such as an Irish night to celebrate St Patrick's Day. Consider developing ideas off the back of national holidays, as families will often anticipate and be ready to support Easter egg hunts and Christmas discos.

▨ Acknowledge key school dates. Perhaps you could sell graduation gifts at the end of the academic year or organise a sponsored readathon during the summer holidays.

▨ Consider any third-party causes your school already supports, such as the Poppy Appeal or Children in Need in November, and factor these into your plans – make sure you aren't asking students and their parents for contributions too frequently.

Try to anticipate which fundraisers will raise the most money and recognise any constraints that may prevent donors from supporting your cause. It might not be a good idea to ask for sponsorship money during the Christmas period, for example, when parents are spending on Christmas presents (a Christmas disco or 'tea with Santa' might go down better instead). Instead, consider timing your appeal for donations to when donors might be feeling most generous – for example:

▨ Ask for raffle prize donations after Christmas when people may have unwanted gifts they are happy to donate.

▨ Ask for donations of foreign coins at the end of the summer break when parents have returned from their holidays and may have foreign currency they no longer need.

▨ Ask for school uniform donations at the end of July when students are leaving school and may have spare clothing.

▨ Ask for financial contributions from businesses when it is coming to the end of the tax year in April.

Identify fundraiser activities that are of genuine benefit to people. For example, you could offer extended after-school clubs (for students and their siblings) on late-night shopping evenings to help parents complete their Christmas shopping, or hold a fitness fundraiser in January when people might want to get fitter after indulging over the Christmas period.

By carefully plotting out fundraising events on the school calendar, schools are not only avoiding the risk of missing out on valuable opportunities to raise money, but they can also identify how these events fit in with the rest of the school year. Make sure you organise a good variety of events across the terms – for example, too many non-uniform days in one school year can infuriate parents! Aim to create a balanced calendar of fundraising events that are spread evenly throughout the year. This will enable you to bring in a regular school income, manage the workload, spread the 'ask' and share the fun!

Here are some fundraising ideas you could plot on your school fundraising calendar:

- January – Appeal for unwanted Christmas presents.
- January – Zumba night to help people get fit after Christmas.
- February – Pancake breakfast, pancake race or sponsored flipathon for Shrove Tuesday.
- February – Valentine's disco and competition for the best-dressed couple!
- March – Non-uniform day for World Book Day (pay £1 or make a donation).
- March – Irish night to celebrate St Patrick's Day.
- March – Sell Mother's Day gifts.
- April – Sell Easter cakes, organise an Easter egg hunt or an Easter bonnet parade.
- May – May Day fair with sponsored dancing and refreshments for sale.
- June – Sell Father's Day gifts.
- June – Afternoon tea to celebrate the Queen's birthday.
- July – Sell refreshments and organise a raffle for sports day.
- July – Summer fete or summer ball.
- July – Appeal for donations of school uniforms.
- July – Leavers party and celebrations.
- August – Sponsored readathon during the summer holidays.
- August – Summer play-scheme.
- September – Appeal for foreign coins or organise a penny drive.
- September – Harvest festival.
- September – Coffee morning.
- October – Halloween disco or Halloween-themed non-uniform day.
- October – Pumpkin carving contest – charge people to enter and ask local businesses to donate prizes for the best pumpkins.
- November – Bonfire night barbeque.
- November – Late-night shopping after-school club for Black Friday.
- December – School disco or Christmas jumper day.

- December – Late-night Christmas shopping after-school club.
- December – Carol singing (take some collection boxes with you) at the local Christmas lights switch-on event.
- December – Raffle and mince pies at the school nativity play.

While the income you generate is very significant to your school, of course, it's also important to consider the educational and entertainment value that fundraisers offer. If students are baking cakes in class to help raise money for your bake sale, for example, then you can use this as an opportunity to teach them about food and cooking techniques as well as numeracy and science.

Don't forget to consider your school improvement priorities, key focus areas and any messages your school is trying to convey. If your school is currently focusing on health and well-being, for instance, then perhaps a sports and fitness fundraiser would be more fitting than a bake sale. Whatever event you organise, make sure it is appropriate for your school and safe for the individuals involved. Always work in accordance with school policies and obtain the necessary permissions first.

If you need any equipment to run your event, then check out Borroclub, where schools can hire a wide range of items such as candy floss machines, fold-up tables and chairs, PA systems, tea sets, decorations, projectors, hot water urns and smoothie bikes. Borrowers are required to pay a security deposit plus a Borroclub fee, and there is a charge for each item per day. Photos of the items offered and fees are displayed on their website. For more details visit: www.borroclub.co.uk.

Chapter 18

Business sponsorship and corporate support

There are many wonderful companies out there that are willing to support good causes. Many larger businesses have a company giving or CSR policy which you can read on their website. This can be a useful way to learn more about the business and their philanthropic priorities.

As mentioned at the start of the book, schools should practise due diligence before accepting money or services from companies or large corporations. Always ensure that your school's culture and ethos are complemented by those of the donor.

Once you are happy that the funder is a good match for your school, there are lots of ways in which businesses can help. This might include:

- Payroll giving (otherwise known as workplace giving or give as you earn schemes): This allows employees to donate money to charity directly through their gross salary, without paying tax on it. These schemes are promoted by the business and administered by a payroll giving agency. Some employers also offer a matched giving scheme, where they match part or all of the employee's donations. Schools can learn more (and download a list of HMRC approved payroll giving agencies) by visiting: www.gov.uk/payroll-giving.

- Charitable grants: Many businesses offer grants to help good causes. Schools are often eligible to apply for these grants, although priority is usually given to good causes located close to the area(s) in which the business operates. While this book provides details of some of the corporate grants available, you can find even more by subscribing to the Funds Online database (formerly Company Giving), which is administered by the Directory of Social Change: https://fundsonline.org.uk. Please note that there is a fee to access the database, but it could be a worthwhile investment since it offers details of over 500 companies giving away over £420 million in cash and in-kind contributions in the UK each year.

- Gifts in kind (also referred to as in-kind contributions): Many businesses are willing to donate other assets aside from money, such as goods or services. This can include free product donations, the use of company facilities, administrative support, expert help, share donations and so on.

- Employee supported volunteering (also called corporate volunteering): Some employers operate a volunteering programme through which they allow employees paid days off to help support charitable causes. Perhaps ask among the parents and carers of students in your school to see if any of their employers are involved in the scheme.

Have you heard of ShareGift? This share donation charity has already donated over £30 million to charities. Donations are given to charities who promote ShareGift and are chosen by their donors. For more information visit: www.sharegift.org.

Schools can also pursue sponsorship opportunities. There are two main types of commercial sponsorship: financial sponsorship which involves sponsors giving the school money towards a specific project, and in-kind sponsorship which involves the company donating goods (e.g. for a prize-giving event) or services in return for advertising exposure within the school. While such partnerships can be very positive, schools should always ensure that they are well-managed to avoid concerns about inappropriate marketing to children and young people. Given that this is a potentially contentious issue, multiple organisations have published advice for schools. For example, the Welsh Government has released a useful document called *Guidance on Sponsorship in Schools*, which sets out a framework to help schools consider whether or not to accept a commercial sponsorship.[1] See also the further reading list at the end of this chapter.

One key point to consider is that acknowledgement of the sponsor should not appear as endorsement of their product or services. Advice from Glasgow City Council to its education leaders points out that logos should not be used for anything other than sponsor identification and should not be larger than the school logo when the two are used side by side – for example, on uniforms or newsletters.[2]

If you would like to encourage businesses to sponsor your school, then here are some tips to help you present an attractive proposition:

- Be clear about what you can offer and what you would like in return. For example, in return for X amount of money you could offer to:
  - Advertise their business within your school.
  - Name a room after the company.
  - Allow them to headline an event.
  - Print their logo on school clothing.
  - Install a commemorative plaque in your reception area.

---

1 Welsh Government, *Guidance on Sponsorship in Schools*. Ref: WG-13137 (2011). Available at: http://dera.ioe. ac.uk/13200/7/111017sponsorshipschoolsen_Redacted.pdf.
2 Glasgow City Council Education and Social Work Services, Management Circular, No. 95 (2007). Available at: www.eis.org.uk/content/asp/glasgow/images/mc95_1207%20commercial%20sponsorship.pdf.

- Install weather-proof display boards within your school grounds.
- Invite them into assembly to acknowledge their support.

▩ Let them know how you can advertise the business within your school community (and across the wider community). Be sure to let them know about your audience reach too. Perhaps you could advertise them:

- In your newsletter.
- On your website.
- Via any communication apps (e.g. ClassDojo).
- On your social media channels.
- In your prospectus.
- By sending a press release to local newspapers.

If your relationship with the business is a very positive one, then you could offer to recommend them to other schools with whom you network.

▩ Pass on key information about your school, such as:

- How big your school is (e.g. is it the biggest in the county?).
- How many students you have on roll (at present and within the next three years).
- How many families you have living within a one-mile radius of the school.

▩ Tell them how you plan to use their sponsorship money and who will be benefit from it – for example, will it be used to fund a new sensory room to support students with special educational needs?

▩ Let them know that partnering with your school is a golden opportunity to make a real difference to the community in which their business operates. Research the company's strategic aims (i.e. their CSR policy) and explain how this opportunity can help them to achieve their priorities.

▩ Let the company know about any awards the partnership can help them to work towards, such as the Education Partnerships Award. To find out more, check out the Business in the Community website: www.bitc.org.uk.

▩ Describe any successful partnerships you have already had with other businesses and the difference this has made to them.

Here is some advice to help you find a new sponsor:

▩ Advertise the opportunity across your school community – perhaps a member of staff, parent or member of the PTA knows of a business that can help.

▩ Send out a press release to communicate the opportunity to local newspapers.

- Review your existing business connections – maybe a current (or recent) supplier is willing to give back to your school.
- Attend a local business networking event. This could be an ideal occasion to discuss the opportunity with multiple businesses under one roof.
- Attend a local CSR forum. These are often set up to help businesses and charities partner together.

It can be worthwhile contacting:

- Any business with a head office in your area.
- Local start-ups with cash to potentially invest and the need to build a brand.
- Any new business that has recently moved into the area and so may be keen on fresh advertising opportunities.
- Any business that is hiring in your area; if they are a growing company, they may have cash to spend.
- Local businesses who have won CSR awards.
- Companies that advertise in local newspapers or magazines – perhaps you can tap into their advertising budget.
- Businesses that sponsor other local schools; they may be willing to sponsor your school too.

It is also a good idea to seek out businesses in sectors that relate to the theme of your project. For example:

- Football stadiums may be willing to host a charity football match to help raise money for new school sports kits.
- Restaurants and bakeries may be prepared to cater for special events or provide ingredients for a school cookery club.
- Theatres and drama companies may be able to help fund end-of-year productions and possibly provide costumes, make-up artists and videographers.
- Employment agencies may be willing to support careers workshops and give career talks.

Don't forget that many supermarkets also offer fundraising opportunities in store, such as bag packing and collection boxes. Many also run 'green token' schemes too, so contact your local supermarket for details (see more on this on page 189).

Always take the time to learn about any businesses you intend to contact and try to find out who the key contact is (you could look on LinkedIn or telephone to ask). Don't forget that other fundraisers may have requested their help too, so you will need to make your pitch for sponsorship as strong as possible.

Here are some tips to help you make a compelling case for your school:

- Be compassionate and show a genuine interest in the business.
- Let them know how keen you are to build a relationship that is mutually beneficial.
- Make the project sound exciting and unusual. Businesses usually prefer to support projects that stand out.
- Don't just simply ask for money; instead talk about the project's needs and the difference you are trying to make.
- Give them different options for how they can support you. Invite them to suggest other ways they may be able to help.
- Describe the difference their support will make.
- Let them know how they will benefit too.
- Tell them what support you already have for the project.
- Explain why you have contacted their business specifically.
- Invite them to come in and see your school.
- Aim to keep it short and sweet!

Once you have found a business sponsor, make sure you have a formal written agreement, so that both parties are clear of their expectations. Take care to monitor the agreement to ensure that the school receives what has been promised. Similarly, make sure you honour your promises and manage the relationship well, with a view to building a positive and lasting partnership.

Nomination schemes

Why not harness the power of your school community and encourage them to nominate your school to win special awards?

Many supermarket chains run community programmes to help local causes with their fundraising activities. The causes they support are usually located within a mile or two of one of their stores because they are keen to be seen to be giving back to the areas they serve. (Most supermarkets have a 'store locator' tool on their website.) The causes have usually been specifically nominated by customers. Some stores have even created a 'community champion' role, a post in which the chosen staff member is responsible for managing fundraising activities on behalf of the store. Schools can usually find the contact details for the local Community Champion via their website or by popping into the store.

The support that supermarkets are willing to give will vary, although most are prepared to give monetary donations. Often, individual stores have a donation budget which is funded from the proceeds earned through the carrier bag levy. Some supermarket chains, such as Waitrose and Asda, operate green token schemes, which enable customers to nominate their favourite causes. Every time a customer completes an in-store transaction, they are given a token to place into the box of their chosen cause (shoppers are usually given the option of supporting one of three causes). Customers who shop online are usually given the chance to vote too. At the end of the voting period (often one month), the store awards a grant based on the number of tokens received. The grant can be spent on things which directly benefit the local community, such as fundraising events, building improvements, day trips, equipment and so on.

To help get you started, here are some popular supermarket schemes for which schools can be nominated by members of the community. It is usually best to contact your local store to find out if and how they can help your school.

Asda Green Token Giving Programme: www.asdafoundation.org/green-token-giving

Co-op Local Community Fund: https://causes.coop.co.uk

Costcutter Local Pride scheme: www.costcuttersupermarketsgroup.com/about-us/local-pride

John Lewis Community Matters scheme: www.johnlewis.com/our-services/helping-our-community

Lidl Community Works (Northern Ireland): www.lidl-ni.co.uk/en/lidl-community-works

Midcounties Co-operative Community Funding: https://community.midcounties.coop/funding

Nisa Make a Difference Locally scheme: www.nisalocally.co.uk/community/make-a-difference-locally

Sainsbury's Local Charity of the Year scheme: www.sainsburyslocalcharity.co.uk

Tesco Community Grants: www.groundwork.org.uk/national-grants/grants_tesco-community-grants

Waitrose Community Matters scheme: www.waitrose.com/content/waitrose/en/home/inspiration/community_matters.html

Further reading

Department for Education and Skills (n.d.) Commercial Activities in Schools: Best Practice Principles. Available at: https://webarchive.nationalarchives.gov.uk/tna/+/teachernet.gov.uk/_doc/7403/commercial%20activities%20in%20schools.pdf.

Glasgow City Council Education and Social Work Services (2007) Management Circular, No. 95. Available at: www.eis.org.uk/content/asp/glasgow/images/mc95_1207%20commercial%20 sponsorship.pdf.

National Union of Teachers (2004) Education not Exploitation: Guidance on Using Commercial Materials in Schools. Available at: www.teachers.org.uk/files/active/0/EXPLOITATION05.pdf.

Raine, G. (2007) Commercial Activities in Primary Schools: A Quantitative Study, *Oxford Review of Education* 33(2): 211–231.

Welsh Government (2011) *Guidance on Sponsorship in Schools*. Ref: WG-13137. Available at: http://dera.ioe.ac.uk/13200/7/111017sponsorshipschoolsen_Redacted.pdf.

Wilkin, A., Kendall, S., White, R., Kinder, K., Bojke, C. and Johnson, F. (2005) *Investigating the Extent of Commercial Activity in Schools* (Edinburgh: Scottish Executive Education Department). Available at: www.webarchive.org.uk/wayback/archive/20180515192259/http://www.gov.scot/ Publications/2005/09/29103216/32167.

Chapter 19

Other income generation strategies

Beyond applying for grants and organising fundraisers for specific projects, there is a lot you can do as a school to draw in a small amount of extra income. If you're savvy, you can join schemes that allow you to earn back a bit of money through routine things like recycling or online shopping. Even small sources of income generation will add up over time.

Hire schemes

Schools can raise extra funds by hiring out facilities and resources, such as conference rooms, drama studios, sports halls, minibuses, equipment and so on. Not only can this provide additional revenue, but it can also strengthen the school's relationship with the individuals, schools, businesses, charities and community organisations that benefit. By renting out your facilities, your school can become a hub for community events. During evenings, weekends and school holidays it can be alive with all sorts of activities – from slimming clubs and car boot sales to drama classes and sports clubs. If this sounds interesting to you, then discuss it with your school governors and find out if it is something they would allow.

If you would like some guidance on the community use of school premises, see the advice produced by the Department of Education in Northern Ireland at: www.education-ni.gov.uk/articles/community-use-school-premises.

Schools can use the SchoolHire website to see what other facilities schools are letting out and how much they are charging. You can also use this platform to advertise your facilities and manage your lettings. Simply upload your details, provide information about what is available and the website will bring potential customers to you. Find out more at: www.schoolhire.co.uk.

We have already seen in Chapter 17 how schools can save money by hiring rather than buying equipment, but web-based platforms like Borroclub can also help you to generate income through the resources your school already owns. If you have spare water urns, catering equipment, gardening tools or musical instruments, for example, then you may like to lend these out to generate an income. It is free to list items and you can take a security deposit too. Borroclub also offers a pick-up and drop-off service, making it convenient to lend. For more information visit: www.borroclub.co.uk.

Recycling schemes

Schools can earn money from recycling waste ink cartridges, stamps, foreign coins, mobile phones, clothes and more. Here are some recycling schemes that your school might like to get involved with to raise funds:

Cash4Coins

C4C Mail Centre, Bayside Business Centre, Sovereign Business Park, 48 Willis Way, Poole BH15 3TB

www.cash4coins.co.uk/schools-clubs

admin@cash4coins.co.uk

0161 635 0000

Simply contact this organisation for a free school fundraising pack and arrange a collection of your foreign coins. Cash4Coins will then make you an offer for them; if you're not happy with the offer they will return the coins at their expense. You can read some school testimonials and find out how much they are raising via their website.

Empties Please

Unit 13, Orion Park, University Way, Crewe, Cheshire CW1 6NG

www.emptiesplease.com/schools

info@emptiesplease.com

0844 879 7179

Empties Please operates a collection scheme for a range of ink cartridges and toners. Postage is free and they pay approximately 50p per empty toner and between 10p and £1.75 for printer ink cartridges. See their website for details of their prices and the brands they accept. They also offer a range of posters to display around the school to encourage parents, students, staff and visitors to donate their empties.

Rags to Riches for Schools

3 Broad Street, Newport NP20 2DQ

www.rags2riches4schools.co.uk

01633 235923

This website offers money for unwanted clothes (including adult's/children's clothes, jewellery, bedding, belts, shoes, etc.), provided they are clean, dry and reusable. They offer 50p per kilo. The old clothes are shipped off to developing countries. Just give them a call to arrange a free collection. They also provide a free media pack to help you advertise this scheme to your school community. You can read some 'success stories' and other school testimonials on their website.

Recycling for Good Causes

The Fundraising Company Ltd, T/A Recycling for Good Causes, 14 Amber Business Village, Amington, Tamworth B77 4RP

www.recyclingforgoodcauses.org
info@recyclingforgoodcauses.org
0800 633 5323

This organisation recycles unwanted items in return for valuable funds. Items accepted include watches and jewellery (anything from plastic beads to broken gold chains), gadgets (such as cameras, games consoles, mobile phones, satnavs and MP3 players), old currency (UK and foreign) and used stamps. Schools keep 75% of the proceeds.

Online and offline commission schemes

Do you realise how valuable your school website is due to its potential to generate income for your school through advertising fees and pay-per-sale schemes? For example, schools can earn a commission by signing up to fundraising websites such as School Angel. If members of your school community like to shop online, then register your school with this website and encourage staff and parents to sign up. They can use this one website to shop with thousands of retailers all in one place. Each time they make a purchase, the retailer donates a commission to your school. It doesn't cost the school or shopper anything to use, and over 4,200 merchants have signed up, including eBay, Argos, Tesco, Boots and Expedia. For more information visit: www.schoolangel.org.uk.

Here are some other fundraising platforms:

Easyfundraising
www.easyfundraising.org.uk
Every time a shopper makes an online purchase using Easyfundraising, the retailer makes a small donation to the school. As well as being a useful fundraiser, it is also a convenient way to shop with over 3,700 retailers.

Give As You Live Online
www.giveasyoulive.com
This award-winning platform enables users to shop at over 4,300 retailers and has helped to raise millions of pounds for good causes since 2010. Universities, schools, pre-schools, playgroups and charities can all register. Give As You Live Online also provides lots of useful resources to administer and market your campaign.

GoRaise
www.goraise.co.uk
Over 3,000 retailers are registered on this platform. School PTAs, local clubs and even national charities can fundraise using this website, and it takes less than a minute to register.

Many individual retailers and businesses also offer their own affiliate schemes (e.g. Clarks, Marks & Spencer, ShoeZone). Although these schemes provide opportunities for schools to fundraise, it is often more prudent to sign up to a commission-based platform instead. Not only do these offer your supporters a greater choice of retailers, but by offering more choice your school cannot be seen to be endorsing or promoting a particular brand.

Schools can also generate income by registering with a fundraising search engine like Easy Search or Everyclick. Like Google, these search engines are free to use but the retailers involved make a small donation. Every time you search the internet with Easy Search, for example, they award approximately 5p to your cause, so just 10 searches a day can generate an extra £95 for your school each year. That may not sound like a lot, but if every person in your school searches the web using this platform it can prove to be a good little fundraiser. For example, you could set up Easy Search or Everyclick as your default search engine on all the school computers (once you have registered your school and created a fundraising page) and encourage your office staff, teachers, students and parents to do the same at home too. For further details see:

Easy Search: www.easysearch.org.uk

Everyclick: www.everyclick.com

There are lots of suppliers of food and drink vending machines that are happy to install and maintain a machine on your site for free, although you might want to ensure that they include a good range of healthy options. Schools receive a commission based on the number of sales. Tea and coffee vending machines can also prove to be useful for parent assemblies and events.

As well as enjoying funds from vending machines, schools can also earn commission by hosting book fairs. By hosting a Scholastic or Usborne book fair, for example, you can receive free books for your school (as discussed in Chapter 2).

Schools can also generate commission through selling Christmas/Easter cards, gift tags, mugs, t-shirts and so on designed by the children. Most firms provide a template and a free sample of each design they receive. There are lots of companies providing this service, so search online for a good deal.

School uniform fundraisers (including further commission schemes)

Schools can also harness the power of school uniforms to help generate money. Some uniform providers offer a cashback incentive for schools, so it's worth shopping around.

Most schools organise the occasional non-uniform day as a fundraiser. Students love the opportunity to come to school not wearing school uniform! Schools usually either charge a set fee or ask them to make a donation. As a variation on this theme, perhaps you could organise a Christmas jumper day, wear a colour to school day or fancy dress costume day. Why not make your non-uniform day even more fun and invite students to come in mufti and teachers to dress in school uniform!

Another way to generate an income for your school is by organising a second-hand school uniform and PE kit sale. Parents may be willing to donate old uniforms because their child is leaving school or because they have just simply outgrown them. Do you have any unclaimed items that have been sitting in lost property for years? If so, why not turn this into cash for the school? By reselling these items you are not only giving them a second home, but it can also save parents a small fortune. Some schools also run a school uniform bank. For an example, check out the Edinburgh School Uniform Bank at: https://edinburghuniform.wordpress.com.

If you have any clothes that are damaged and unsellable, then be sure to recycle them. Schools can recycle school uniforms, but if items include a badge then ask your uniform supplier for advice or visit RecycleNow: www.recyclenow.com/what-to-do-with/school-uniforms.

Crowdfunding

Many schools are turning to crowdfunding as a way of encouraging lots of small donations from a large number of donors. If there is something specific you are fundraising for and you have a target figure in mind, then crowdfunding can be the way forward. Many people like to know what they have helped to buy rather than donating to a general fund.

There are hundreds of crowdfunding websites. Schools can either use a general platform or one specifically designed for schools or the type of project for which they are fundraising. For example, Rocket Fund (discussed in Chapter 6) is a platform specifically designed for technology-related projects. Most platforms charge a commission or fee to cover costs, but Rocket Fund receives grant funding from Nesta and other partners which means they pass on 100% of donations.

When comparing crowdfunding platforms, assess the requirements for signing up, what tools are on offer, fees/commissions and what additional services they can provide (if any). Have you also thought about creating a fundraising page on your own school website to encourage donations?

Here are some crowdfunding platforms you might like to explore:

CrowdFunder
www.crowdfunder.co.uk

This social platform helps fundraisers to request donations. They have a variable fees model, so the fee you are charged depends on the type of project for which you are raising funds.

DonateMySchool

https://donatemyschool.com

DonateMySchool helps state schools to fundraise for one-off or ongoing projects. It is free to use, although a marketing fee of 3–5% is deducted from the money raised.

JustGiving

www.justgiving.com

This platform can help schools to raise money for equipment, facilities, support staff, repairs and so on. Since 2001, JustGiving has helped to raise over £4 billion for good causes.

Here are 10 tips to help you run a successful crowdfunding campaign:

1. Research similar projects by other fundraisers for inspiration.

2. Make sure your goals are reasonable and that any targets you set are realistic.

3. Aim to connect with potential supporters by sharing your story with them. Remember that not all potential donors will be familiar with your school, so try to communicate the importance of the project and the difference it will make.

4. Consider creating a fundraising team to share the workload – you could involve teachers, governors, PTA members and so on. Also try to involve the students, and use this as an opportunity to help them gain skills and experience in marketing, finance and project management.

5. Plan ahead and begin marketing your campaign a month or so before it is officially launched. Try to get some pledges lined up before it goes live to encourage others to donate.

6. Get supporters involved from an early stage and celebrate the start of your campaign. Hold a launch event and create an instant buzz.

7. Offer incentives to inspire people to donate. For example, if supporters donate X amount towards your project, then in return you could give them a thank-you card, a special mention on social media or the opportunity to name something new (for the most generous donation). You could offer different perks based on the amount each person donates: the more they give, the better the reward!

8. Spend time promoting your campaign and endeavour to keep it interesting. You could use social media, write a blog post, seek out guest bloggers or create a short inspiring video. Make sure you do something that targets all the different donors, including students, parents, alumni, suppliers and local business owners. Start

off by contacting those closest to your school (and those who are most likely to donate) and then work out to wider networks.

9. Make sure you thank every donor, regardless of the size of the contribution.

10. At the end of your campaign, celebrate the achievements with everyone who has been involved and let them know what they have helped to raise.

School PTAs

PTAs can be a valuable asset to any school. Although they can assist in many ways, if given the right support they can help to raise thousands of pounds. Does your school have a PTA or friends group? Is the group active and successfully engaging parents? Do staff support the group? Are you offering them enough backing, training and guidance? Are they applying for grants as well as organising fundraising events?

It is worth conducting regular surveys to uncover stakeholders' views about your school's PTA. For example, some parents might like to get involved with the PTA but avoid doing so because they don't like the way it is being run. Sometimes those who do help end up stepping down because they feel undervalued and that their contribution is unrecognised. By conducting a survey (which could be anonymous), you can find out how people really feel about the PTA and use this to help you determine any extra support they may need to help it thrive and be successful.

Another good tip is to collaborate with other schools and find out how much money their PTAs are raising. This will give you a benchmark and help you to find out if your PTA is reaching its full potential.

There are lots of tools, training opportunities and sources of information available online to help you support your PTA. Parentkind (formerly PTA UK) is a charitable organisation which offers advice, training and resources for PTA leaders. (Please note that there is a membership fee based on the size of your school.) To find out more visit: www. parentkind.org.uk.

Have you thought about creating a simple PTA induction pack to help your PTA run effectively? A clear set of ground rules can make all the difference to how the PTA is run and the support it attracts.

It is a good idea for the head teacher to pop into PTA meetings regularly (even if this is just for a few minutes). Being present and acknowledging everyone who supports the PTA can make a real difference to the people involved.

Don't forget that there are lots of benefits to your school PTA becoming a registered charity, including tax exemption and eligibility for Gift Aid and Payroll Giving. By having charitable status, your PTA will also be eligible to apply to many more grant-making trusts. For more information about charities and tax, please visit: www.gov.uk/charities-and-tax.

Fundraising clubs

Why not encourage students to get involved with fundraising by setting up a dedicated lunchtime or after-school club? As well as raising money, it can give students the opportunity to play an active role in fundraising, develop a range of skills and give them a sense of achievement when they see the end result.

Perhaps members of your alumni may like to meet up regularly and fundraise too? Past students (and even their families) often love the opportunity to support their old school.

Chapter 20

Money-saving ideas

Saving money is an effective way to free up cash that could be used to fund vital resources. The Department for Education states that 'all schools must do their part in securing value for money in public spending'.[1] Although this is a book about income generation, it seems sensible to offer some suggestions for how schools can save money too.

Don't buy unless you need to

Keep an up-to-date inventory of what assets you already own and refer to this when planning your budget. Not only can a good inventory can save you from making any unnecessary purchases, but it can also help you to make the best use of what you have.

Track all of your assets (e.g. computers, electrical items, instruments, teaching aids, furniture) and make sure you know their exact location. If you don't know what you have, how will you know if anything has been stolen? How will you know whether you are overpaying on your insurance premiums if you don't keep accurate records? You can also avoid costly late return fees if you keep a tight rein on the resources you are leasing and return them on time.

Make sure you're not wasting money by misplacing or losing things. Store commonly used items (such as unused pens, highlighters and exercise books) in a central storage cupboard rather than having them scattered in classrooms, so that all teachers can benefit.

Borrowing, renting and leasing

Schools can look for opportunities to borrow resources from other schools or community sharing platforms like Borroclub (see Chapter 17). To reduce upfront costs, schools can also explore rental agreements and operating leases. Not only can these help schools to access goods they may not be able to afford to buy, but they can also provide piece of mind – for example, if maintenance costs are included in the package then this is one thing you won't have to worry about. Leasing ICT equipment, which can soon become old and outdated, can also help schools to stay current with the latest developments in technology. Renting equipment can also be sensible if you only need the item short term.

---

1 Department for Education, *Review of Efficiency in the Schools System* (June 2013). Ref: DFE-00091-2013, p 3. Available at: https://assets.publishing.service.gov.uk/government/uploads/system/uploads/attachment_data/file/209114/Review_of_efficiency_in_the_schools_system.pdf.

Make sure that any rental or leasing agreements you enter into comply with the law with regard to school borrowing. If you're unsure, ask a legal expert to look over the contract to identify any potential risks. Ask for confirmation of the exact end-of-lease costs and be clear of any extra charges. For example, are there any additional charges if you return an item late?

Purchasing tips

Here are some ideas to help you save money. Although some of them may sound obvious, sometimes the simplest ideas are the best!

- If you need to make a purchase, then remember that cheaper isn't always better. When it comes to buying products or services, always do the maths and assess the quality of the product against the price (never go on price alone). For example, it is often more economical to pay more for something that will last longer, whether that is paint, washing-up liquid or a vehicle.

- Don't be deceived by brand names or fancy packaging. Although buying a branded item can feel like a more attractive offer, less well-known or supermarket own brands can be just as good. If the actual product inside doesn't represent the best value, then question why you are making the purchase. Don't be put off from considering more budget-friendly options – many shops offer their own good-quality 'value' ranges. Consider carrying out your own market testing to assess the quality of the products yourself.

- Only buy what you need. Don't be fooled by clever marketing and stay focused. If you only need one product, then don't be tempted into buy one, get one half-price offers.

- Never be pressured to buy.

A good tip is to ask staff for feedback on the products you buy and use this to guide your future purchases. Do staff feel those pencils you ordered last time represent value for money? What do they think have been the best and worst purchases you have made over the last couple of years?

Discounted items

If you do need to make a purchase, then consider the benefits of buying discounted items rather than paying the full price. New clothes, furniture, equipment and even food items are often sold at discounted prices if they are:

- End of line.
- End of season.

- Short shelf-life.

- Excess or surplus stock (due to overproduction).

- Ex-display.

- Returns.

- Perfect items with damaged packaging.

- Slight seconds.

Ask manufacturers and suppliers about any discounted stock they may have available – perhaps they have a clearance area in their store or on their website. Contact clearance wholesalers too. Before you commit to buying, always inspect the items to assess the quality and ensure they are safe and suitable for your needs. Remember, not everything can be bought second-hand, especially if health and safety is compromised.

Another way to buy discounted goods is by shopping with redistribution organisations which aim to connect businesses with good causes. Many are run by charities or community groups which collect and receive donations and sell them on at reduced prices.

Here are some examples of redistribution organisations:

Community RePaint Network

https://communityrepaint.org.uk

repaint@resourcefutures.co.uk

0117 914 3452

This organisation is sponsored by Dulux. They collect usable leftover paint and redistribute it to community groups and organisations.

Giving World Online

www.givingworldonline.com

0116 251 6205

Giving World redistributes new and discontinued business stock. Items are available for free (provided they are used directly by your organisation). Recipients are only responsible for costs associated with the collection or delivery of items.

In Kind Direct

www.inkinddirect.org

info@inkinddirect.org

0300 302 0200

In Kind Direct is an HRH Prince of Wales charity, redistributing new and usable consumer goods which have been donated by major manufacturers and retailers in the UK. A whole range of items are available to buy, from sanitary products to cooking equipment.

Of course, you will need to ensure that any purchases you make are in line with your school's procurement policy, which will be informed by Department for Education guidance (in England).[2] For larger, higher-value purchases you will need to tender quotes or use an agreed framework, but shopping online might be a good option for small ad-hoc purchases. The Money Saving Expert website (founded by Martin Lewis) has a wealth of up-to-date information, tools, offers and other useful ideas to help you save money. See also the Cheap Online Shopping page to gain over 40 useful tips for shopping online: www.moneysavingexpert.com/shopping/cheap-online-shopping-shopbots.

If you shop on Amazon or eBay, then check out the following websites to find the best discounts and offers:

Auction Lot Watch

www.auctionlotwatch.co.uk

Auction Lot Watch offers tools to help shoppers access better deals on eBay: the Auction Misspelling Tool helps you to find listings that are spelled incorrectly (and therefore less likely to attract bids) and the eBay Sniping Tool helps you to bid on an item at the very last minute.

Money Saving Expert

www.moneysavingexpert.com/shopping/cheap-amazon-loopholes

This website has an Amazon Discount and Deals Finder page which is dedicated to helping consumers find the best deals on Amazon. It provides information about current offers and a range of useful tools to help you save even more money.

Promotional offers

It is not uncommon for school furniture, stationery and educational suppliers to have promotional offers, so try to stay up-to-date with special deals. Of course, the aim is to incentivise schools to buy and so increase sales, but this can often mean better prices.

Promotional offers can include:

- Temporary price drops.
- Buy one get one … (BOGO) offers.
- Free returns.
- Free gifts with purchases.
- Limited time offers.

---

2 For more guidance see: www.gov.uk/guidance/buying-procedures-and-procurement-law-for-schools.

- New launch offers (e.g. when a new store opens the first 100 customers may get a free item).
- Purchases that automatically enter schools into a free prize draw.

If you shop with a supplier frequently, then be sure to sign up to their newsletter and email alerts and/or download their app (if they have one) to stay informed about offers and promotions. Sales deals are also advertised in magazines, newspapers and online, and don't forget that product packaging may contain coupons or vouchers.

Third-party savings

Are there any offers you can access through organisations with whom your school partners? Trade associations, membership organisations and training providers, for instance, often run offers to help their members access savings and discounts through bulk deals they have organised. For example, if you are looking to run a forest school and are a member of the Forest School Association, then you can benefit from discounted insurance with Birnbeck Insurance: www.forestschoolassociation.org/member-benefits.

Timing your purchases

If you have some flexibility when making a purchase, think carefully about the right time to buy. Could you wait for a sale (when items could be reduced by 10–75%)? Sales can happen at any time of the year, although in general they tend to happen:

- At the end of each season.
- During bank holiday weekends.
- In January.
- On Cyber Monday (online) in November.
- On Black Friday (online and in store) in November.
- At the end of a big event.
- When businesses update their stock.
- When businesses are newly opened or are closing down.

If you spot a sale taking place and shop with the business often, consider jotting this date on your calendar as it may be something the business repeats every year.

Another way to save money is buying out of season when prices may be cheaper. Forward buying can help you to achieve greater savings if you buy at the right time of year.

Try to beat price rises too by anticipating when this is likely to happen (such as the new tax year) and timing your purchases just right.

If you tend to make lots of small purchases throughout the year, then consider making one large order instead. Companies often offer better unit cost deals when you buy in bulk. It can also reduce the amount of work you need to do and can potentially help you to save on delivery costs. It may not always be practical (or financially feasible) to forward buy all of your school resources, but it is a cost-saving strategy that you may like to explore.

Collective procurement

If buying in bulk can help you to achieve greater savings, then consider increasing your order size by joint purchasing with other schools. All schools are in the same boat when it comes to looking for ways to save money and achieve greater buying power, so be pro-active, collaborate with other schools in your area (including feeder schools) and arrange opportunities to procure together. Exchange ideas with other schools online, attend school leadership events or join a local networking group.

Here are some tips to help you network with other schools:

- The Institute of School Business Leadership has published a useful list of networking groups to help school leaders collaborate: https://isbl.org.uk/Regional-Groups.aspx.
- Check out the Department for Education's guidance on professional networking for school business professionals: www.gov.uk/government/publications/join-or-create-a-network-for-school-business-professionals.
- Don't forget that Twitter is a powerful social media tool to help schools connect: check out #SBLtwitter, #SBLchat and #SBM.

While schools can manage their own tendering process, you can speed this up by working together with other schools or by using an existing procurement framework. In this way, your school can access deals that have already been arranged, which can instantly save time and money that would have been incurred arranging this yourself.

Schools can access Department for Education approved frameworks at www.gov.uk/guidance/find-a-dfe-approved-framework-for-your-school. Alternatively, you can partner with a professional purchasing organisation such as YPO. YPO works with suppliers across the UK to offer the latest products and services to schools at the most competitive prices. There are over 30,000 products on their website. Find out more at: www.ypo.co.uk/education.

If you would like to manage your own procurement process, then make sure you follow the relevant procurement laws. You can reduce some of the workload by using templates, forms and model documents provided by the Department for Education. You can also access advice and guidance on running and implementing your own procurement processes at: www.gov.uk/guidance/buying-for-schools.

Volunteers

Lots of businesses (and councils) run employee supported volunteering (ESV) schemes, which give staff the chance to take paid 'special leave' to volunteer or fundraise to help local good causes. ESV schemes provide opportunities for schools to connect and work with the local community. Schools can potentially use these schemes to access employees' skills and expertise – for example, if your school needs help with an ICT or health and safety related issue, perhaps the relevant expert at your local council could help? This can save your school from paying consultancy fees and give the helping organisation a better insight into any problems your school may be facing.

Once you have recruited volunteers, look for ways to retain them – nurture them, help them grow and make them feel valued and part of the team. Perhaps you could establish an annual award to recognise volunteers within your school? There are also external awards and schemes for volunteers – for example, volunteering can count towards the Duke of Edinburgh's Award: www.dofe.org.

Staffing costs

Employee costs are usually the highest outgoing expense for most schools, so it's worth reviewing your staffing structure regularly and monitoring the amount you are spending. Take a look at school benchmarking data to compare your expenditure with other similar schools. Schools in England can use the Schools Financial Benchmarking Service at: https://schools-financial-benchmarking.service.gov.uk.

If your staffing costs are high, perhaps you are paying more than you should on supply teacher agency fees when it might be cheaper to add them to the pay-roll. The government has launched an online tool to help schools (in England) to get the best deal on agency staff: www.gov.uk/guidance/deal-for-schools-hiring-supply-teachers-and-agency-workers.

If your costs for supply teachers are high, then consider training up teaching assistants to become higher level teaching assistants so they can cover when teachers are absent. Not only can this help you to save money, but it also supports career progression for staff and offers continuity to students.

If you are overstaffed, then look at reducing hours or sharing staff with other schools.

If you need extra staff, then here are some ideas to help you save money:

◼ Rather than hiring a permanent member of staff, collaborate with other schools and identify opportunities to share teaching talent.

◼ Could it be cheaper to upskill an existing member of staff rather than making a new appointment?

◼ Consider taking on postgraduate teaching or teaching assistant apprentices. Apprenticeships are also available in fields such as administration, catering, facilities management and finance. For more information on apprenticeships in schools, see the Department for Education's *A Guide to Apprenticeships for the School Workforce*.[3]

You can also save money by reducing staff absence. Here are some tips to help you improve attendance:

◼ Identify why staff are off and develop an action plan to get them back to work as quickly as possible.

◼ Monitor trends in attendance, sickness, paid and unpaid leave and so on. Consider offering free flu jabs to staff.

◼ Use absence management software (instead of a manual spreadsheet) to analyse data and generate reports.

◼ Identify any improvements the school can make to support staff and manage their duty of care. If staff are off work due to stress, for example, then perhaps you need to create a well-being plan, conduct a workload audit or introduce mindfulness into the workplace.

◼ Offer a return to work programme to help staff transition back into work, such as training, support, return-to-work interviews, reduced working hours or phased working patterns.

You could also consider conducting exit interviews when staff leave to help identify any problems or improvements the school could make.

Recruiting and inducting new staff costs time and money, so schools benefit financially by holding on to employees and volunteers. Here are some ideas to improve retention:

◼ Put systems in place to value and recognise people (e.g. rewards).

◼ Be approachable and operate an open-door policy – invite staff to come to you with any concerns.

◼ Conduct regular appraisals to ensure staff are happy and feel supported.

---

3 Department for Education, *A Guide to Apprenticeships for the School Workforce* (June 2018). Available at: www. gov.uk/government/publications/a-guide-to-apprenticeships-for-the-school-workforce.

- Monitor performance to help staff grow and develop.

- Offer training and development opportunities.

- Provide a positive working environment to enhance staff well-being.

- Organise social events for staff to encourage teams to come together.

- Consider offering flexible working hours to help staff achieve a good work–life balance.

- Organise mentoring and induction programmes to help support new employees.

- Offer perks such as health benefits, bonuses, retirement plans and employee benefit schemes.

Some schools go the extra mile to make employees feel valued and happy. For example, they reward staff by sending them a card or gift, celebrate milestones by ordering in treats, run a scheme to celebrate staff birthdays and organise 'shout out' meetings to acknowledge staff. Some schools run a 'staff star of the week' system to recognise employees and give them a reward – for example, the privilege of using the school's VIP parking space for the week! Many of these things cost little or nothing, but can make a big difference to workplace satisfaction.

Sustainability

Not only can reducing your energy usage help your school to save money, but it is also good for the environment as it helps to reduce carbon emissions, so aim to adopt good energy-saving practices in your school.

When making a new purchase, don't just think about the short-term savings you can make but consider long-term savings too. For example, energy-saving light bulbs may be more expensive to buy initially, but they can save you money in the long run because they use up to 80% less energy and last up to ten times longer than traditional light bulbs. Solar panels can also be a great long-term investment and can even generate profit for your school. (For more on this see Chapter 10.)

Most electronic devices come with an energy label, so make sure you choose one that has a good energy rating. Don't forget that appliances like dishwashers also come with a water efficiency label too.

Some products incorporate cost-saving features. If you need to replace the taps in your school, for example, then taps with water-saving features can be a great long-term investment.

Also look out for products that enable you to monitor and control how much energy you are using and therefore how much you are spending. For example, the most efficient printers have security tools aimed at cutting costs and reducing waste.

There are lots of other money-saving techniques that schools can implement. The Department for Education has published a *Review of Efficiency in the Schools System*, which provides an insight into how schools are currently spending money and suggests strategies for how to achieve better efficiency.[4]

---

4 Department for Education, *Review of Efficiency in the Schools System*.

Conclusion

This book has aimed to highlight a range of grants, schemes and other sources of help which are available to schools. There is a lot of other help out there too, so try to stay up-to-date with opportunities as they emerge and evolve, and continue raising awareness of the causes you need help with.

While grants potentially offer the biggest source of funding, this book has also described other ways in which schools can boost their income, such as crowdfunding, sponsorship schemes, commission schemes, improving the uptake of pupil premium and so on. Always choose the fundraising method most relevant to your project and keep planning ahead to ensure continuing success.

As well as applying for grants, this book has highlighted ways in which schools can save money, whether that is by making better use of the resources the school already owns, installing solar panels to reduce long-term energy costs, buying refurbished equipment or sharing resources with other schools. It is important that each opportunity is explored carefully, as not every option will be suitable for your school. Always work in line with your school's policies and procedures, and ensure that your school's culture and values are complemented by those of the donor or scheme.

Aside from fundraising, thousands of schools across England are campaigning to protest against cuts to school funding. If you would like to learn more about this campaign, or take action, then visit the National Education Union's School Cuts website at: https://schoolcuts.org.uk. This national campaign is ongoing and gives teachers, school staff and parents the opportunity to have their voice heard. There are lots of ways in which your school can get involved, from sharing the website and raising awareness of the campaign to joining marches and protests. You can also follow the campaign on Twitter by using #SchoolCuts and following the account @SchoolCuts, or on Facebook at: www.facebook.com/schoolcutsuk.

Good luck with your fundraising projects. Please feel free to connect with others and share opportunities and experiences via this book on Twitter – simply use the hashtag #SchoolFundraisingHandbook.

Notes

Notes

Notes

Notes

Notes